EMPOWERED PARTICIPATION

REINVENTING URBAN DEMOCRACY

Archon Fung

PRINCETON UNIVERSITY PRESS   PRINCETON AND OXFORD

Copyright © 2004 by Princeton University Press
Published by Princeton University Press, 41 William Street,
   Princeton, New Jersey 08540
In the United Kingdom: Princeton University Press, 3 Market Place,
   Woodstock, Oxfordshire OX20 1SY

Second printing, and first paperback printing, 2006
Paperback ISBN-13: 978-0-691-12608-1
Paperback ISBN-10: 0-691-12608-9

The Library of Congress has cataloged the cloth edition of this book as follows

Fung, Archon, 1968–
Empowered participation : reinventing urban democracy / Archon Fung.
p.   cm.
Includes bibliographical references and index.
ISBN 0-691-11535-4 (CL : alk. paper)
1. Political participation—Illinois—Chicago—Case studies. 2. Chicago
   Public Schools. 3. Chicago (Ill.). Police Dept. I. Title.
JS717.A2F86 2004
323'.042'0977311—dc22   2003055635

British Library Cataloging-in-Publication Data is available

This book has been composed in Sabon

Printed on acid-free paper. ∞

pup.princeton.edu

Printed in the United States of America

10 9 8 7 6 5 4 3 2

Contents _____

Figures and Tables _____

Figures

Tables

Preface

I BEGAN this project with the straightforward notion that examining actual institutions and practices of political participation and deliberation at the meso- and microlevel might contribute to our understanding of how deliberation actually works and so tell us something about what it is. I also wanted to explore whether the complexities and wickedness of contemporary public problems have made these deeply democratic, somewhat old-fashioned ideals obsolete. Or, to the contrary, can these concepts be updated to meet modern challenges to direct democracy, even in the most depressed areas and for the poorest people?

As I tromped around Chicago's South Side for several years in search of answers to these questions, I was privileged to meet many parents, residents, police officers, teachers, and school principals for whom democracy is not just an abstract idea, but a living practice that they struggle to use and improve. It was humbling to watch these people work with one another, sometimes against each other, to better their collective lot. If you want to find democracy's heroes, look in the streets. They do not receive the recognition they deserve in the following chapters because I changed their names to "protect the innocent," as they used to say. The people who went far out of their way to help me understand the design and reality of neighborhood governance in Chicago are too numerous to credit here, so I name only a few representatives. They allowed me to observe, ask stupid questions, poke, and otherwise prod when they had serious work to do. Anything worthwhile in the pages below was spied through lenses that they provided.

Anthony Chiesa, Mary Hansen, and Mary Glynn-Johnson at the Chicago Police Department (CPD) and Lynette Fu and Denise Ferguson at the Chicago Public Schools (CPS) helped me to see how the Byzantine workings of these agencies sometimes advance larger democratic aims.

Chicago wouldn't be the city it is, or have taken the course that it has, without an extremely rich ecology of activist organizations committed to civic engagement and resident empowerment. Warren Friedman, Ani Russell, John McDermott, Ralph Rivera, Kwame Porter, and many others at the Chicago Alliance for Neighborhood Safety (CANS) corrected many of my conceptual and factual errors in the course of our occasionally heated discussions. Julie Woestehoff, Sheila Castillo, Don Moore, and Andrew Wade are just a few of the school-reform movement leaders who let me into their world.

Beyond its administrators and activists, Chicago is blessed by extremely capable research groups dedicated to evaluating and improving public policy. The dean of policing, community and traditional, is Wesley Skogan. He and his colleagues at the Chicago Community Policing Evaluation Consortium, especially Susan Hartnett and Justine Lovig, were kind enough to teach me much of what I know in that area by sharing their wisdom and their data. Similarly, this project would have been impossible without the continuing research of those at the Consortium on Chicago School Research.

   Whether you are a street-level public servant or citizen, the most difficult work occurs in the neighborhoods. There is no thanks or glory there, only commitment, perseverance, and the desire to make things a little better for you and yours. Among those who showed me how they try to make things better in their own corners of Chicago are Hanif Shakir, Sandra Munoz, Vivian Medios, Susan Evans, Eleanor Hollander, Larry Knowlin, Karen Hoover, Jacqueline Mitchell, Nathaniel Bowden, Andrea Waters, Ellyn Cronin, Neil Glynn, Mary Ellen McWilliams, John Bradley, Mary Scannell, and Kathryn Kemp.

   This book, like much academic research, fosters the illusion of having been a solitary intellectual endeavor, but of course resulted from countless collaborations and conversations. I owe the deepest substantive debt to Joshua Cohen and Charles Sabel. Their impact on my approach and method runs deeper even that their particular ideas. Josh showed me how rigorous political philosophy and social theory can be. Chuck taught me, despite much unwitting resistance on my part, that improving one's ideas often requires going out into the world. From Noam Chomsky, I learned that the gap between democracy's values and its reality is wide and paradoxically hard to comprehend, but demands a response nonetheless. The manuscript improved immensely as a result of Erik Olin Wright's painstaking reviews. Dara O'Rourke provided immense intellectual feedback and emotional support throughout. Steve Ansolabehere, David Barron, William Boyd, John Gerring, Lani Guinier, Gary Herrigel, Linda Kaboolian, Linda Kato, Taeku Lee, Jane Mansbridge, Steve Page, Robert Putnam, Martin Rein, Joel Rogers, Tom Sander, Debra Satz, Theda Skocpol, Guy Stuart, Cass Sunstein, and David Thatcher gave me generous feedback. Taimur Samad provided valuable research assistance. I owe special thanks to many graduate students, especially those of Chuck and Gary, who provided critical comments that required me to rethink much of the proposal and research agenda for *Empowered Participation*.

   The John F. Kennedy School of Government generously supported the completion of this project.

   Finally, without the boundless love, understanding, and affection of my parents, Bing and Mildred, and my wife, Deborah, none of what follows would have been possible or worthwhile.

Abbreviations

CANS	Chicago Alliance for Neighborhood Safety
CAP	Corrective Action Plan
CAPS	Chicago Alternative Policing Strategy
CBE	Chicago Board of Education
CPD	Chicago Police Department
CPS	Chicago Public Schools
CSC	Citizens Schools Committee
CSLC	Chicago School Leadership Cooperative
CTU	Chicago Teachers' Union
CU	Chicago United
DFC	Designs for Change
DI	Direct Instruction
EPG	Empowered Participatory Governance
IGAP	Illinois Goals Assessment Program
IPR	Institute for Policy Research
ITBS	Iowa Test of Basic Skills
JCPT	Joint Community-Police Training Program
LSC	Local School Council
NEA	National Education Association
PCER	People's Coalition for Educational Reform
PCS	Possession of a Controlled Substance
PURE	Parents United for Responsible Education
RESPECT	Reconstruct Education with Students, Parents, Educators, and Community Together
SIP	School-Improvement Plan
TAPA	Traxton-Area Planning Association
TRUE	Taxpayers for Responsible Education
UCPP	Urban Crime Prevention Program
UNITE	United Neighborhoods Intertwined for Total Equality

EMPOWERED PARTICIPATION

1

Democracy as a Reform Strategy

IN 1996, the parents, staff, and principal of Southtown Elementary School[1] executed a coup to make the neighborhood school their own. They won permission from the Chicago Board of Education to change the name of their South Side school to Harambee Academy, after an ancient North African kingdom renown for its scholarly achievements. To the community of the newly dubbed Harambee Academy, the name was the appropriate face of a broad initiative to reorganize the school around a coherent, common, and Afrocentric vision. Of Harambee's some seven hundred students, after all, 99 percent were African-American and 92 percent were from low-income families.[2] How better to forge a shared vision than to reclaim academic excellence as a distinctive component of their racial and cultural tradition?[3]

Changing a name, of course, cannot itself raise test scores, make classes more orderly, build classrooms, or increase children's readiness for middle and high school. In the months and years ahead, the parents and personnel of Harambee would attempt to advance their historical and cultural commitment to scholastic achievement through a variety of programs that included technology labs, prekindergarten programs, physical plant upgrading, curriculum changes, and a host of instructional innovations.

Those versed in education reform will find these projects familiar and recognize that they are by no means distinctive to Afrocentrism. For many low-income urban schools, however, mustering the leadership, organization, staff motivation, and community commitment to imagine and implement such changes is itself more difficult than any particular change. Without commitment to their shared and culturally specific vision, many of these initiatives might not have been launched and perhaps none of them would have enjoyed the support and devotion needed to carry them through.

The school continued to face daunting obstacles—the poverty of its families and decaying family structure, neighborhood migration that resulted in the turnover of 42 percent of its students each year, and a building that was constructed before the turn of the century (Chicago Public Schools 1996). Despite this challenging environment, the staff and community set in place two of the basic components necessary for school improvement: students, parents, staff, and managers were broadly committed to a com-

mon educational vision and these groups developed capacities to formulate and implement a variety of promising school-reform strategies.[4]

Several miles to the north of Harambee, residents of a Chicago neighborhood called Lakeville were plagued by intimidation, narcotics trafficking, prostitution, and suspected gang activity.[5] They met with police
for several months to understand these problems and develop strategies
to mitigate them. In these meetings, they determined that most of the
undesirable activity originated in a large park nearby. Analyzing patterns
of behavior there over several weeks, they found that most of the illicit
activity occurred at night around an unfinished sunken concrete structure
deep within the park. They dubbed this area, obscured from the street by
trees and elevation, as the "pit."

In the short term, residents and police worked together to mitigate disturbances. Police patrolled the area more frequently at peak times identified by residents, conducted foot patrols, and enforced loitering and cur-
few laws. Neighbors living next to the park organized themselves to
watch for illicit activity and summon police response via a phone tree. In
the longer term, residents followed Jane Jacobs's (1993) wisdom that
"eyes on the street" can prevent crime and nuisances in public places.
They began with simple measures such as trimming tall trees to make the
park's interior visible from the street. More ambitiously, residents sought
physical improvements to make the park more useful, attractive, and inviting to legitimate users in the hope that they might drive out illegal ones.
Through social connections, they contacted an architect who redesigned
the park to include a community garden, a multi-use athletic field, and
plenty of lighting. Residents secured approval to make these modifications from the Parks Department. They also raised more than $20,000
from the Chicago Cubs and local businesses to implement their new design. After construction was completed, unlawful activities and nuisances
all but disappeared and residents used the park more frequently.

1.1. Empowered Participation as an Administrative Reform Strategy

Why were citizens and officials at Harambee and Lakeville able to improve
their local circumstances and public institutions when those in thousands
of similar urban neighborhoods in dozens of other cities seem unable to
move forward? At the most proximate scale of school and neighborhood,
local heroes like the principal, committed teachers, police officers, and
parents deserve the credit. But the choices, powers, and motives of those
inside schools and other local institutions are deeply determined by the
institutional terrain around them. Both schooling at Harambee and policing in Lakeville benefitted from an institutional environment that created

a certain kind of participatory democracy. Several years earlier, both the Chicago Police Department (CPD) and the Chicago Public Schools (CPS) were reorganized to create new channels through which residents could exercise their collective voice and influence. Extensive powers were devolved from their headquarters out to the neighborhoods. These initiatives transformed the CPD and the CPS into the most participatory-democratic public organizations of their kind in any large American city.

In 1988, the General Assembly of Illinois passed a major piece of education legislation that turned the hierarchical structure of the CPS on its head. The legislation shifted governance power to individual schools by creating some 580 Local School Councils (LSCs), one for each elementary and high school in the city. LSCs are bodies elected every two years by members of the school community. Each consists of six parents, two community members, two school staff persons, and the principal. These bodies are empowered to select principals, develop school-governance plans and visions, and spend discretionary funds. These powers and responsibilities enabled the Harambee LSC and school community to develop its Afrocentric educational vision and to pursue a variety of innovations outside the school as well as within it.

The CPD embarked on a similar strategy of reform in 1995 when it rolled out its Chicago Alternative Policing Strategy (CAPS). While many other cities had experimented with forms of community- and problem-oriented policing for several years (Wilson and Kelling 1989; Sparrow, Moore, and Kennedy 1990; Kelling and Coles 1996), CAPS is quite distinctive for the extent to which it involves ordinary residents and street-level police officers in determining policing priorities and approaches (Skogan et al. 1999). Unlike the situation with respect to local school governance, residents who participate in CAPS cannot hire and fire police officers; however, the police officers in each of the city's some 280 neighborhood "beats" hold monthly open meetings with residents to discuss neighborhood safety issues. In these sessions, police and residents jointly select priority public safety issues and develop wide-ranging strategies to address them. These community-policing arrangements form the institutional structure through which residents, police, city officials, and nonprofit organizations rebuilt Lakeville's dilapidated park. Beat meetings created new spaces in which police and residents could together and develop a range of solutions addressing various problems at the park. CAPS's grant of operational autonomy liberated police officers to implement some of these ideas.

These reforms set into place some central features of a kind of participatory democracy that is appropriately called Empowered Participatory Governance (Fung and Wright 2003). In the crucial areas of public education and policing, the CPS and CPD reforms advance the central tenet of participatory democracy: that people should have substantial and equal opportunities to participate directly in decisions that affect them (Pateman 1970, 22–44; Pitkin and Shumer 1982). Despite many complexities and limitations, these reforms have made the CPS and CPD much more *participatory* in that they invite ordinary individuals to take part in crucial governance decisions about the goals, priorities, and strategies of policing and public education. Furthermore, this participation is *empowered* because, unlike the case with regard to many advisory panels, public hearings, and discussion groups, decisions generated by these processes determine the actions of officials and their agencies. Finally, decision-making around local education and policing has become much more *deliberative* in that members of Local School Councils and beat meetings make decisions through a process of structured reasoning in which they offer proposals and arguments to one another. The chapters that follow elaborate these concepts of participation, empowerment, and deliberation; analyze the political and administrative institutions that translate these abstract concepts into actual practices; and explore the empirical experience of those institutions to assess the promise of participatory democracy in these challenging contexts.

Of the many objections to participatory democracy, perhaps the most common and compelling is that the ideal is irrelevant in the face of modern governance challenges. The problems of scale, technical complexity, the intricate division of labor of government, and the privatization of public life all decisively weigh against any straightforward implementation of the New England town meeting (Bryan 1999) or the Greek assembly to most modern political contexts (Cohen and Sabel 1997). This book responds directly to the objection of irrelevance by counterexample. The following chapters show how two large urban bureaucracies, operating under very challenging background conditions, did in fact transform themselves in substantially participatory-democratic directions.[6]

Even if some version of participatory democracy is feasible, it might not be very desirable as a path of reform. The core argument of this book is that troubled public agencies such as urban police departments and school systems can become more responsive, fair, innovative, and effective by incorporating empowered participation and deliberation into their governance structures. The experiences of Harambee and Lakeville suggest several ways in which neighborhood participation and devolution might improve the quality of public action compared to centralized agencies. Foremost, centralized programs may be effective in some places and under some circumstances but not others. Decentralization, by contrast, allows localities to formulate solutions tailored to their particular needs or preferences (Tiebout 1956). Harambee's effort to develop a school mission and vision suited to the culture and background of their student body illustrates this advantage. Devolution can also free residents, teachers, and police officers to imagine and implement innovations that depart from conventional wisdom and routine, and are therefore unlikely to come from the central office. Police supervisors, for example, were much more likely to offer intensified patrol than environmental redesign as a solution to the problems at Lakeville Park because of their professional training and administrative capacities. Third, residents and officials may have local knowledge that can usefully inform policy strategies but that may not be systematically available to or easily usable by centralized organizations. Residents' and police discovery of the "pit" in Lakeville Park and their knowledge of the best way to reshape its grounds to enhance use and visibility illustrate the importance of such local knowledge. Fourth, citizens who depend on these public services have strong motivations to contribute to their improvement through civic engagement. Given opportunities to participate in school governance or community policing, they can contribute distinctive resources and expertise, as they did in the architectural redesign and fundraising around the park. As we will see, they can also use these opportunities to hold principals and police officers accountable when they shirk, lie, or act incompetently.

1.2. Accountable Autonomy: An Institutional Design for Empowered Participation

If these intuitions about the contributions of participation to public action sound familiar, it is because they stem from a long tradition of those who favor participatory decision-making (Pitkin and Shumer 1982; Barber 1984) in local democratic forms such as New England town meetings (Mansbridge 1980), community controlled public offices (Arnstein 1969; Kotler 1969), and workers' cooperatives (Pateman 1970; Whyte and Whyte 1988; Gastil 1993). Proponents of this view favor local autonomy from centralized authority in part because they fear that central power tends to encroach on local prerogatives, to crowd out civic initiative and engagement, and to disregard crucial local knowledge. The constructive forms of civic-official action at Harambee and Lakeville suggest that these fears are sometimes warranted. But local autonomy often encounters its own difficulties. Scholars who have examined participatory small-group decision processes have found that they are often no more fair than other kinds of governance and decision-making (Mansbridge 1980; Gastil 1993; Sanders 1997). Voices of minority, less educated, diffident, or culturally subordinate participants are often drowned out by those who are wealthy, confident, accustomed to management, or otherwise privileged. Liabilities such as parochialism, lack of expertise, and resource constraints may impair the problem-solving and administrative capabilities of local organizations relative to centralized forms.

Such pathologies may not be intrinsic to empowered participation and deliberation. Rather, the extent to which such criticisms apply may depend upon the details of the institutions that render the abstract notions of deliberation, participation, and empowerment into concrete practices. In particular, the devolution of authority to autonomous local bodies is frequently taken to be the natural institutional form of participatory democracy (Arnstein 1969; Kotler 1969; Mansbridge 2002). It may be, however, that a judicious allocation of power, function, and responsibility between central authorities and local bodies can mitigate these pathologies of inequality, parochialism, and group-think and so better realize the ideals empowered deliberation and participation. To their credit, the CPS and CPD reformers tried to address the defects of decentralization and localism by developing just such hybrid arrangements. They did so by moving toward an institutional design of administrative and democratic organization that is appropriately called *accountable autonomy.* Though the two parts of this term may seem to be in tension, consider how they work together in the context of municipal and neighborhood governance.

Officials and citizens working together in Harambee and Lakeville illustrate the importance of autonomy. Within the broad charge of improving education and public safety, these two groups set their own agendas regarding both ends and means. The Harambee LSC and community forged an institutional vision that centered on educational excellence in an Afrocentric setting, developed a host of school-level programs to realize that vision, implemented those through internal resources, and were afforded the latitude to act under the 1988 state education-reform legislation. Similarly, it was Lakeville's residents and police, not central authorities, who designated the park as the most urgent problem area, devised unconventional tactics to address it, and mustered the wherewithal to execute their plans.

These renditions, and the local democratic tradition generally, improperly conflate two distinct senses of autonomy. In one sense, autonomy entails independence from central power. In a second, it stresses the capacity of local actors to accomplish their own ends, such as school improvement or neighborhood safety. Accountable autonomy stresses the latter sense, which requires retreating from autarky to a conception of centralized action that counterintuitively bolsters local capability without improperly and destructively encroaching upon it. Support and accountability are two pillars of a reconstructed relationship between central power and neighborhood action that can reinforce local autonomy.

Successful local action, especially in depressed urban contexts, frequently requires external support. This support can come in multifarious forms such as financing, other direct resources, expertise, or cooperation from larger entities. In Lakeville Park's cleanup, for example, residents and police were aided by numerous external public and private actors such as the streets and sanitation department, the parks department, a friendly architect, private foundations, and local businesses. Harambee's LSC also benefited from friendly partnerships with downtown elements of the CPS and helpful local parties. While these examples for the most part illustrate ad hoc forms of support, central authorities of both the CPS and CPD have organized themselves to provide quite systemic forms of assistance for local planning and problem-solving. These mechanisms, analyzed in detail in the chapters that follow, include extensive training for both participating residents and street-level officials, changes in the legal and regulatory environment of these efforts, the pooling of knowledge and experience, and provision of technical assistance.

A second and perhaps more perplexing problem with local independence is that groups may lack the wherewithal, goodwill, or motivation to come together as the professionals and residents at Harambee and Lakeville managed to do. While proponents of participatory forms of decision-making tend to presume that the greatest threats to democratic values lie outside the boundaries of community and locality, many of its critics point to the dangers within. Internal divisions among participants, for example between factions of residents or between residents and officials, may paralyze the group or allow some to dominate. Or, even in the absence of conflict, groups may be unmotivated to utilize local discretion to innovate and advance public ends through problem-solving. Many beat groups and LSCs in Chicago certainly seem imprisoned by habit and have continued with ineffective but comfortable routines in the years following the devolutionary reforms there. Group divisions, domination by particular factions, and lethargy all reduce local autonomy, when autonomy is understood as capacity rather than license.

Centralized authority in "accountable autonomy" can reduce these internal obstacles through mechanisms to safeguard both local processes and substantive outcomes. To check domination and faction, external reviews and audits can verify the integrity of local decision-making processes and intervene when procedures seem suspect. For example, both the CPS and CPD require local groups to document and justify their missions, agendas, strategies, and particular actions and then subject these plans to supervisory review. To assure that local groups utilize their discretionary latitude constructively, outside bodies monitor the relevant outcomes—through student test scores, truancy rates, incidents of crime, and more discerning measures—to detect trends of improvement, stasis, or decline in performance. While efforts to establish substantive accountability are fraught with the difficulties of developing sensitive performance metrics and judiciously associating observed performance with internal effort, both the CPS and CPD have begun to develop such monitoring programs.

Accountable autonomy, then, offers a model of how reformed public agencies such as schools and police departments might interact with citizens that stands in contrast to visions of local democracy and community control on both conceptual and institutional dimensions. This model emphasizes the positive and constructive face of autonomy—the capacity, indeed responsibility, of groups to achieve public ends that they set for themselves—as much as the emancipatory aspect of shedding centrally imposed constraints and demands. Beyond this, it reduces potential pathologies that afflict social choice within small groups. These two considerations support alternative institutional relationships between center and periphery. Far from withering away, central authority serves two important general functions in this model. The first is to provide various kinds of supports needed for local groups such as beat teams and LSCs to accomplish their ends, yet would be otherwise unavailable to these groups in isolation. The second is to hold these groups accountable to the effective and democratic use of their discretionary latitude. Somewhat paradoxically, realizing autonomy requires the sensitive application of external guidance and constraint. When factions inside a group dominate or paralyze planning processes, outsiders can step in to break through jams and thus enable the group to better accomplish its ends. When the indolence of these groups results in subpar performance, external interventions and sanctions can transform license to innovation and problem-solving.

1.3. Paths More Traveled: Markets and Public Hierarchies

Reformers of many stripes agree that public policies and administrative organizations should instill the kind of coherence and problem-solving capacity exhibited by those at Harambee and Lakeville. Indeed, fostering that self-motivated, innovative drive is a prime objective of public-sector management and organizational reform. Experts disagree vehemently, however, about how best to generate these qualities. While they frequently acknowledge the importance of citizen empowerment, often understood as customer satisfaction (Osborne and Gaebler 1992), strongly participatory variants of citizen engagement, such as community control or accountable autonomy, seldom arise. Instead, this debate roughly pits two general positions against one another. In one camp are thoughtful defenders of the public bureaucracies, who seek to repair their obvious defects and failings by improving the effectiveness of the hierarchy through modern management techniques and accountability mechanisms. Those in another camp argue that the failures of large public-sector organizations are so deep and incorrigible that they require radical evisceration. These reformers, impressed by the efficiencies and accomplishments of firms in the private sector, would inject healthy doses of competition and consumer choice through market mechanisms to improve the performance of the public sector.

Empowered participation is a third path of reform that takes its inspiration from the traditions of civic engagement and participatory democracy rather than public-management techniques or competitive markets. The concepts, experiences, and analysis that follow show that this course has already yielded many benefits for the substantive objectives of public safety and education while advancing important democratic values of participation and deliberation. Empowered participation, and other reform models that spring from democratic roots, therefore merit serious exploration and consideration alongside the prevalent choice between hierarchies and markets. For some problems in some places, like public safety or school improvement in central cities, democratically inspired strategies may offer decisive advantages.

A definitive analysis of these three alternative reform paths would detail their relative strengths and pitfalls across various cultural, political, and organizational contexts. Which strategy, or mix of them, yields the largest improvements in public performance? Unfortunately, no one can offer such a comprehensive analysis because the experience with each of them is too short and sporadic. Indeed, taken on its own terms the intense controversy surrounding each of these reform paths indicates that systematic comparisons must await their maturity. Juxtaposing the justifications that motivate hierarchical and market-reform strategies, however, clarifies the terms of comparison and highlights the distinctive promise of accountable autonomy.

Some of the most visible and hotly debated efforts to transplant market mechanisms appear in the reform of public education (Chubb and Moe 1990). School-choice programs allow children to attend public schools outside of their neighborhoods and then reward schools that attract more students, thus fostering competition among public schools. Charter-school programs—a second variant adopted by many jurisdictions, among them Arizona and Massachusetts—begin from the desire for entrepreneurship. They enable individuals or groups to form and manage new public schools. School vouchers constitute yet a third variant that goes further in its degree of privatization. For example, programs in Milwaukee, Cleveland, and many other cities grant vouchers that enable parents to send their children to private schools.

Though these variants differ in important design details, their supporters share three common commitments. First, they believe that hierarchical management of schools—top-down efforts to improve them by imposing particular curricular or instructional requirements, for example—are misguided. Improvement must come from the personnel of the school itself. This requires rescinding many of the procedural requirements that commonly direct public-school operations. Second, they believe that children should not be forced to attend particular schools simply because they live near that school, but rather their parents should be able to select from among a range of schools that match their quality requirements and curricular preferences. Improved parental choice drives a third commitment to competition among schools. While some believe that emancipation is sufficient because it will unleash the entrepreneurial energy, craft, and compassion of principals and teachers (Meier 1995, 2000), most favor competition among schools as a way to motivate educators. Hence market-based reform strategies link financing to the number of students that choose a given school.

Like these strategies, the accountable autonomy approach relies upon bottom-up innovation rather than wisdom that flows down from on high. But it differs in three important respects. First, accountable autonomy emphasizes the importance of citizen participation and voice before exit.[7] In both LSCs and beat meetings, the first recourse of unhappy parents is not to move to another school or neighborhood, but rather to contribute to governance efforts to improve the situations in which they find themselves. Some parents and users of other public services may not—for reasons of time, distance, expense, inconvenience, or allegiance—wish to abandon their neighborhood school as quickly as they might switch between telephone companies or brands of soda. When they do engage in partnership and joint governance with local officials rather than play the role of consumers selecting between different service offerings, they can contribute to innovation and institutional improvement. Most market-based reforms rely upon the efforts of professionals. As we have seen with both Harambee and Lakeville, the engagement of citizens can add distinctive resources, ideas, and talents to governance and problem-solving endeavors.

A second difference concerns the need to link local units like firms and police beats together. By eschewing central authority in favor of consumer and producer sovereignty, market-based reform strategies rely upon competition and price to diffuse innovations and to solve coordination and equity problems. If one school hits upon an innovation that works well for its students, for example a truancy-reduction strategy or effective reading program, market-based mechanisms may be quite slow to spread this good news to other schools that might benefit from it. Indeed, if education markets were quite competitive, the most successful schools might prefer to hoard their techniques as a kind of intellectual property for competitive advantage. Similarly, market-driven systems have difficulty redistributing their resources where they are most needed. While many voucher proponents favor distributing them to poor students first, and perhaps even giving larger vouchers to the most needy, other helpful interventions outside the realm of market-style reform might instead channel resources to the most needy schools or neighborhoods. In accountable autonomy, by contrast, central authorities are redefined and revitalized to perform such functions.

A third concern revolves around the extent to which market-based reform strategies advance the public mission of the institutions they seek to reshape. John Chubb and Terry Moe have argued that public-school systems are paralyzed by a surfeit of missions generating contradictory and burdensome regulations that ultimately thwart effective school operations (1990). Their prescription is that schools be subject to market disciplines and insulated from these self-defeating political pressures. But, as public outrage over a Kansas Board of Education decision to inject creationism into its program shows, collective social concern for the curricular content and substantive vision of public schools is perhaps unavoidable and probably desirable. Market mechanisms, aspiring as they do to automatic self-regulation though consumer choice and producer response, offer no direct solution to this steering problem. By contrast, the model of accountable autonomy holds local groups, such as those in schools and police beats, to more general procedural and performance standards. So, Harambee Academy's staff justified its adoption of an Afrocentric vision and school environment on the grounds that this would create a more effective school as measured by the general criteria—themselves determined through ordinary political and administrative processes—under which schools are generally evaluated, such as test scores and graduation rates.[8]

In addition to these market-based mechanisms, another well-trodden path of reform recommends enhancing performance within the public sector through modern management techniques, among them decentralization, careful monitoring of subordinates, and accountability. Some areas, for instance police operations and the provision of public safety, may be widely regarded as too critical to be privatized or left to the vagaries of market governance. Others may harbor criticisms of market mechanisms like the foregoing, or they may see reform within the public sector as a more rapid path of transformation in light of both political resistance to the imposition of market competition and the difficulty of creating enough independent providers to replace existing public capacity. Though there are many prescriptions for improving public management, a prevalent and salient strain resembles accountable autonomy in that it combines the devolution of authority with careful performance-monitoring and accountability mechanisms. As a managerial approach, this path differs from accountable autonomy in that it makes no special provisions to engage citizens. It does not rely substantially on their voice, insight, or energy, nor does it seek to establish direct channels of accountability between public officials and the citizens they serve.

In modern policing, for example, this path of reform is well articulated under the heading of "problem-oriented policing" and exemplified by the reforms led by William Bratton and supported by then-mayor Rudolph Giuliani in New York City (Goldstein 1992). This new policing responds to perceived failures in the ability of centralized and hierarchical methods to cope with the complexity and multiple modern threats to public safety. In response, it calls for ordinary frontline police officers to become more informed about the particular problems they face, assume responsibility and "ownership" for addressing them, and attempt more innovative approaches. Following the adage that responsibility requires authority, this reform recommends enhancing the discretionary power of officers in the streets by liberating them, in the manner of market reforms, from regulatory minutiae.

In the New York City Police Department, for example, performance accountability has replaced loose procedural supervision. Through a now well-known and highly regarded procedure called COMPSTAT ("comparative statistics"), precinct commanders meet regularly to review crime incidents, reports, and response patterns as generated through a centralized information-management system.[9] Supervisors congratulate their commanders when rates drop. In high-crime precincts, however, they castigate commanders and demand that they develop more effective abatement measures. In subsequent meetings, these commanders are called on to report steps taken and assess their success by considering COMPSTAT data. This city-wide procedure is mirrored in many of the precincts, with commanders using more localized data to motivate and assess their captains and sergeants. At multiple levels, supervisors encourage subordinates to creatively engage and solve problems and evaluate their efforts through statistical monitoring. Proponents of COMPSTAT credit it with not only contributing to the widely noted decreases in violent crime in New York City, but also with consolidating fundamental and lasting reform of the department (Buntin 1999; Silverman 1999).

In some manifestations, high-stakes standardized testing is the educational analog to COMPSTAT. In recent years, a movement for accountability based on standardized testing has emerged as the main alternative to market-based education reform. In states like Massachusetts, North Carolina (Jones et al. 1999), Texas, and many others, student performance on standardized tests of basic knowledge and skills is becoming the fulcrum of educational change.[10] An array of programs seeks to evaluate students, teachers, and schools based on these tests and to punish those who perform poorly with grade retention, loss of merit pay, and administrative sanctions. Many of these initiatives are accompanied by teacher training and support. Critics of high-stakes testing contend that this accountability restricts the creativity and professional discretion of teachers and disproportionately punishes schools that serve minority and poor student populations (National Research Council 1999; McNeil and Valenzuela 2000; Orfield and Kornhaber 2000). Supporters contend, to the contrary, that these accountability arrangements motivate teachers and principals to explore instructional methods that improve their students' test performance. Though research has not yet settled this controversy, testing proponents rest their faith on the efficacy of a managerial combination of professional discretion at the school and classroom levels and direction via performance accountability from above.

Problem-oriented policing and high-stakes testing illustrate three important respects in which these new public-management strategies differ from the participatory path of accountable autonomy. First, accountable autonomy relies much more heavily upon direct contributions of citizens and users of public services. As we saw in the cases of Harambee and Lakeville, the participation and partnership of parents and residents figured centrally in the formulation of overall agendas and visions and the development and implementation of specific strategies. While new public-management strategies claim to invite citizen participation—in the form of community-policing outreach or parental consultation and support associations, for example—they depend predominantly on the resourceful action of professionals at the street, school, and headquarters levels.

Second, accountable autonomy entrusts local groups that include both citizens and professionals to develop their own agendas and set their own ends, whereas the new management strategies leave line officials to determine the best ways to advance ends, whether higher test scores or lower crime rates, that are set for them from above. Harambee Academy developed its Afrocentric course to improve student test scores, but also to bolster staff morale, engender student commitment to education, increase parental involvement, and enhance school discipline. Its LSC and school community set these goals for the school after substantial reflection on its context and particular strengths and weaknesses, and in response to the centralized requirement that each school construct a coherent mission as part of its plan. Similarly, the residents and police of Lakeville targeted the park in part because of incidents of crime, but also because they knew that it could become a rich addition to the public life of the neighborhood. Much more than new managerial strategies, whether high-stakes testing or COMPSTAT, accountable autonomy encourages the incorporation of local values and knowledge into public decisions.

A third difference stems from considerations about the trustworthiness of public officials and the mechanisms that hold them accountable to the broader public. The new managerial strategies rely upon the integrity and efficacy of highly placed officials who establish the standards of success and stipulate the consequences of failure. In environments where agency heads and their staffs are highly effective and well respected, this delegation and confidence may be warranted. In contexts where the rifts between the government and the public are greater, however, and marked by distrust or a history of failure and disappointment, reentrusting central authority to control subordinates and transcend ignominious legacies may seem less prudent. The history of policing and many other public services in Chicago and numerous other cities certainly contains many scandals, complaints, and failures that feed such distrust.

Accountable autonomy meets this trust deficit by building direct avenues of communication and oversight between local officials and the citizens they serve. The principal of Harambee Academy answers to an elected LSC that writes, monitors, and chooses whether or not to renew his contract. The officers in Lakeville meet monthly with residents and report on actions taken to implement various public-safety strategies and their outcomes. Low-level officials are thus doubly accountable. From above, supervisors monitor their performance and techniques and call them to account when necessary, as with the new managerial strategies. From below, citizens and clients participate directly in determining, implementing, and reviewing the problem-solving strategies in partnership with local officials.

1.4. Origins: Civic Engagement, Pragmatism, and Deliberative Democracy

While market-based reforms stem primarily from insights in economics and new methods of public organization derive from the field of management practice and related scholarship, empowered participation extends three traditions centered on investigations of society and democracy: civic engagement, pragmatism, and deliberation.

Interest in society's contribution to democratic governance in America dates famously to Alexis de Tocqueville's celebration of citizens' propensity toward self-help and habit of "forever forming associations" in the nineteenth century (Tocqueville 1969, 513). Recent work examining social capital and civic organizations, perhaps most notably that of Robert Putnam (1993, 1996, 2000) and Theda Skocpol (1999), importantly has brought the associative habits of citizens back into the forefront of scholarly and public concern. Though their findings are not without controversy, both of these scholars contend that in recent decades Americans have become more private and less social. In Putnam's language, stocks of "social capital"—norms, networks, and associations—are drying up. One main contribution of their work is to track the rise and decline of associations and individual participation in them. This research also argues that civic participation offers a kind of social education in which citizens learn to trust and work with one another that better enables them to act collectively for common ends. Since healthy democracy is itself composed of a multitude of such collective efforts and transactions, they argue that the ebb of civic-engagement decreases the quality of public life and state action (Putnam 1993).

With a few important exceptions, civic-engagement scholarship has not yet generated compelling accounts of how public policy and institutional design might reverse these trends of civic deterioration (Hirst 1994; Cohen and Rogers 1995). Reforms in the direction of empowered participation attempt to reciprocally connect public policy with civic engagement at points where particular social problems arise. The police and school-governance reform strategies in Chicago open up previously insular municipal agencies to public input. In doing so, they invite residents to generate and deploy social capital to make their neighborhoods safe and improve their schools. As we shall see, many people respond to this call, engaging with officials and other community members in attempts to solve public problems, because they believe that they may be able to make a difference through participation. Reforms that foster voice and empower citizens to solve problems urgent to them may thus increase the public returns from social capital by generating concrete and highly valued public goods.

While many scholars of social capital treat engagement as a highly fungible and multipurpose good, this account of empowered participation also extends pragmatism, a second tradition that emphasizes contexts, the impact of particular problems, and how efforts to address them often transform citizens, their associations, and public policies. In *The Public and Its Problems*, John Dewey laid out an ideal form of governance in which democratic institutions and cultural habits of thought enable citizens and experts to act publicly to solve their collective problems, and to recognize and comprehend the surprising consequences of their actions (1927). Since the effects of joint actions in complex environments can never be completely foretold, perhaps the most crucial capacity of a modern democracy is its ability to reformulate strategies, policy instuments, frameworks, interests, and even values and ends in light of such surprises. For him, this participatory, social, and creative feedback was the essence of democracy: a democratic public exists when individuals in society can collectively recognize and sensibly respond to the problems that arise from their interactions with one another.

Critically, however, he lamented the stagnancy and inability of political forms to enable this feedback in the face of rapidly changing economy and society. Citizens in preindustrial America may have been able to keep abreast of public affairs and express their will through the machinery of parties and elections, but these institutions had proven woefully inadequate to the challenges of modern governance with its large scale, diversity, and technical complexity. The problem of the modern public—and the cause of its incoherence—was that citizens, alone and together, were for the most part bewildered when they contemplated affairs of state and their relationship to it. An effective and democratic public would be one in which citizens felt the actions of government, understood the relationship of polities to these effects, discussed the connections between these ends and means, and in turn were connected through democratic arrangements to a state that respected their discussions. In contrast to this ideal of civic engagement, he thought that available social and political institutions did not enable citizens to organize themselves into publics capable of understanding, responding to, and directing their state in this way, and so governance—now largely the province of experts—was cut loose from the tether of democratic guidance. The spheres of state and society had lost their reciprocal linkages.

Despite a recent renaissance of interest in Dewey's pragmatism and his public philosophy, this "problem of the public," as he put it, remains largely unanswered (Westbrook 1991; Bernstein 1992; Stever 1993; Evans 2000). Though it was the central puzzle for Dewey and his progressive cohort, contemporary scholars have for the most part shied away from answering, or even asking, how state and society might be pragmatically reconnected. That is, what public policies can improve the capacity of citizens to sense and understand the effects of state action, on one hand, and empower them to improve it by incorporating its lessons, on the other? The institutional design of accountable autonomy offers one potential answer. Public action organized through participatory planning—rather than through hierarchy, market, or expert devolution—allowed the residents and officers in Lakeville, for example, to develop highly tailored local strategies based on their reflective understandings. A feedback loop that was compact in terms of time, geography, and levels of administration allowed these residents to observe the consequences of their strategies, learn from those though collective discussion, and thereby improve the quality of their problem-solving.

If empowered participation draws from civic-society research answers to questions about who should act and from pragmatism suggestions about what reform designs might be appropriate and effective, deliberative democracy suggests how strategies ought be formulated and collective decisions made. In different ways, political theorists such as Jürgen Habermas (1989, 1992, 1996), Joshua Cohen (1988, 1989, 1996), John Dryzek (1990), and James Fishkin (1991, 1995) offer an attractive formulation in which public decisions ought to be made, or at least steered, by citizens reasoning and persuading one another about the values or course of action that they should pursue together. This deliberative view contrasts with decision processes that attempt to aggregate individual opinions or preferences into a single choice, for instance through voting, majority rule, and other adversarial processes (Riker 1982; Cohen 1988). It also clearly differs from arrangements in which power is delegated to authoritative experts.

Proponents of deliberation argue that enabling those who must live with the consequences of a decision to make it together—struggling to reach mutual understanding, if not agreement, through discussion—offers several advantages over both adversarial and expert decision-making. For instance, the information and creativity that often grows out of discussion may improve the quality of decisions. Outcomes that take into account the reasons why participants support various courses of action—rather than simply tallying votes, money, or power—may thereby become more fair and just. Citizens themselves may become wiser and more understanding and accepting of different views and preferences after encountering them in discourse. Finally, even when some participants disagree with group deliberations, they may be more easily reconciled to the outcomes because others have justified the bases of their positions in good faith. The Harambee and Lakeville experiences illustrate how local participatory planning can reap some of these benefits.

As an empirical investigation of a concrete set of institutional reforms that utilize direct deliberation, empowered participation extends this line of research in two main ways. First, many of these theorists have thought that fair deliberation requires demanding and rarely realized preconditions—as economic or social equality, wealth, or shared values and a homogenous culture, for example. By examining deliberation in the context of Chicago's poor and often conflicted neighborhoods, this investigation explores whether the often distant ideal of deliberative democracy can be applied fruitfully to urgent contemporary public dilemmas. Second, the conceptual development of deliberative political theory has come at the expense of investigating the practical institutional forms that might realize the ideal in actual organizations and agencies. The chapters that follow begin to fill this gap by examining a range of institutional mechanisms in Chicago school and police reform that sometimes help, while at other times hinder, deliberation.

1.5. Mechanisms of Effectiveness

Those sympathetic to the radical democratic tradition may find account-able autonomy attractive because of its provisions for citizen voice, influ-ence, and deliberation. This institutional design, compared to those of markets and public hierarchies, increases the opportunities for citizens to exercise voice in decisions that are important to them. It may also yield psychological and educative benefits often attributed to participation, such as contributing to participants' political skills, sense of efficacy, and solidarity (Pateman 1970). In dealing with critical institutions like schools and police departments, however, many will gauge the desirability of par-ticular reform proposals according to practical consequences that are less directly associated with participation and deliberation. The democratic benefits of citizen voice and political socialization may be purchased at too high a price if empowered participatory-governance methods turn out to be less effective than market reforms or new managerial strategies.

Therefore, empowered participation must offer a practical account of how its organizational prescription will generate effective public action. Insights from research in civic engagement, pragmatic participation, and deliberative democracy contribute to such an account. In public-action environments where there is a history of distrust between officials and citizens, or where conditions are diverse and unstable, four mechanisms may offer decisive advantages over markets and hierarchies: directed dis-cretion, institutionalized innovation, cross-functional coordination, and studied trust.

As a consequence of diversity in their problem environments, tasks nec-essary to achieve a given broad public aim vary from one situation to another. In the field of primary education, the most urgent task for one school might be teaching English-language skills, for another computer literacy, and for yet a third dealing with truancy and discipline issues. The optimal pedagogical method for one school might be a progressive, Deweyan, "whole-language" approach, while rote methods of Direct In-struction better suit a second (Gardner 1993; Druffin 1996). Policing situ-ations are just as diverse—residents of some communities may perceive the police as little more than an occupying army, while residents from other neighborhoods might see them as an ally against encroaching disor-der. Such variation makes it difficult for a centralized body of experts or managers to accurately specify a uniform set of tasks or procedures that will effectively advance even the most general of public ends. Due in part to these complications of diversity, hierarchical attempts to direct street-level actors frequently cannot guide action because their rules are either overdeterminant and contradictory or underdetermined and dependent upon the skillful use of discretion. Michael Lipsky writes that

Rules may actually be an impediment to supervision. They may be so volumi-
nous and contradictory that they can only be enforced or invoked selectively.
In most public welfare departments, regulations are encyclopedic, yet at the
same time, they are constantly being changed. With such rules adherence to
anything but the most basic and fundamental precepts of eligibility cannot be
expected. Police behavior is so highly specified by statutes and regulation that
policemen are expected to invoke the law selectively. . . . Similarly, federal civil-
rights compliance officers have so many mandated responsibilities in comparison to their resources that they have been free to determine their own priorities.
(Lipsky 1980, 14)

If tasks cannot be specified, then routines cannot be formalized and relevant performance cannot be monitored. As is commonly known by students of bureaucracies and subordinates who work in them, low-level
agency staff fill the gaps in these formal procedures through their own
discretion (Downs 1967; Lipsky 1980; Wilson 1989). Sometimes managers have the foresight to grant discretion; at other times operatives seize
it. Such discretionary gaps are inevitable in any bureaucracy, but grow
larger with the increasing diversity of problem environments because formal routines loose prescriptive purchase.

The standard response to such discretion is professional indoctrination
and training. If successful, indoctrination reduces the need for close supervision by instilling enthusiasm and codes of ethics in ground-level agents.
This training attempts to enable agents to cope with diverse situations by
providing them with a wider repertoire of routines than can be specified
through bureaucratic routine and by developing senses of professional
judgment.

But there are at least two reasons to think that a hybrid scheme of well-
trained professionals organized in a bureaucracy of loose formal routines
will be hampered in conditions of diversity. First, the professional model
still presumes a body of experts who possess effective routines and can
train others in these techniques. Perhaps due to radically diverse conditions, there are many areas of public action in which expert prescriptions
seem irrelevant or ineffective. Thus, "many novice [teachers] look back
at their training and complain it was insufficient for the challenges they
face" (Catalyst Staff 1996). Standard advice to rookie cops on the first
day of the job from veterans is to "forget what you learned in the police
academy" (Wilson 1989, 37). Absent a set of master routines, then, professional bureaucracy has no generative mechanism for practical knowledge beyond informal training provided by experience on the street. And
since the reasons for bureaucracy's effectiveness stand on its capacity to
implement articulated routines, informal experience is simply an explanation of how bureaucracies (don't) work, and not a justification for them.
Presuming that this source of incapacity could be overcome, discretion

also erodes democratic accountability. Emancipated from the strictures of the center, organizations in which street-level officials enjoy wide discretion may become more effective. But since professional socialization can never be complete, some may use their discretion to shirk or otherwise abuse the public's trust.

The design of accountable autonomy responds to these difficulties with the mechanism of *directed discretion*. It recommends increasing discretion for street-level officials with respect to formal rules and centralized oversight, but harnessing that discretion to the achievement of public ends through internal and external direction. Internally, citizens should be invited to deliberate with street-level officials, in forums like beat meetings and local school councils, on how public power and resources should be deployed. Externally, these group deliberations, subsequent actions, and the results of those actions should be fully documented and available to the wider public. These two provisions create avenues of accountability from the bottom up—through local citizen participation—and from the outside in—through public transparency—to help assure that street-level officials utilize their irreducible discretion to advance public ends.

To *generate innovations and diffuse them*, conventional bureaucracies rely upon policy specialists, markets utilize entrepreneurs driven by competition, and the new public management employs well-trained, but closely watched, line officials and their supervisors. Several institutional features of accountable autonomy create potentially superior capacities for responsive innovation. Devolution and heightened local authority liberate operational units from headquarters' constraints, thus creating the space and potential for constructive innovation. At the local level, deliberative problem-solving encourages constant reevaluation of received procedures to identify more effective strategies; in James Fearon's (1998) terms, deliberation may help decision-makers to overcome their constraints of bounded rationality. Furthermore, the feedback loops connecting decision, action, and results are quite small, and so enhance the potential for rapid trial-and-error learning compared to lengthy chains of hierarchical command or the relatively slow responses from price and demand signals.

At the level of the participants, accountable autonomy reduces the alienation that accompanies demands for change from centralized authority by fusing task conception and execution at the level of the individual operator. In hierarchical schemes, waves of innovation devised at the top wash down on a rank-and-file that often receives them as ill-considered and often impractical (Lipsky 1980). It is unsurprising, therefore, that lack of ground-level "buy-in" often hampers the implementation of innovations in bureaucracies. Agent participation in deliberative problem-solving sets the content of innovative strategies. Having emerged from discussions between citizens and local officials, strategies and policies are more likely to enjoy grassroots support and enthusiasm. Innovation becomes part of the core job responsibility rather than being an occasional idiosyncratic requirement. In accountable autonomy, part of being a good teacher, policeman, principal, other public servant, or citizen requires being able to continuously envision how the job or the organization might do better, explain that vision, and then help implement it.

Finally, accountable autonomy potentially diffuses successful innovations quite rapidly to enable a kind of system-wide learning. While its provisions for devolution liberate indigenous creativity, its centralized apparatus can identify local successes and make their techniques known to others by pooling disparate experiences and making them accessible to others who might benefit (Dorf and Sabel 1998; Sabel, Fung, and Karkkainen 2000). This device is widely known in other contexts as the benchmarking of best practices.

A third mechanism in accountable autonomy might be called *cross-functional coordination*. Every organization and system must deal with complexity by breaking daunting tasks into more manageable parts, and then by developing divisions of labor and expertise appropriate to those subtasks. So, the public tasks of city management might be broken up into fire, police, schools, transportation, sewers, sanitation, and other agencies, each with their core competencies. Solutions to many urban problems, however, require jointly coordinated action on the part of two or more agencies, or between public agencies and private actors in civil society or the economy. The logic of rigid division and specialization, constraining both new management and market-based reform strategies, makes these kinds of problems seem complex and even insoluble. Deliberative local problem-solving, however, can facilitate the recombination of public and private parties necessary to overcome these barriers of complexity.

Problems that lie between the core competencies and responsibilities of several agencies are complex because effective remedial action requires coordination between horizontally separate agencies. Because no particular agency centrally bears official responsibility, all lack motive and opportunity to solve such problems. In this way, bureaucracies purchase economies of scale at the expense of scope; each specializes in a particular policy area and develops a stock of procedures and techniques to address the canonical problems that arise in that arena. Problems seem complex, then, when they do not fit these canonical types. In accountable autonomy, however, public action often acquires a more open approach, in which the scope of a solution is determined (on the fly, as it were) by the particular problems to be addressed. In Lakeville, for example, residents developed a solution involving the architectural redesign of a city park to what began as a policing issue.

A fourth way in which this democratic reform path enhances the effectiveness of public action is by creating a framework of discussion and action in which participants, citizens and officials alike, can earn each others' *trust through tests of collaboration.* The bureaucratic principle of professional autonomy demands insulation from public, politicized, nonprofessional "interference." In many urban areas, this insularity has fostered mistrust and conflict between citizens and public servants by hardening the identities and interests of each and pitting them against one another. From the perspective of officials, citizens seem unreasonably demanding, their suggestions uninformed, desires contradictory (e.g., civil rights and safe streets), their engagement unconstructive, whiny, and clueless. Several close observers of law enforcement, for example, identify these beliefs as constitutive of police culture: (1) "No one understands the real nature of police work. . . . No one outside police service . . . can comprehend what we have to do. The public is generally naive about police work"; (2) "We have to stick together. Everyone else . . . seems to be out to make our job difficult"; and (3) "Members of the public are basically unsupportive and unreasonably demanding. They all seem to think they know our job better than we do. They only want us when they need something done" (Sparrow, Moore, and Kennedy 1990). Though the levels of public trust in government varies widely, broad segments of the public hold large public agencies such as schools and police departments in low esteem and lack faith in them.

Accountable autonomy offers deliberative problem-solving to citizens and public servants as a method for reconstructing their trust in one another and modifying their respective behavior in ways that warrant trust (Sabel 1993). In contrast to the bureaucratic separation of state from society, it throws citizens and their agents together at the grassroots level. Joint problem-solving is an occasion for participants to probe each others' agendas, motives, and commitments and to identify and expand real regions of overlap. In the context of public safety, citizens may not trust police because they perceive a wide gap between what police should be doing and what they actually do. In the process, citizens can demand that police justify particular actions, or, more commonly, that they take action. If police cannot justify a particular course, reasonableness demands that they change future behavior. When such demands arise under bureaucracy, street-level agents can "pass the buck" by claiming that rules and red tape do not permit them to change dysfunctional routines. Accountable autonomy, however, removes this excuse by empowering grassroots agents to implement results of deliberation. On the other hand, police may be able to justify apparently unreasonable behaviors by providing additional information or deeper explanations.

Similarly, repeated interaction between citizens and officials in deliberative problem-solving allows each to ascertain the others' commitment to a shared goal—say, public safety or education—by observing levels of follow-through. Anecdotes about such studied trust-building—following the dictum to "trust but verify"—recur frequently in tales of participation in community policing and school governance. Initial meetings between police and residents begin as shouting matches, where each suspects that the other side had no real commitment to supposedly common goals, and then transform slowly and tentatively into problem-solving. Often, citizens and officers surprise one another by fulfilling their commitments, sometimes tenaciously. In this way, citizens and public officials can gradually and verifiably build the mutual confidence necessary for partnership and cooperation.

1.6. Sources of Fairness

Apart from the effectiveness of these public-sector organizations, a second crucial axis of evaluation concerns the fairness of their policies and actions. In the ideal, fairness in a public-school system would mean that every child enjoys an equal opportunity to gain a high-quality education for his later educational, professional, and personal pursuits. In public safety, the ideal might be that residents, regardless of location or personal characteristics, face similar and low risks of criminal victimization or nuisance. No urban area comes close to meeting these ideals of fairness. Because accountable autonomy prescribes substantial devolution of power to decentralized groups, however, some may suspect that this reform path will exacerbate unfair and inequitable outcomes.[11] The first risk is that decentralization will amplify the gap between differently situated groups, for instance those in wealthy neighborhoods versus those in poor ones. It may, for example, create opportunities for voice and creativity of which wealthy or well-educated residents make good use, but that are inaccessible to poorer citizens. Beyond intergroup inequities, decentralization may facilitate the domination of vocal or entrenched factions within particular groups.

Much of the inequality in service provision, opportunities, and outcomes across different neighborhoods stems from the background of social and economic disparity that characterizes all urban environments in the United States. Children from disadvantaged families and neighborhoods face much greater barriers to obtaining decent education and their parents suffer greater risks of criminal victimization due to social factors that stand quite apart from the details of how school systems or police departments are organized, governed, or even financed. It is worse than wishful to think that any administrative reform could approach the ideal of fairness without broader measures to alter this background. Some social choices, such as the practice of funding education from ad valorem taxes on real estate, no doubt reproduce these differences (*San Antonio v. Rodriguez* 1972; Gutmann 1987). The appropriate question for administrative reform, however, is whether some paths might dampen the effects of background inequalities between neighborhoods and groups and so move toward the goal of fairness despite these daunting socioeconomic obstacles.

Accountable-autonomy reforms attempt to advance intergroup fairness through two distinctive routes. First, it should be recognized that effectiveness within school and police systems is itself an important component of fairness. One primary source of urban inequality is precisely the existence of effective schools and policing in some areas but not others. To the extent that these reforms improve the quality of service in disadvantaged areas, therefore, they contribute importantly to fairness. While bureaucratic, market-based, and new management methods also seek to enhance the fairness of public systems in this way, accountable autonomy distinctively creates channels for the least advantaged to act constructively against this unfairness. It attempts to reverse the adage that those who need democracy most use it least by creating space for efficacious voice at the most basic levels. Those low on the socioeconomic ladder, it is hoped, will use these channels to articulate demands for effective service, and for resources that they themselves can use to help direct and provide that service.

Through centralized mechanisms of support and monitoring, agencies that adopt the accountable autonomy–reform course can prioritize the neediest groups for various kinds of assistance. Given the limited resources of public organizations, they must make important choices about allocation and redistribution. A natural principle to guide this allocation in accountable autonomy is to redistribute centrally pooled energies to assist the least capable groups. In the Chicago school-governance reforms, one manifestation of this principle is the central-office policy of identifying the schools whose students perform least proficiently on standardized tests and then channeling additional supervision and resources to them. In a similar vein, the least capable neighborhood groups and police beats might be prioritized in the allocation of personnel and material for training, mobilization, and technical assistance. Finally, the mechanisms that diffuse innovations in accountable autonomy link the most successful to the least by making the creativity and good fortune of the former available to the latter. The extent to which particular agencies enact this distributive principle of channeling assistance to the most needy of course depends upon numerous contingencies such as political will, social mobilization, and committed administration. In this regard, it resembles the conditional character of fairness in other reform strategies, for example the generosity of vouchers in market-based education proposals and the ethical disposition of high and low public officials under new public-management reforms.

A second kind of unfairness, less noted in administrative-reform discussions but equally important, concerns the character of action within groups. More difficult to evaluate than intergroup equity, the fairness of decision-making within localities is determined by the extent to which the perspectives of relevant parties are taken into account and their interests advanced. On this understanding, it would be unfair if the principal of Harambee Elementary had, for example, reorganized the school along Afrocentric grounds over the objections of staff and parents. It would have been unfair for a police commander to decide that speeding was Lakeville's priority policing concern if beat officers and residents worried most about drug activity in the park. Note that this conception of fairness differs from both market-driven and new-management perspectives. In the former, these administrative decisions pose no particular problem of fairness because consumers of public services can choose another school. The latter typically privileges the official judgments of correct agendas and strategies above the views of untrained citizens and users.

The participatory approach of accountable autonomy, however, puts professionals and citizens on an equal footing by charging them to develop problem-solving strategies and priorities together. This process is deliberative in that each must try to convince the other of the wisdom of its preferred course of action. It is often the case that principals and teachers offer greater contributions than parents in the formulation of instructional and curricular strategies, but these strategies often improve in the course of justification to and reflection with parents and others. One danger of this kind of deliberative problem-solving is that the outcomes will be no more fair, or substantially different, from choices made under market-driven or purely expert arrangements. Professionals may dazzle the untrained or uninitiated and assert their programs without any genuine discussion. Quite a different threat is that troublesome factions of citizens or professionals will obstruct the constructive, and perhaps wiser, recommendations of principals or police commanders. Both courses lead to unfair outcomes—the former because the views of some are improperly discounted and the latter because a faction prevents progress from which most would benefit.

Accountable autonomy addresses both of these kinds of domination by attempting to create open deliberative processes of agenda-setting and problem-solving. It does so first by altering basic administrative routines not only to devolve authority and open new channels of access to nonprofessional citizens, but also to ensure that procedures and norms of deliberation govern the exercise of local power. This effort begins with the creation and diffusion of training for deliberation, facilitation, and problem-solving methodologies to groups like LSCs and beat teams. After equipping groups and individuals to deliberate, it then relies upon them to utilize these tools and take the norms of reasonableness and receptiveness seriously rather than pursuing narrow interests and goals. Doing so may be enough to avoid the expert domination or factional paralysis that often characterizes small-group interactions. When the self-regulation of local groups through deliberative norms and procedures fails, however, centralized methods should detect these outcomes and attempt to correct them. External review of problem-solving procedures, for example, can help detect the undue influence and control of professionals or factions, especially when those who are excluded voice procedural complaints. Performance monitoring can help to detect paralysis or inaction. In both cases, external sanctions and supportive interventions can help set deliberation back on track.

1.7. Exploring Accountable Autonomy, in Theory and Practice

The sections above contend that empowered participation offers an attractively democratic course of institutional reform that departs from the received organizational templates of hierarchical bureaucracy, marketization, and the new public managerialism. This contention is composed of three general linked claims: (1) institutional reforms that follow the design of accountable autonomy can spur (2) robust direct citizen participation and deliberation that (3) contributes to the fairness and effectiveness of governance outcomes through a variety of mechanisms. The chapters that follow explore each of these stages. A first set of questions relates the concepts of participation and deliberation to institutional designs. How do the institutional-design features of the CPD and CPS constitute deliberation, participation, and empowered voice for Chicago residents? In other words, how do organizational changes, new rights, and novel procedures translate these abstract, potentially attractive, notions into opportunities for citizens and street-level bureaucrats to join in urban governance: to exercise influence, learn about each other and their environment, and solve problems? And, as a matter of institutional history, why did the CPD and CPS develop in this participatory-democratic direction when their counterparts in other cities pursued new-managerialist or market-oriented strategies? A second set of questions concerns the quality of the democratic processes established by these institutional reforms. In particular, what is the character of participation and deliberation within these new institutional forms? Is participation highly biased toward better-off citizens, or unsustainably low, as some critics might expect? Does decision-making approach the ideal of *reasoned* decision-making, or do participants simply rely on their numbers, status, or expertise to exercise control? Finally, is there evidence that these reforms generate fair or effective outcomes by, for example, improving the quality of schools or safety in the streets?

The next two chapters establish the historical and conceptual foundations for this investigation by answering three questions. First, how did the CPD and CPS, which appeared to be quite hide-bound hierarchical agencies in the mid-1980s, come to embrace deliberative and participatory-democratic reforms in the 1990s? For both school reform and community policing, sophisticated nongovernmental organizations that were expert in education and public safety issues leveraged popular discontent to advance a reform agenda that focused on neighborhood involvement. Those who traditionally controlled the urban educational agenda—the Board of Education and the Chicago Teachers Union—were initially quite hostile to this reform course. With community policing, by contrast, police officials and the mayor embraced community policing and championed it as their own initiative.

In what ways did the 1988 LSC legislation and the development of CAPS in 1995 constitute empowered participation and deliberation? The model, even to the level of its central concepts of deliberation and civic engagement, contains theoretical abstractions that attempt to distill the underlying design principles and features of actual reforms. These are not part of the vocabulary that officials and citizens have used to describe their own efforts. Chapter 2 thus elaborates the idea of accountable autonomy by showing how the powers, procedures, and responsibilities that were placed upon citizens and street-level bureaucrats in individual schools and police beats by the reorganizations of the CPS and CPD do indeed formally institute devolution, citizen participation, and deliberative problem-solving at the neighborhood level.

The third chapter then explores the second part of accountable-autonomy institutions by describing the roles and functions of central authorities both conceptually and as they actually operate in the CPS and CPD. Whereas central powers in conventional bureaucratic models formulate, direct, and supervise subordinate units such as school personnel and beat officers, central authorities in both the CPS and CPD have developed mechanisms to support, monitor, and selectively intervene to bolster the problem-solving efforts of local deliberative bodies. This chapter shows how, as a design solution, these arrangements can address classic pitfalls of deliberative and participatory democracy such as parochialism, factionalism, elite domination, and paralysis. In their operationalization, however, both the CPS and CPD fall short of the ideal. One obstacle has been the difficulty of developing novel and effective management, support, and oversight mechanisms that depart from the conventional wisdoms of hierarchical supervision or market-like decentralization. A second, more fundamental block is that the reform visions and commitments within these organizations have oscillated between the distinctive Chicago path of deliberative participation and more conventional and insular managerial methods.

Given these formal provisions for grassroots engagement, who actually participates? As with any scheme for civic engagement and direct democracy, success depend upon the character of actual participation. The generation of fair and effective decisions and actions in accountable autonomy relies upon the involvement and collaboration of ordinary citizens and street-level officials. Outcomes depend not only upon the presence of citizens in the aggregate, but also upon the representativeness of those who choose to participate. The absence of citizens from poor neighborhoods or minority groups, for example, would indicate serious systemic malaise. Chapter 4 explores the quantitative shape of participation under the CPS and CPD reforms. Surprisingly, citizen engagement under Chicago school and police reform defies conventional explanations of political engagement that rely on socioeconomic status or resources as central predictors. People from poor neighborhoods, for example, participate as much or more than those from wealthy ones. Contrary to expectations of some critics of deliberation, women participate more than men. The chapter then presents city-wide participation data to develop an explanation that relies upon policy design: people from low-income neighborhoods participate when doing so yields tangible results in areas of urgent concern to them.

Though substantial levels of participation and the absence of severe bias are necessary conditions for fair and effective deliberative problem-solving, they are far from sufficient. Chapters 5 and 6 offer a more textured understanding of the strengths and pitfalls of deliberation by examining the course of participatory problem-solving as it unfolded over several years in six Chicago South Side neighborhoods. Generally, these case materials contribute much-needed empirical texture to the predominantly abstract and theoretical content of current debates about deliberative democracy. Specifically, these studies explore the micromechanisms, processes, and outcomes of actual deliberations. When, for example, is deliberation inclusive and reasonable? What conditions, on the other hand, generate factions, domination by elites, paralysis, or ignorance? Aside from the democratic quality of discursive local processes, these case studies also afford some purchase on questions about the administrative and technical contributions of accountable autonomy. Sections 1.5 and 1.6

above put forward some mechanisms through which institutions of accountable autonomy might generate fair and effective outcomes. When do actual deliberations about school and police governance employ such mechanisms to produce innovative solutions? When, on the other hand, does popular participation hamper the efforts of capable professionals or unfairly divert their energies to serve powerful constituencies at the expense of weaker ones?

Chapter 5 offers insight into these questions by examining actual problem-solving processes in three cases that differ along the dimension of economic wealth. Two cases analyze school-improvement planning and community policing in poor neighborhoods, and the third probes similar efforts in a wealthy school. Confirming the expectations and findings of previous inquiries, poor residents and their public servants do indeed find it more difficult to deliberate and solve public problems than do wealthy professionals. Even citizens and officials from poor neighborhoods act effectively under certain conditions, however. When they do, participatory opportunities and powers yield greater benefits for them than for their more well-off counterparts.

Beyond poverty, several political theorists have criticized deliberative democracy because it can allow culturally or economically advantaged participants to dominate and exploit vulnerable ones in diverse or socially conflicted contexts. Chapter 6 uses ethnographic evidence to explore the dynamics of deliberation in three internally diverse and balkanized environments. The first case study examines community policing in a neighborhood that is segregated between one group of professional and middle-class white residents and another of lower middle-class African-Americans. In a second neighborhood, all of the residents are relatively poor, but the relevant differences fall along racial and cultural lines: one group is African-American while the other is Hispanic. In the third, factions of parents and staff fought each other to a stalemate that paralyzed school governance. One central finding from these cases is that unguided laissez-faire discussion does indeed often result in domination of one group by another, but that facilitated and structured deliberation can generate improbable but constructive alliances between wealthy white professional residents, their lower middle–class African-American neighbors, Hispanic residents, and the local police that serve all of them.

The final chapter concludes by assessing Chicago's experiments with participatory and deliberative democracy and then turning to the question of generalization. Is the design of accountable autonomy limited to specific urban policy problems or even to the unique political conditions and history of Chicago? Or, it is applicable to a much broader range of governance challenges? Beyond the arenas of public education and policing, reforms that embrace many of the principles and elements of accountable autonomy have begun to emerge in arenas such as environmental regulation, municipal budgeting, and economic and social development. These diverse experiments illustrate how accountable autonomy, as a strategy of participatory-democratic, administrative reform is applicable to many areas of public concern in which market-based or hierarchical models seem inappropriate or ineffective. If the scope of accountable autonomy can be extended to an array of policy arenas, its multifarious application would create diverse opportunities to improve the quality of governance though citizen engagement. This, in turn, suggests an ideal of citizenship that lies between a fantastic ancient participatory ideal, in which every citizen ought to be engaged in all public matters, and the modern reality, in which few deeply or frequently participate in the affairs of state at all. The ideal of citizenship in accountable autonomy is one that respects the contemporary constraints and complex realities that prohibit a person from engaging all of the public problems that merit attention. It asks, however, that each consider at times stepping away from purely private pursuits to participate in public problem-solving around urgent issues of common concern. It does so by striving toward institutional reform that leverages such participation to amplify the wisdom and impact of public action. Simultaneously, this engagement empowers people to make governance an endeavor that is in part their own rather than a distant set of actions from which benefits are extracted or burdens suffered.

2

Down to the Neighborhoods

IN THE SHORT SPAN of a decade, the organization of two crucial Chicago administrative agencies—the police department and public schools—underwent fundamental transformations. They moved from insular, hierarchical bureaucracies in the Weberian cast to admit new and empowered forms of citizen participation, public deliberation, and street-level discretion. Charting the course of that transition shows how the top-down administrative structures set in place by Progressive reform were unable to cope with the increasing challenges and demands placed on city government. These crises of organizational performance opened windows of opportunity for reformers. Many other public agencies in America experienced similar performance gaps, but responded to them through market-based or professionalized strategies outlined in the previous chapter. Chicago embarked on a different course, however, in part because reformers there—especially those associated with community and civic organizations—argued that these difficulties would be best addressed through a kind of participatory democracy and community control. From the perspective of historical transformation, these parallel developments in policing and public education illustrate one path along which democratic reform movements can transform bureaucratic organizations. Reflecting upon the design of these concrete institutions, developed in the name of civic engagement, also illuminates how abstract ideals like deliberation, participation, and citizenship might be advanced under the decidedly nonideal conditions of contemporary urban governance.

2.1. Perils of Patronage: School Governance in the Machine Era

At the roughest level of detail, the story of Chicago's public schools over the first half of this century follows that of the other big-city school systems. Various schooling models—sometimes locally controlled, sometimes volunteer, most often dominated by local "machine" politicians—gradually and painfully converged into the "one best system" as judged by a rising class of professional educators (Tyack 1974; Katz 1987). This model borrowed its major elements from what were widely regarded as the most efficient practices of the modern corporation at the beginning of the century: centralized supervision and direction of personnel; staff qualifications based on standards and common tests; functional hierarchical differentiation and specialization; careful measurement of administrative inputs and outputs with particular attention to costs; and insulation of the educational organization from political control and public scrutiny (Callahan 1962; Tyack 1974, 126–76; Katz 1987, 60–65). To be sure, the diffusion and consolidation of this model took place over decades, perhaps beginning in Boston and finishing in Chicago (Katz 1987, 58–100).

The most common historical interpretation of this diffusion, which we accept here, is that two powerful opposing forces fought over whether to adopt this model. On one side stood city politicians, for whom control over school lands (Herrick 1971, 75–79; 104–6) and the teaching, clerical, and maintenance work within burgeoning school systems provided rich spoils that could be given to political supporters. On the other side stood Progressive reformers, led by a growing cadre of professional educators, who argued that these school systems would operate effectively only if they ran according to an autonomous professional logic and not at the behest of local politicians. By the midpoint of the twentieth century, educational professionals had largely wrested control from city and ward politicians and then used that control to establish the hierarchical bureaucracies that they viewed as the most efficient form.[1]

At the close of the nineteenth century, however, city politicians accurately considered the rules and resources of the Chicago school system as theirs to manipulate and allocate. According to an 1893 law, the Chicago schools were to be administered by a Board of Education consisting of twenty-one individuals appointed by the mayor and confirmed by aldermen on the city council. One of the major duties of this board was to select a superintendent of schools, charged with overseeing day-to-day operations. For decades after the 1893 provisions, however, the superintendent's office was subordinated to a school board that did not hesitate to terminate uncooperative school executives. These institutional arrangements created a system that served the needs of political officials but not necessarily those of education. At the time, one close observer of the Chicago schools noted two deficiencies in this system. First, an appointed board of lay citizens would inevitably serve partisan political, not educational, interests:

> [The Board of Education's] members continued to be appointed by the mayor with the consent of the common council. That this practice has borne evil fruit the analysis in the subsequent pages will prove. It has bound the school system to the city hall and has subordinated the interests of education to the vagaries and vicissitudes of partisan politics. It has fostered the tradition that board members are creatures of the mayor and must either do his bidding or resign. (Counts 1928, 39)

In addition to a subservient lay board with no special educational expertise, these arrangements also created a school superintendent, who was in most cases an educational professional, without power:

The appearance of a vigorous superintendent has always meant trouble. Since the opening of the century, the two outstanding personalities to stand at the head of the Chicago schools have been Mrs. [Ella Flagg] Young and Mr. [William] McAndrew. Both combined courage and energy with a high sense of professional obligation; both sooner or later were forced into a bitter struggle with the board in defense of their schools; both were ultimately ousted from the superintendency. Although they differed radically in their educational philosophies and school policies, their careers while in office were equally unhappy, and they shared the same fate. (Counts 1928, 52)

These official positions on the Board of Education and in the office of the superintendent, the laws regulating the Chicago school system, and school policy itself were spoils of political battle to be won by the forces of partisan political machines seeking to stabilize their base of support, on one side, and the forces of Progressive municipal reform—educational professionals, good-government groups such as the Chicago Women's Club, and the city's business interests in the Chicago Association of Commerce—on the other. To be sure, there were cross-cutting issues and associations that spanned both sides on particular issues; vocational education (Counts 1928, 166–68) and teachers' voice in educational policy (Herrick 1971, 115–20), but the principal enduring cleavage in these decades, especially in the public eye, concerned the professional autonomy and organization of the school system. These battles between the Progressive forces and the political machines manifested themselves most visibly in the scandals, critical blue-ribbon reports, and brief, violently terminated tenures of school superintendents by machine-controlled boards.

In 1898, for example, Carter H. Harrison, then mayor of Chicago, appointed a commission of local notables to study the organization of public schools. The commission's report became known as the Harper Report for its chair, the first president of the University of Chicago, William Rainey Harper (Harper 1898). Chief among its recommendations were measures that would quickly become common to the Progressive movement for municipal reform: insulate school-system operations from nefarious political influences. The commission recommended that the board be reduced from twenty-one to eleven members, that the terms of board members be extended, and that they should represent the city at large rather than specific sections of it. Furthermore, the board should concern itself with policy matters and delegate all administrative functions to the superintendent of schools. The term of the superintendent should be extended from one year to six, and he should only be removed from office on the basis of specific, written charges, and then only with a two-thirds vote of the board (Herrick 1971, 83–87). The board also recommended that teachers be hired and promoted on the basis of objective examinations and took issue with existing politicized hiring practices.

Interestingly, many of the Harper Report's recommendations departed from the command-and-control, bureaucratic measures that would characterize more mature Progressive thought. Like much of the rest of the Progressive movement at this early moment, there was no clear commitment to a single organizational form. While one tendency leaned toward a more participatory democratic mode (Mattson 1998), the other tended to the hierarchical bureaucratic model that eventually dominated (Callahan 1962; Tyack 1974; Katz 1987). The Harper Report moved ambiguously between these two poles. Toward the former, for example, it recommended the establishment of a system of teachers' councils throughout the city that would advise the Board of Education on matters of school organization, administration, and curriculum. Very few of the recommendations of the Harper Report would be implemented for decades after its release.

The report did very little to protect the school board or superintendent from partisan attack. In 1898, the year of the report's release, a democratically appointed board refused to renew the appointment of Superintendent Anthony Lane, whom without evidence they accused of having misused his influence. His successor, E. Benjamin Andrews, opposed the board on several appointments and promotions and for his troubles was also fired several months before the end of his term. His successor, Edwin J. Cooley, made himself known as a creature of the board, and served until his voluntary resignation in 1909 (Herrick 1971, 80–81). During Cooley's tenure, however, the mayor removed several board members for insubordination in 1907; they were later reinstated through court action (Counts 1928, 12). Ella Flagg Young, a respected veteran of the Chicago schools and student of John Dewey, served as the system's superintendent from 1909 until 1915, when newly elected mayor William Hale Thompson opposed her renewal due to her independence and support for organized teachers.

Following a series of public scandals, Democrat William Dever was elected Mayor in 1923. He appointed seven reform members to the school board, who in turn chose William A. McAndrew to be school superintendent. McAndrew had served as teacher and principal in several Chicago schools, but then had moved on to posts around the nation and eventually to deputy superintendent of the New York City school system. In McAndrew, Chicago had its first fully formed advocate of the hierarchical, bureaucratic model of school organization derived from the efficiency experts of industry. Counts, writing just after the end of McAndrew's tenure, observes that:

The ideal of business efficiency seems to have dominated the entire administration. Mr. McAndrew entered upon the duties of his office with the definite assumption that slackness, indolence, and general inefficiency characterized the conduct of the schools of Chicago. . . . He adopted the slogan, "Every man on the job"; he reduced the number of holidays and dismissals; he introduced the time check for all employees . . . . he emphasized the use of objective tests in the appraisal of the work of teachers and principals. . . . he brought about a fundamental re-organization of the administrative system. (Counts 1928, 73)

McAndrew himself writes that, "A system directly touching a total of 545,929 pupils and paid members must [of necessity] work clumsily on the old village conception. It must adopt the motto of other big businesses: 'Organize, deputize, supervise' " (Illinois Department of Education 1924, 10). McAndrew set about implementing this model of educational reform immediately and autocratically. He abolished the teacher's council system that had been recommended by the Harper Report and initiated by Ella Flagg Young. He instituted a system of "close supervision" of teachers under which they clocked-in on a monitoring sheet four times a day, and he constantly berated their indolence and sloth in public addresses (Herrick 1971, 154–55). "Supervision became one of the watchwords of Mr. McAndrew's administration. This again was part of the program of efficiency, for it recognized the virtues of special professional training and subordinated the inexperienced and the unskilled to the direction of the expert," writes Counts (1928, 78). Furthermore, he instituted the "Platoon Plan" of school operation, pioneered in Gary, Indiana, that aimed to increase the efficiency with which the school building would be utilized. Under this system, the building would be used for a greater percentage of the day and accommodate more students through the use of rotating classes and the extension of the school day into shifts (Callahan 1962, 126–47). Finally, in accordance with Progressive reform tenets, McAndrew sought to insulate the operations of the school system from political influence:

Perhaps to be classed with his policy of business efficiency . . . was Mr. McAndrew's steadfast opposition to all political influence in schools. One of the cardinal principles of his theory of administration was that professional decisions should not be subservient to politics. Strict adherence to this principle in any large city is extremely difficult; strict adherence to it in Chicago is all but impossible. Yet that Mr. McAndrew sought vigorously and with temporary success to enforce this principle, few informed persons would deny. (Counts 1928, 82).

McAndrew lasted until 1927, when the former Mayor Thompson ran again and defeated the Progressive incumbent Devers. A school board appointed by Thompson pressed charges against McAndew in the board's own chambers, and voted to dismiss him in 1928. A circuit court later ruled that McAndrew had been unjustly dismissed, but the process had stolen his desire to serve. While several of his administrative reforms took root, patronage needs of the machines continued to dominate school operations. Teachers enjoyed tenure privileges, but three thousand jobs in clerical, maintenance, and janitorial duties were available for patronage functions. When the depression years brought a fiscal crisis for the Chicago school system, Thompson's board responded by cutting instructional services while leaving most of the nonteaching patronage jobs intact (Herrick 1971, 187–90; 209–25).

From 1933 until 1947, Chicago politics was dominated by the Kelly-Nash machine, named for its principals Mayor Edward J. Kelly and Democratic County Chairman Patrick A. Nash. This organization was one of the "country's most powerful and longest lasting machines" (Erie 1988, 109). Over this period, Democratic bosses continued to utilize the school system to feed their political bases. In order to divert city funds to more pliable areas of public expenditure, the board gutted the school system in 1933 by passing a measure that reduced kindergarten classes by 50 percent, dismissed 10 percent of the teaching force, mandated that each principal supervise two schools, halted textbook purchases, and discontinued athletic, music, special education, printing, and physical education programs. In 1936, investigators revealed a scheme to rig principals' tests to secure jobs for machine supporters. In the same year, a University of Chicago study revealed that the ratio of business-administration spending—the main pool of patronage employment—to instructional spending was approximately four to one in the Chicago school system, but only one to two in the New York schools and one to three in the Philadelphia system (Herrick 1971).

Though the Kelly-Nash machine exerted enormous influence, it was by no means all-powerful. Progressive forces mounted sustained protests, criticisms, and investigations against these abuses. Their persistent reform efforts were finally rewarded in 1945. In that year, a reform group called the Citizens Schools Committee (CSC) organized a host of Progressive educators and their allies, including the Chicago Teachers Unions (CTU) and the Illinois State Teachers' Association, to investigate a decade of abuses by the Chicago Board of Education and Superintendent William Johnson. Their final report summarized dozens of serious misdeeds involving the personnel and finances of the school board. The CSC paid for wide distribution of the report and used it to mobilize against the Kelly-Nash board of education. In a subsequent unprecedented measure, the NEA voted to expel Chicago Superintendent Johnson for unprofessional conduct. The city council held highly attended public hearings, but the aldermen ultimately voted to reject the report's findings (Herrick 1971, 272–75). Finally, the body charged with accrediting Chicago high schools, the North Central Association of Schools and Colleges, responded to the report by warning the Chicago superintendent that further accreditation of Chicago schools would be dependent on two measures: centralizing system control under the office of the superintendent and insulating the board from undue political influence (Chicago Tribune Staff 1946).

Seeking to avert political disaster, Mayor Kelly appointed yet another blue ribbon educational advisory committee—composed of area university presidents—to develop reform recommendations. This time, however, he pledged to implement the recommendations of the panel no matter what they were. As a result of this panel, the superintendent and half of the Board of Education were immediately dismissed and replaced by reform-minded individuals. More importantly, however, several groups including the CTU and CSC joined to draft state legislation that created an empowered and insulated general superintendent of schools. In 1947, almost fifty years after the Harper Report recommended largely the same measures, the governor signed legislation that would shift control over personnel, budget, and contract decisions from the Board of Education to a general superintendent of schools (Peterson 1976, 21).

2.2. Progressive Reform and Bureaucratic Administration, 1947–1980

Herold Hunt, head of Kansas City schools, was appointed general superintendent of the CPS in 1947 and thus became the first reform leader to enjoy the autonomy of the new 1947 law. As Orlando Wilson would do for the CPD a decade later, this outsider and those who followed him used their new freedom from machine control to reconstruct the CPS along hierarchical, command-and-control bureaucratic lines that had embodied professional notions of efficient organization since Superintendent McAndrew's tenure in 1923. This bureaucratic organizational form had three main components (Weber 1946, 196–204; Katz 1987, 60–73). First, it insulated major operations of the bureaucracy from public and political control and reserved them instead for trained and certified career professionals. Second, authority over determination of tasks and organizational routines, as well as supervision of implementation, were centralized according to a hierarchical scheme. Finally, bureaucratic organizations became increasingly differentiated according to specific areas of function in which additional areas of expertise were created.

Progressive reformers finally reduced political influence over education with a 1947 law that again entrenched the superintendent through tenure and granted him much of the Board of Education's powers. Beyond this, additional laws and procedures were soon enacted to protect superintendent decisions and school-system operations against board control. In a reversal of the pre-1947 pattern, these laws and routines seemed to shield school professionals from any effective board oversight at all. For example, school-board members were prohibited from meeting outside of their regular bimonthly meetings to discuss school policy. Annual budgets and other matters were submitted to the board, composed of lay citizens, in documents numbering thousands of pages, and were often approved without substantial amendment due to the incomprehensibility of the documents themselves (Peterson 1976, 120–23).

Hunt also established new departments within the central school office to centralize and apply expertise to areas of the school program. He revamped the Department of Personnel to professionalize hiring decisions. He created a new Department of Instruction and Guidance to develop uniform curriculum for the CPS. Soon after, the central office assumed power for school budgeting, purchasing, and personnel decisions.

Almost as soon as the last bricks of the public-education hierarchy had been laid, this edifice in turn suffered rebukes for inefficiency and unresponsiveness. By the mid-1960s, outside consultants and evaluators began to criticize the extreme centralization of the Chicago school system. In 1963, Robert Havighurst of the University of Chicago was commissioned by the Board of Education to conduct a comprehensive survey of the CPS. He acknowledged the superintendents' achievement of establishing an effective bureaucracy, but then went on to criticize the inability of those measures to keep pace with the increasing complexity of the Chicago educational environment (Havighurst 1964). In particular, the study found that "curriculum planning is done for the entire school system through the Central Office" (94) but that the diverse needs of schools and districts might be better served by decentralizing curriculum-design functions. Textbook selection was also determined in lengthy cycles by staff of the central office, and this practice impeded the efforts of school principals to support their teaching staffs (111). Echoing a complaint that teachers had voiced for decades, the survey revealed that existing routines and central-office requirements maximized actual teacher classroom time and thereby did not budget sufficient allowances for course planning, grading, and school staff discussions (176–78).

A confidential study conducted in 1967 by the consulting firm of Booz, Allen, and Hamilton for the Board of Education reiterated these dysfunctions (Booz, Allen, and Hamilton 1967). This study criticized both machine and bureaucratic domination of the school system:

> The Board has, at times, been deeply involved in the administrative and educational matters of the system, holding a tight rein on the general superintendent. During the 1950's and early 1960's, on the other hand, the general superinten-

dent clearly was the dominant figure. . . .

   [This] relationship between the board and the general superintendent . . . has
had significant organizational impact on the Chicago school system. Out of it
has emerged an organizational structure where responsibility and authority are
concentrated in a relatively small number of people who administer the programs of the school system on a highly centralized basis. (1–2)

And:

**The Operation of the School System is Almost Completely Controlled
by the Central Office**
From an organizational viewpoint, the Chicago school system is highly centralized. Central office personnel have responsibility for the development of educational and administrative programs, and direct the implementation of these programs in the schools. Relatively few decisions of substance are made in the field.
Generally, only routine action is taken without central office approval. (11;
emphasis in original)

   A host of popular protests against the school system's racial segregation
and general unresponsiveness compounded these professional criticisms
(Peterson 1976). Officials and activist organizations in other cities had
responded to similar challenges by decentralizing their school systems.
The state legislature of New York decentralized its schools into a governance system of some thirty districts (Ravitch 1974; Gittell 1994) in 1969
and Detroit divided its system into eight regions in 1970 (Mirel 1990;
Hess 1991, 87–88). The Chicago system, however, resisted these pressures
for change and remained largely intact as a single, highly centralized, and
increasingly unwieldy bureaucracy throughout this period and well into
the 1980s.

2.3. Legitimation Crisis to Accountable Autonomy, 1980–1988

While education-reform and watchdog groups continued to launch criticisms against the school system from the 1960s through the 1980s, the
entrenched administration successfully rejected reform overtures.[2] Just as
the machine-dominated Board of Education had resisted Progressives in
the beginning of the century, so the new school administration fought
outsiders' demands for change. Just as the forces of reform won their
long battle at midcentury, many of the hierarchical institutions that they
installed would in turn be again transformed near the century's end. In
1988, the Illinois legislature enacted school-reform legislation for Chicago that broke apart the CPS into a decentralized, participatory system.
The law devolved control of many aspects of school operation to parents

and local staff, it opened operations to popular participation, and problem-solving became the core task of these school governments. Like the
midcentury Progressive reforms, this sweeping institutional change followed the gradual accumulation, over decades, of popular complaints
against the failures of the CPS.

The case that, by the mid-1980s, the CPS had more or less completely
failed in its educational mission hardly needs to be made. By that time,
some 43 percent of students who entered high school dropped out before
graduation; in some inner-city schools, that rate reached 67 percent. Of
those that remained in school, slightly less than one-third could read at
the fifth-grade level by the time they graduated; 11 percent of graduates
could read at or above the national average. Standing behind these statistics was a swelling administrative apparatus. Though total school enrollment had dropped from 458,497 students in 1981 to 430,000 in 1988,
the number of CPS staff working in central and district offices (not
schools) grew from 2,884 to 3,708 over the same period (Hess 1991, 24–
27). Furthermore, some $42 million in state and federal monies ear-
marked for disadvantaged students was being used to support the central
school administration over the same period. Though they no doubt had
other motivations, many in the downstate Illinois legislature had good
reason to see the "city's schools as a 'black hole' absorbing everything
that came near it and putting out nothing in return" (O'Connell 1991,
19). In 1987, U.S. Secretary of Education William Bennett called Chicago
schools "the worst in the nation," and in May 1988 the *Chicago Tribune*
published a seven-part, 70,000 word (!) investigative series to document
that claim (Chicago Tribune Staff 1988).

Against this background of failure and fiscal crisis, several very different policy organization and advocacy groups offered their respective di-
agnoses and eventually converged upon a common prescription. Chicago
United—a business group concerned with public education and formed
by influential executives from corporations such as Inland Steel, Com-
monwealth Edison, International Harvester, and First National Bank of
Chicago—began its reform effort by hiring management consultants to
conduct a sweeping study of the CPS in 1979. The final report, released
in March 1981, recommended 253 specific changes that covered nearly
all aspects of school operations (Special Task Force on Education 1981).
The document found that the central administration was bloated while
instructional capacity in the field was sorely lacking; that daily administration nevertheless did not function smoothly; that the board attended
too much to administrative details and consequently could not formulate
policy; and that CPS had no capacity to relate system-design choices to
measurable goals. Though most of these findings couched the problem
in terms of inefficiencies in central administration, one of the group's

were able to channel this anger and frustration into a groundswell of support for their decentralizing reform proposals. Observing presciently,

> Clark Burrus, a member of the Chicago school board, said before the strike began . . . that such a confrontation could backfire, and that he feared the result could be a legislative restructuring of the system.
>
> "If we have a prolonged strike, I am fearful of what the legislature would do in a crisis situation," Burrus said. "There is talk of decentralization, elected school boards, turning power over to the parents.
>
> "We don't want anything like that," he said, shuddering. "That's one place where we and the unions are in agreement—we don't want any restructuring." (Griffin and Hardy 1987)

As crystal balls go, his turned out to be quite accurate. The strike invigorated an array of parent, community, and local political groups, and they continued to demand school-system reforms even after the CTU and the board struck a deal. Some favored reorganization of CPS into some twenty smaller districts along the lines of New York's much-touted and derided 1967 decentralization program, others favored centralized accountability mechanisms such as school-wide inspectorates, groups like RESPECT stressed funding-equity issues, and some just wanted to slash the budget of the administrative center.[4] In an extraordinary legislative moment, Michael Madigan, the powerful Speaker of the Illinois House of Representatives, invited interested parties—not only board of education and CTU advocates, but also representatives of groups like DFC and Chicago United—to use his office as a space to draft a major piece of school-reform legislation that would enjoy the support of all interested parties. Outside of Madigan's office, hundreds of parents and community members trekked from Chicago to Springfield—the state capital—to demonstrate support for reform, while Chicago United brought business leaders down in their corporate jets to press the flesh with legislators (O'Connell 1991, 21).

Over the next sixteen weeks, parties deliberated, cajoled, and bargained over reshaping the CPS in a moment—albeit writ quite small—that resembled Bruce Ackerman's (1991) description of higher lawmaking through wide-open public debate at the founding of the American Republic, its Reconstruction, and, later, in the era of the New Deal. Don Moore and the proposals first conceptualized by Designs for Change unmistakably carried the day in this debate. Due largely to alliances with the business community that DFC had forged through years of careful research and persuasion, and in no small measure to the energy of DFC staff during these meetings in Springfield, Madigan's draft legislation enacted the major elements of the DFC proposals for participatory site-based governance. It called for the creation of one LSC for each of Chicago's 560 elementary (K-8) and high (9–12) schools. Eleven elected members—six parents, two teachers, two community members, and the principal—would compose each elementary school LSC, while high school LSCs would add a nonvoting student member. The legislation empowered each LSC to hire and fire the principal, approve school budgets, and develop comprehensive three-year School-Improvement Plans (SIPs). Departing from DFC proposals based on local control, the business community demanded a centralized accountability mechanism, and so the legislation also included provisions for an oversight body to monitor system-wide implementation of the decentralizing reform.

After some log-rolling, partisan conflict over less central provisions, and interest group bickering, the bill passed the Illinois General Assembly in special session with a majority vote supplied by Democratic support. At the last minute, Reverend Jesse Jackson and Operation PUSH—calling the legislation "education deform"—fired off telegrams urging legislators to vote against it, members of the Board of Education railed against the bill, and the Principals' Association attacked the bill for removing principal "property rights" in tenure. By November 1988, however, negotiations over minor provisions gained the support of the Black Caucus, the CTU, and all major reform groups. Both houses of the legislature passed the bill by very wide margins in December 1988–56 to 1 in the Senate and 98 to 8 in the House. The first LSC elections were held in 1989; 17,256 candidates stood for election, including 9,733 parent candidates, 4,944 community-resident candidates, and 2,579 teachers. Approximately 5,400 of them were elected to govern some 540 Chicago schools (Designs for Change 1989).

2.4. Progressive Reformers and Machine Policing

A similar decades-long narrative of change—from machine domination to Progressive centralization to decentralized democracy—describes the evolution of the Chicago Police Department (CPD). At the beginning of the twentieth century, Progressive reformers' notion of good policing matched that of their contemporaries and the modern public. According to one prominent historian of policing, most assumed and expected that police

> enforced the law, kept the peace, and served the public; they suppressed vice and eradicated crime, preserved order at the polls and in the street, and aided citizens in distress. Underlying this notion were two assumptions. One was that most policemen did their job. The patrolmen, who were assigned to precincts, walked the beat looking for a complaint or a call for help. . . . The detectives

... investigated serious crimes and watched well-known criminals. And the special details maintained order at the courts, theaters, docks, railway stations, and other public places. The other assumption was that most policemen used little or no discretion . . . they should be guided only by the language of the law and the constraints of a policed society. (Fogelson 1977, 31)

Progressive efforts over the next fifty years sought to bring actual street-level policing behavior in harmony with the first expectation through management techniques built upon the second assumption.

This disjunction between expectations placed upon police departments and their real-world performance motivated the reform efforts of good-government activists. They waged their campaigns by publicizing the dimensions and extent of poor policing. A survey of Chicago policemen in 1904 revealed, for example, that "they spent most of their time in saloons, restaurants, barbershops, bowling alleys, pool halls, and bootblack stands. They were everywhere except the beat" (Fogelson 1977). It did not require sophisticated social-science methods to show that patrolmen did not enforce vice laws uniformly, but instead often used their public powers for personal gain or to support their machine patrons (Royko 1971, 102–11). From the turn of the century through the 1920s, Progressive reformers generated reports, staffed commissions, published newspaper articles, conducted official inquiries, and sponsored legislation that exposed corruption forces, drew the links between machines and police, and argued for professional, depoliticized police forces.

One particularly critical and prominent investigation began in 1911 in response to the complaints of angry onlookers who reported seeing police take protection bribes from bookies outside of Comiskey Park during a wrestling match. Subject to increasing public pressure from this and similar violations, then-Mayor Carter H. Harrison appointed three civil service commissioners to investigate reports of collusion between the police and organized perpetrators of vices such as gambling and prostitution (Lindberg 1991, 106–7). The commissioners conducted a sweeping three-month probe into the activities and organization of the CPD and published their results in a highly critical report that found:

(a) That there is and for years has been a connection between the Police Department and the various criminal classes in the City of Chicago.

(b) That a bi-partisan political combination or ring exists, by and through which the connection between the Police Department and the criminal classes above referred to is fostered and maintained.

(c) That to such connection may be charged a great part of the inefficiency—disorganization and lack of discipline existing in the Department.

(d) That aside from such connection, inefficiency also arises through faults of organization and administration.

(e) That the Police Department, as now numerically constituted, can enforce any reasonable regulation . . . if honestly and efficiently administered.

(f) That with the Department as now organized, efficient administration cannot be expected nor secured. (Chicago Civil Service Commission 1912, 52)

Specific findings brought rather severe personnel discipline: "One captain resigned under charges, and three inspectors, three captains, one sergeant, and six plain clothes men have been discharged" (Chicago Civil Service Commission 1912, 8). More generally, the report's constructive recommendations followed the standard good government formula for professional, hierarchical administration: completely reorganize the department along "logical and scientific lines"; remove "the service as far as possible from the influence of politics"; "simplify and modernize" the records; consolidate the executive officers into a central facility; and establish standards and professional training capacities (Chicago Civil Service Commission 1912, 52–53). Predictably, those at the apex of political and administrative police power ignored these blue ribbon recommendations.

Between 1890 and 1930, Progressive reformers outside of police departments launched similar attacks against many urban machines. Their efforts met with gradual, cumulative success in large cities across the nation. In 1894, Chicago reformers raised standards for police personnel by putting the department under civil-service regulation and otherwise stiffened entrance requirements. They raised officers' salaries an average of 50 percent between 1919 and 1929 in Chicago in order to attract more qualified candidates (Fogelson 1977, 82). By the 1930s, most big-city departments had founded professional training academies. Over this period, Progressives had managed to implement important parts of their program, but left many of the basic, dysfunctional operations of the departments untouched—city-wide chiefs exercised little real authority over precinct-level commanders or rank-and-file officers, and the daily operations of the police were still very much under the local control of ward machines.

A second round of reform between 1930 and 1960 transformed big-city police departments around the country into the large bureaucracies with which we are familiar today. In contrast to the earlier Progressive movement, forces from within the police community led this wave. Perhaps progressivism's most effective action lay not in its political skirmishes with machines, but in sowing two ideological seeds that grew within professional communities: that the purpose of municipal agencies was to provide the most effective public service at the lowest possible cost and that the organizational form that best achieved this end was rationalized bureaucracy (Carte and Carte 1975; Fogelson 1977, 90, 144; Sparrow, Moore, and Kennedy 1990, 34–41). Chiefs who led the second wave of reform imbibed and then developed these ideas in the community of police discourse formed by new institutes and professional associations: the International Association of Police Chiefs; American Association for the Advancement of Criminology; state police associations; the University of Louisville's Southern Police Institute; Florida State University's Southern Institute for Law Enforcement; and seminars sponsored by Harvard University or the Operations Research Center of the Massachusetts Institute of Technology, to list but a few (Fogelson 1977, 144). Wherever a member of this new generation came to power, he sought to remake his department in the shape prescribed by these professional discussions.

2.5. Building the Modern Police Bureaucracy in Chicago

In Chicago, the ax fell in 1960 when Orlando W. Wilson became police chief. His appointment followed persistent disclosures of low-level corruption combined with a series of highly publicized scandals that left no doubt in the minds of Chicago residents that some substantial fraction of the police department was involved in serious criminal activity. These revelations created a kind of legitimation crisis for the first Mayor Daley, and he responded with the appointment of a nationally respected police reformer.

In the decade of the 1950s, writes one Chicago police observer,

> Inefficiency and corruption still undermined the detectives' bureau and the police squads. . . . Any wise motorist who owned a car in the 1950s knew that the best way to beat a traffic ticket was to keep a $10 bill wrapped around the driver's license at all times. Typically, a patrol officer would pull an offender over to the curb and ask the driver to accompany him to the front seat of the squad car, where the money would be passed (Lindberg 1991, 287).

Another investigation in the late 1950s resulted in the indictments of thirty-five court officers involved in ticket-fixing for money and favors (Peterson 1959). Several months after this already serious revelation, a far greater criminal conspiracy surfaced. In the "Summerdale Scandal" of 1958, a burglar confessed that eight police officers were his associates in crime; for over two years, they had been helping him carry his loot away in their squad cars. Stolen property was recovered in the homes of the officers, and there was talk that many more officers could be involved (Lindberg 1991, 295–304). Mike Royko (1971, 122) noted that "the public was genuinely shocked. It's one thing to take a few bucks to overlook an illegal U-turn; but even Chicagoans could become indignant at the thought of policemen jimmying the locks of appliance stores and loading up their trunks, on city time yet."

Daley, who had previously accepted police corruption and local-ward control of the police department, adopted an extreme reform program designed to regain public confidence. He began by searching for a new chief, one with impeccable, nationally recognized credentials. He found Orlando W. Wilson, whose qualifications included running police departments in both Berkeley and Fullerton, California, and Wichita, Kansas, serving as professor of policing and dean of the School of Criminology at Berkeley, and consulting for some dozen police departments across the country. Well aware of the obstacle that Chicago's political-police links would pose to reform, Wilson demanded carte blanche inside the department and political support from the mayor beyond it, and Daley gave it to him. Over the next ten years, Wilson implemented a stunning series of changes that completed the program of Progressive institutional reform within the CPD. The department adopted state-of-the-art techniques and technologies: motorized patrol using one-man cars; efficient centralized radio dispatch; specialized functional squads, including intelligence and vice; vastly improved record-keeping; and improved training, recruiting, and promotion practices. Lindberg (1991, 314) credits Wilson with forcing the CPD "to break from its historic nineteenth century roots. [Under him] the period of modernity had at last begun."

These modernizing reforms included three fundamental planks constitutive of professional bureaucracy: *professional autonomy, hierarchical command*, and the *development of expert sources of practical knowledge*. Each of these bureaucratic characteristics stood on its own as part of a larger scheme of efficient police-service delivery, but each can also be understood as a contextual strategy for wresting control of police from the political machine.

Wilson's predecessor, Timothy O'Connor, "was never in any position to reform, or even control, the police force. The day-to-day management of the department was conducted by the seven aged and canny assistants in his office who took their orders from the politicians while O'Connor went through the motions of being in charge" (Royko 1971, 113; Lindberg 1991, 274). Wilson's first task, then, was to increase the professional and organizational autonomy of the police department at the expense of these local politicians. With the support of Daley, Wilson shattered ward control by moving more operations to the headquarters, reducing the number of police districts from thirty-eight to twenty-one, breaking the alignment between police-district and political-ward boundaries, and instituting strict procedures for hiring and promotion that would insulate police employment from political manipulation (Royko 1971, 117; Fogelson 1977, 175–82, 226). He won an Illinois law that shifted discipline procedures from the Civil Service Commission to a five-member police board. Any other police reform, Wilson correctly supposed, depended upon first transferring control over the police from machine politicians to professionals inside the law-enforcement community.

Beyond organizational autonomy, Wilson favored the model of centralized command and coordination that had proved its mettle not only in other municipal agencies, but also in the military and large private corporations. This hierarchical model of police organization first of all demanded the separation of task-conception from task-execution (Wilson 1950): the details of organization and routine were to be determined at headquarters, passed down to the districts, and then finally passed on to the patrol officers who would execute them. A 1964 report on the progress and direction of CPD reform advertises its management philosophy:

> A core of 62 officers now constitutes the top command of the Chicago Police. It is to these men that the task of successful implementation has fallen. Each has the job of interpreting plans and policies in frequent face-to-face contact with the men under his command. His subordinates must be kept fully informed, understand the reasons for change, and be properly motivated. (Chicago Police Department 1964, 7, 14)

Strict hierarchy and supervision made sense not only as an organizational embodiment of efficiency, but as a way to combat the widespread corruption that had brought Wilson to Chicago. He imposed stricter regulations on the behavior of patrol officers both on and off duty and he established the Bureau of Inspectional Services to monitor these regulations (Chicago Police Department 1964, 8). In line with professional recommendations, he reorganized the department along functional rather than geographic lines by moving many of the patrolman's responsibilities to centralized special units.

Finally, Wilson institutionalized the generation of expert knowledge within the department and cultivated sources outside of it. The police organization was to be guided not by politics, but by a body of practical knowledge called "policing," or, more expansively, "criminology." Like all other big-city police departments, the CPD has its own section devoted to research and development that generates usable knowledge about local departmental matters. Nationally, expert knowledge comes from groups like the National Institutes of Justice, the FBI, and numerous centers and departments in universities. One enduring achievement of the reform period was the establishment of the FBI's Uniform Crime Reports, which collect, centralize, and then report incidents of crime and police response across the country. It is worth noting two aspects of this expert knowledge that would be reversed in the participatory reforms to follow. First, those who generated theoretical knowledge and practical recommendations were, for the most part, divorced from the day-to-day operations of policing, and they had only quite tenuous connections to street-level operators. Second, expert prescriptions propagated downward through the bureaucracy. Research-and-development departments transmitted their results to chiefs, who then ordered their subordinates to follow these recommendations.

Through this bureaucracy, police became quite adept at implementing the three crime-fighting strategies that together form the core of modern policing: preventative patrol, rapid response, and retrospective investigation. Each of these strategies was based upon reasonable, but quite speculative, theories about crime abatement. Preventative patrol is the practice of maximizing police visibility—first by putting officers in automobiles and then by monitoring to ensure that they are indeed patrolling—in order to reduce opportunities for criminal behavior. An early 1970s experiment in Kansas City cast doubt on the efficacy of preventative patrol and shocked the law-enforcement community. Patrol areas were divided into three sections. In one section, patrol manpower remained at its previous level, in a second it was doubled, and in a third area, patrols were removed altogether. Researchers found no discernible impact on crime rates (Kelling et al. 1974; Fogelson 1977, 231–32; Sparrow, Moore, and Kennedy 1990, 15–16).

The second basic anticrime strategy is rapid response to citizen calls for police service. Everywhere in the United States, this has been instituted through the 911 emergency system and radio dispatch. The theory of rapid response holds that minimizing the time between the occurrence of a crime and the arrival of police will increase the probability of apprehending the perpetrator. Two findings about police operations cast doubt on this theory. First, the vast majority of 911 calls and patrolmen's time is spent on noncriminal matters—traffic directions, domestic disputes, and the like (Fogelson 1977, 231). Second, even the shortest response times have been shown to be insufficient to allow police to catch criminals because "the chance of arresting a villain at the scene became infinitesimal if victims waited more than five minutes to call the police. Unfortunately, most waited far longer" (Friedman and Matteo 1988).

The third crime-fighting strategy is ex post facto investigation and apprehension of criminals by detectives and patrolmen. Inside police departments, the ratio of apprehended suspects to reported crimes is known as a "clearance rate," and it is a figure of substantial managerial merit (Simon 1991). Assuming that criminals are rational actors, increasing the probability of arrest (and severity of punishment) will deter crime (Wilson 1983). Like most hypotheses about rational action, the evidence for this one is mixed. Without engaging too much in the debate, evidence suggests that apprehension is insufficient as a crime-control measure; crime rates have soared right along with incarceration rates since the 1970s.

2.6. Legitimation Crisis in Policing

By the 1960s, Wilson and others across the country had largely completed their bureaucratic-reform project. The CPD weathered disturbances of the late 1960s and 1970s; its basic institutional design and practical theory remained intact until another legitimation crisis that dates from the mid-1980s. Whereas the first crisis consisted of disjunction between widespread notions about the ideal form of policing and its actual corrupt, machine-serving practice, the latest crisis concerned the inability of police—irrespective of organizational form—to maintain safety and social order in urban neighborhoods. The precise dimensions of the crisis in law enforcement are difficult to establish, as are the levels of performance anxiety and outside pressure necessary to induce change in insular bureaucracies like police departments (Downs 1967). Yet, two kinds of gross evidence—attitudinal and epidemiological—support the case that those inside the law-enforcement community had good reason to feel some performance anxiety and that outsiders demanded change.

Consider first trends in national attitudes toward crime. Along with economic issues like unemployment and the high cost of living, since the 1970s Americans have consistently and frequently named crime as "the number one problem facing this country" in national surveys. If survey results are at all indicative of the national sentiment, then Americans' anxiety about crime has increased dramatically since 1985. The Gallup polling organization frequently administers a national survey that asks, "What do you think is the most important problem facing this country today?" It provides a menu of responses that includes "crime," "inflation and the high cost of living," "unemployment," and, since the 1970s, "drugs." Figure 2.1 plots the percentage of Americans who responded that "crime" or "drugs" was the nation's most important problem.[5] In the absence of recession, since roughly 1970 between 5 and 15 percent of Americans have identified crime as the nation's most important problem, outstripping all other concerns—education, health care, welfare, and the environment among them. Only economic issues such as unemployment and inflation have competed with crime as *the* national priority over the last quarter-century. Since 1985, however, crime concerns sharply surpassed even the economy, with between 20 and 60 percent of respondents naming it as the nation's most important problem. It should be noted that I have considered "drugs" as a part of overall concern about crime due to the close linkage between drug trafficking and crime, both in reality and in the popular perception. So, the steep rise in crime and drug concern between 1985 and 1992 can be largely attributed to mass media—refracted images—the

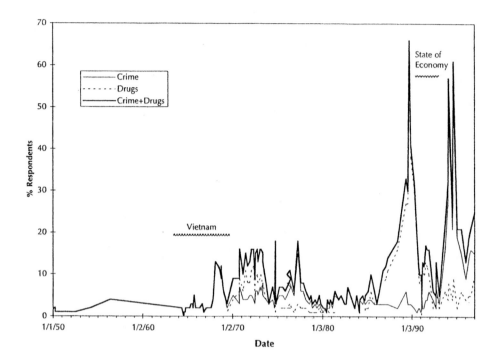

2.1. Crime as a National Priority, 1950–1997.

"crack epidemic" and the "war on drugs"—that are inextricably fused to notions about crime.

Locally, Chicagoans were very concerned about crime and public safety. In 1991, when asked in surveys if there was a place in their neighborhood where they were afraid to go after dark, more than half responded affirmatively. Almost 40 percent responded that concerns about crime prevented them from engaging in some activities in their neighborhoods (Skogan et al. 1999). By 1996, more than half of survey responded highlighted crime when asked about their neighborhood's greatest problem (Skogan et al. 1999). These concerns prompted officials in city hall and the police department to consider new approaches and departmental-reform options.

Furthermore, this rise in public concern about crime is not *merely* a perceptual shift; the rate of crime itself has also increased. Figure 2.2 depicts trends in the four major categories of violent crime as collected by the FBI in its Uniform Crime Reports (U.S. Department of Justice, various years), together with the rate of incarceration, our primary institutional response. Like all crime figures, these data should be treated with caution. They are based upon crimes reported to police, and so the actual crime rate is higher—especially with regard to rape—than FBI figures reflect. Part of the increase in crime over time may, therefore, be attributable to

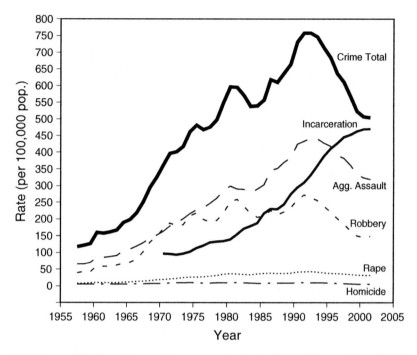

2.2. Rates of Violent Crime and Incarceration in the United States, 1957–2001.

increases in propensities to report crime. The crime of homicide, however, is far less subject to reporting bias, as the vast majority of dead bodies are eventually located. As shown above, homicide rates reflect increasing trends in crime and demonstrate that threats to personal security reached all-time highs in recent decades. Setting these figures in an epidemiological context, the Centers for Disease Control (CDC) reported that overall homicide was the eleventh leading cause of death nationally in 1995 (National Center for Health Statistics 1996). The problem is of course much greater in urban areas, for blacks, and for men. In Chicago, in 1990 homicide was the third leading cause of death for black males, just behind heart disease and far outstripping HIV infection (Epidemiology Program 1994, table 4). Figure 2.3 depicts homicide rates in Chicago[6] and in the United States through time.[7]

2.7. Toward Community-Centered Community Policing

In the 1980s, these trends of increasing crime and public concern about personal security sparked tremors of police reform that continue today in many cities across the United States. Reformers struck deeply by questioning the cardinal strategies of policing discussed above—preventative

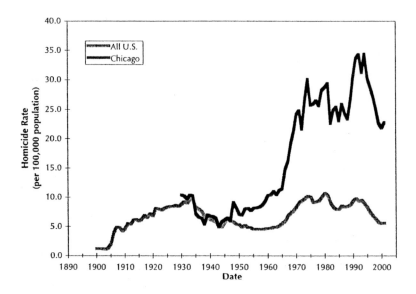

2.3. Homicide Rates in Chicago and the United States, 1900–2001.

patrol, rapid response, and investigation—and suggested that alternative, admittedly vague strategies like "proactive problem-solving" and "community partnership" might do better (Sparrow, Moore, and Kennedy 1990; Goldstein 1992; Chicago Police Department 1993). By 1997, a survey by the National Institute of Justice found that 54 percent of police departments had adopted some variant of community policing, and another 28 percent were in the process of doing so (Skogan et al. 1999, 21). Departments that chose these sorts of strategies as a way out of their legitimation crises would quickly find their accustomed centralized, hierarchical, paramilitary organizations incompatible with the effective implementation of these alternatives.

The Chicago Alliance for Neighborhood Safety (CANS) was among the earliest proponents for this wave of police reform in Chicago. It began in 1980 as a public-safety and crime-prevention technical-assistance group that aided Chicago neighborhood organizations with federal funding under the Urban Crime Prevention Program (UCPP). Adhering to an ideology of community organizing common to both the New Left and Saul Alinsky, CANS stressed indigenous neighborhood capacity, autonomy from state power (though ironically itself a creature of the state), and confrontational tactics. By the late 1980s, the limitations of their microorganizing strategy had become apparent, and CANS reinvented itself into an advocacy group that pushed for institutional reforms that would make the police department more responsive to neighborhood residents. In the words of longtime CANS Executive Director Warren Friedman:

The organizations [we helped] were supposed to take these resources, organize residents, develop action plans and, *when necessary*, work with the police to make the neighborhood safer. . . . There was no hint of policy participation or institutional change. With the lack of police cooperation, this strategy began losing credibility. CANS . . . began to evolve in response to the clear limits of its community safety strategy. (Friedman 1997; emphasis added)

Its revamped organizing strategy was to be twofold. First, it agitated for reforms to the CPD that would make police more responsive to community voices. Retaining its ideological and organizational commitment to local participation, community involvement would always figure prominently in its reform proposals. Second, it would organize community groups and residents—it would capacitate them—to take advantage of the institutional permeability that it demanded from the police.

CANS waged its campaign to change the police department with reports that explained national best practices in community policing and criticized the CPD for failing to adopt these practices (Friedman and Matteo 1988; Friedman 1996). Using a kind of carrot-and-stick approach, it first discussed these reports with high-level police officials. When it felt officials were unreceptive, they mobilized public criticism. In 1991, CANS organized a city-wide Community Policing Task Force comprising some one hundred community-based organizations, as a forum to discuss and push for these ideas. It also conducted a Leadership Institute for Community Policing that consisted of six seminars led by professors of criminology and policing. It sponsored field trips, attended by Institute participants as well as CPD personnel, to New York and Seattle to see other community-policing efforts at first hand. Foreshadowing the intensive provisions for community participation that would later distinguish Chicago's program, Friedman writes that, "most evenings [during the field trips], . . . we met to discuss what we had seen and heard that day. Over and over, the question was raised, 'Where's the community?' In both cities, they saw that little thought had been devoted to or investment made in community participation, education, or training" (Friedman 1997).

Inextricably connected with, but independent from, this campaign, the upper echelons of the police department and city hall also began making reform motions in the early 1990s. For a sticker price of $475,000, the city commissioned a study of the CPD from the consulting firm of Booz, Allen, and Hamilton that was completed in 1992 (Spielman 1992). In addition to an array of management techniques to increase the number of patrol officers per city dollar, Booz, Allen, and Hamilton recommended that the city experiment with various community-policing devices in five of its twenty-six police districts. Many of these devices would resemble the community-policing efforts of other cities. Reforms in Chicago, however, would create much more extensive provisions for community involvement. While the substance of most of the policing reforms can be attributed to an evolving professional (police) consensus about community policing, CANS deserves credit for the reform's participatory emphasis. Because they were loud, because there was no fundamental conflict of interest between the community organizers and the police reformers, and because police professionals believed that CANS's ideas might actually enhance the effectiveness of policing, their suggestions were smoothly integrated into the early rounds of police reform.

As the first step of a city-wide policing initiative dubbed "Chicago's Alternative Policing Strategy" (CAPS), the five prototype districts went on-line in January 1993. They incorporated devices that broke with traditional policing tenets. Against the principle of hierarchy, the new policing directed street-level police officers to proactively identify and solve problems. To make room for this activity, units in prototype areas were divided into "beat" and "response" sections, with the former solving problems and the latter responding to 911 calls for assistance. Against the principle of centralization, prototypes built the capacity of operational "beat" units. The geographic atom of policing in Chicago is the beat—the city itself is divided into 279 beats, each of which delineates the patrol area served by one squad car at any given time.[8] Prototype districts stressed "beat integrity," which meant that individuals officers focused service on their patrol areas—they did not patrol areas outside of the beat and individuals were assigned to particular beats for sustained periods so police officers could familiarize themselves with the problems and residents of their beats and residents could get to know them.

Prototype areas opened channels for resident participation at both the beat and district levels. At monthly meetings in each beat, police met with residents to jointly identify, strategize, and eventually solve the most urgent problems of crime and disorder in their neighborhoods. Beyond this, each district created an advisory body of community leaders to present larger concerns to each district's commander. The program was hailed as a success (Chicago Community Policing Evaluation Consortium 1994) and expanded to cover the entire city beginning in fall 1994 (James 1994). Approximately 80,000 people attended beat meetings during 1995 and the first four months of 1996 (Chicago Community Policing Evaluation Consortium 1996).

2.8. Administration as Pragmatic and Participatory Neighborhood Deliberation

By the mid-1990s, then, strong currents of neighborhood control and citizen participation were visible in both the CPD and CPS. Compared to the underlying logic of the bureaucracies that preceded them, these reforms contained radically different notions about the local role of citizens, the autonomy and discretion of front-line officials, and how public action should be mobilized in grappling with complex problems. Whereas those prior bureaucratic arrangements pushed the balance of policy formation, decision-making, and problem-solving to higher levels of supervision and administration, these reforms decentralized decision-making. Whereas the prior strategies sought to insulate agencies from popular voice and control, these reforms created opportunities for just such participation. These reforms created hundreds of neighborhood-level structures for problem-solving in the hope that this combination of civic engagement and administrative decentralization—participatory devolution—would be better able to improve neighborhood safety and school quality than the preceding bureaucracies. While some have described these participatory structures in the familiar coordinates of community control (Bryk et al. 1998), the language of deliberative democracy offers several advantages for understanding the deeper implications and democratic potential of the Chicago school and community-policing reforms.

In community-policing beat meetings and local school-council sessions, citizens and officials come together to address common concerns about safer neighborhoods or more effective schools. Characteristically, participants are unsure about what they ought to do to address such concerns. They are uncertain, for example, about which areas are most dangerous or about which school programs are most promising for their students. Since they know that, despite this uncertainty, they must proceed, and the reforms give them the authority to do so, these groups' activities are a kind of practical *inquiry* about appropriate actions: specification and prioritization of problems facing the groups, analysis about the causes of those problems, and formulation strategies to solve the problems that take account of the groups' limited capabilities. They analyze, however, only in order to guide the collective actions that will satisfy their common need. Since both their analyses and actions will inevitably be imperfect, collective action is also *experimentalist*—implementation reveals flaws in analysis that then feed back into the mill of inquiry.[9]

Ideally, these groups make decisions through *deliberation*. Participants aim to identify the most promising strategy to satisfy that need which is shared with the rest. If authoritative experts could develop optimal strategies, command rather than deliberation might be the appropriate method of decision. If participants had deeply opposed interests, and the goal of the group was to advance the greatest happiness of the greatest number, then the aggregation of interests through voting might be more appropriate than practical deliberation. But since the goal is to find solutions to common problems rather than to aggregate opposing preferences and since there is often no dispositive expert, then deliberation—full and open discussion of available options—seems appropriate not only to decide the best course, but also to gain the allegiance necessary to implement it. If, after ample deliberation, participants still hold conflicting opinions regarding the optimal course of action, voting may appropriately settle the divergence and, at least tentatively, arrive at the single opinion that collective action requires.[10]

To further fix the flavor of deliberation that has been created by the Chicago school and police reforms, consider the deliberations of each group as an ideal problem-solving procedure. As we shall see in the chapters that follow, participants in some groups approximate this procedure well while others depart far from it. Laying out the ideal procedure, however, sets a benchmark and norm for what practical deliberation should look like. Furthermore, it suggests ways in which the institutionalization of this procedure would advance important core democratic values of inclusion, participation, voice, and control. Finally, the procedure offers a way of conceptualizing the kind of practical deliberation that appears in Chicago neighborhood meetings about public safety and education. This practical deliberation differs both in process and goal from types of deliberation aimed at settling fundamental value conflicts (Gutmann and Thompson 1996), resolving basic questions about political and economic structure (Rawls 1993), or capacities for political criticism (Habermas 1992, 1996). In the ideal, then, participatory neighborhood deliberation is a process of inquiry that aims to solve collective problems through the following five-step (D1–D5), iterated procedure.[11]

D1. *Identification and Prioritization.* Participants are taken to share a common but vague concern, for instance the perception that their neighborhood is unsafe or that their school could do better. Participants begin by dividing this general, daunting concern into component problems, for instance a crack house on the corner or a dilapidated school building. Prioritizing these component problems builds a consensus on what exactly the problem is and yields a schedule that will assist in the allocation of collective resources.

D2. *Proposal, Justification, and Selection of Provisional Strategies.* These steps are taken with respect to the concrete concern developed at D1. The rational capacity—the instrumental reason—of participants is called into play here. At this stage, the deliberative process should forge a number of robust proposals, or strategies, to address the common concern. Each of these proposals constitutes a hypothesis about how best to address the concrete problem. This stage also requires parties to be reasonable. Some may attempt to disguise their private interest as the general interest by making proposals geared to advance their private interests, at the expense of other parties, even as these same proposals may solve the general problem. Since parties are called on to justify their proposals, and proposals which cannot be justified in terms of the common good are excluded, deliberation can generate a menu of strategies, each of which seems (prospectively) effective and fair by the lights of everyone.

A complete proposal will have at least these elements: a set of tasks to be done, a division of labor that assigns tasks to parties, a set of expectations about what each of the tasks will accomplish vis-à-vis the concrete issue before the group, and provisional methods with which to assess whether or not parties completed assigned tasks and whether successfully accomplished tasks yielded expected effects. With a set of seemingly effective proposals before them, the parties deliberate again to select one that seems more promising than the rest. Deliberation again is geared toward choosing an effective and fair proposal, and toward achieving a working consensus. Since a menu of proposals, all of which seems both fair and effective, is before the group, there is no reason to suppose that consensus can be achieved. Each proposal is, after all, a guess about what the world is like and how it will respond to various problem-solving strategies; these are complex matters about which reasonable and bright people often differ. One reasonable way to proceed, therefore, is to vote on the proposals and adopt the majority or plurality winner as the provisional hypothesis for the group. In giving her vote, each participant gives her guess about which of these solutions is most effective, and all participants realize that the social choice that results is their best guess and nothing more.

D3. *Implementation.* Parties attempt to carry out the tasks assigned to them by the proposal selected in D2. Each may fail to carry out her task for a variety of reasons, for instance she may shirk or the task itself may be more demanding than anticipated.

D4. *Monitoring and Evaluation.* Following implementation, parties deliberate about how things went. It is hoped that the resources for intersubjective agreement on assessment will have been progressively constructed at D1 and D2.

Working backwards, they first assess the degree to which component tasks of the solution were successfully implemented. Thus, the group assesses whether or not particular parties failed to deliver on their commitments and whether the tasks assigned were too demanding. This level of assessment yields information about the reliability and capacities of various parties.

The group then evaluates whether or not the accomplished tasks yielded expected benefits. Each task in the solution adopted at D2 itself represents a hypothesis about the intended effects of various courses of action. The action at D3 can be viewed as executing experiments formulated at D2, and one of the points of evaluation is to attempt to ascertain the validity of those rough hypotheses. Finally, the agenda (D1) is only a provisional guess about the components that make up their common concern and may itself require revision in light of evidence. With a full evaluation in hand, parties can assess their entire solution in parts: what worked, what did not, whether new strategies need to be formulated, and whether the agenda itself needs to be revised.

D5. *Reiteration.* The experience of D1–D3 made public through deliberation at D4 equips the group to attempt another round at the solution of its common problem. Since we expect the solution to be neither a complete failure nor a complete success, participants will be motivated to continue some process of cooperative action to the extent that they still have a problem in common. So the ideal procedure is iterative.

We can expect the quality of later iterations of the stages wherein proposals are formulated and selected (D2) and thereafter evaluated (D4) to increase for three general reasons. First, previous rounds generate *more public information* about each of the parties and about the common problem. Thus so, initial expectations about the skills, reliability, and trustworthiness of each is subject to revision through the addition of information. Also, experience and public reflection upon attempts to address the problem yield information about its contours. Second, we can expect the limited practical *rationality* and *reasonable* capacities of all parties to improve because of the principle of learning by doing. Since these three features—the amount and quality of information, the rational capacities of parties, and their reasonableness—largely determine the character of deliberation, we can expect future rounds of proposal generation and evaluation to improve.

Implementation (D3) may improve for two reasons. First, the parties themselves, again through the principle of learning by doing, will gain the knowledge and skills required for various implementation tasks. Second, public knowledge of the skill level and reliability of each increases with future iterations, and so the tasks assigned to parties will become more suited to individual interests and skills.

How has this abstract procedure appeared in the participatory, deliberative, and decentralizing reforms of the police and public schools in Chicago? The next two sections show how those organizations have implemented deliberative problem-solving in their local units of public action. We can think of community-policing reform as creating 279 communities of inquiry—one in each beat, and educational reform as creating some 560 school-based communities of inquiry. These examples show not only how the abstract procedure can be operationalized to solve complex public problems, but also demonstrates how agencies that until quite recently appeared to be among the most hierarchical and insular have indeed embarked upon this reform trajectory.

2.9. Deliberative Problem-Solving in Chicago LSCs

Recall that a 1988 Illinois law radically decentralized the governance structure of the CPS. For each of the 560 elementary schools, the legislation created an elected Local School Council composed of the principal, two teachers, six parents, and two community members. Each LSC was empowered to hire and fire the principal, allocate the school's discretionary monies, and help determine the allocation of staff resources. The law also required each LSC to develop a School Improvement Plan (SIP) that guides the exercise of these powers:

> [t]he local school principal shall develop a school improvement plan in consultation with the local school council, all categories of school staff, parents and community residents. Once the plan is developed and after the local school council has approved the same, the principal shall be responsible for directing implementation of the plan, and the local school council shall monitor its implementation. (*Illinois Code of Compiled Statutes*, 10, 5/34–2.4).

According to the general language of the enacting legislation, each school's SIP is a three-year plan "to improve educational quality."[12] In practice, it is a working document, updated yearly, that states a school's vision of itself as an excellent educational institution, lists the most urgent steps necessary to move the institution to that point, and assigns those tasks to particular individuals in the LSC or staff. The principal of a school typically develops the plan in consultation with school staff, the LSC, and other members of the community, and the LSC must approve the document each year. SIPs are modified annually according to changing circumstances and results of implementation efforts, and so compose part of a "continuous planning" process.[13] The changing activities of staff, LSC members, and others who work with the school can be broadly viewed as the actualization of this ever-changing plan.

In order to ease the task of composing SIPs, an office of the CPS recommended a format that nearly every school has chosen to follow; though some schools have much better SIPs than others, they all look similar. This paperwork reflects the structure of deliberative problem-solving in LCSs. The form has four sections. In the first section, a school states its vision for itself and in the final section records budgeting decisions. Sections two and three document a school's problem-solving activities and thus are most salient here.

In the second section of an SIP, titled "Analysis of Current Conditions," each school lists its priority activity areas, and then reflects upon the strengths and weaknesses of that area. This section corresponds to the prioritization (D1) and evaluation of previous strategies (D4) of the ideal

SECTION 2   ANALYSIS OF CURRENT CONDITIONS

SUPPORT AREA: Quality Instructional Program

FOCUS OF ANALYSIS	WHAT IS WORKING	WHAT NEEDS WORK
Language Arts	Model of Preferred Reading Instructional Practices established Procedures adopted to assure greater Time on Task New Reading Series purchased K-5 Computer generated Accelerated Reader on line Four hundred new Accelerated Reader books grades 4-9 purchased for library SQUIRT ALERT (Super Quiet Uninterrupted Reading Time) implemented in all classrooms ...	Classroom libraries need to be updated Networked system not reliable therefore Accelerated Reader tests are not available Determine Language Arts resource and text needs for grades 6, 7, 8 Consider using common basal in upper grades for continuity of language arts Remediate present decline in recreational reading by intermediate and upper grades Large class sizes in upper grades limit quality of instruction Need additional staff and volunteers to meet all students needs ...

2.4. School-Improvement Plan, Excerpt A.

deliberative experimentalist procedure. Figure 2.4 reflects one elementary school's analysis of its own language-arts program.

The third section of the SIP form, labeled "Establishing Goals, Plans, and Monitoring Progress," lists strategies, tasks necessary to implement them, assignment of those tasks, and monitoring provisions; it documents each LSC problem-solving plan at stages D2–D4. Figure 2.5 shows part of the same school's SIP, which addresses the aspects of the reading program identified as weak earlier in its SIP. Thus, lack of reading comprehension is one priority problem (D1) and the school has selected Accelerated Reading and SQUIRT (Super Quiet Uninterrupted Reading Time) programs as its strategies to address that problem (D2). To implement this strategy (D2), classroom teachers will emphasize students' reading aloud, more time will be devoted to silent reading, and use of the existing computerized "Accelerated Reader Program" will be increased. If this computerized instruction seems fruitful, the school will expand its facilities. The second column lists multiple monitoring activities, again devised by school personnel, that involve student testing, teacher self-assessment, and principal supervision (D4). Finally, the third column lists target dates for monitoring and implementation (D4).

Updated annually, SIPs serve as baseline plans to guide staff and LSC activities throughout the school year. LSCs monitor plan progress at their

SECTION 4 ESTABLISHING GOALS, PLANS, AND MONITORING PROGRESS

PRIORITY GOAL #: Improve reading comprehension by revisiting "Readers are Leaders" theme through the Accelerated Reader Program and SQUIRT reading.

WORK PLANS/PERSON(S) RESPONSIBLE FOR 1996-1997	ACTIVITIES FOR MONITORING PROGRESS	MONITORING TARGET DATES
Place a strong emphasis on reading aloud to students/all classroom teachers grades K-8	-lesson plans -principal's observations -teacher reports	Middle and end of marking period
Place a strong emphasis on having students SQUIRT read daily since studies have proved students who read show tremendous growth in reading and improved math scores/all classroom teachers grades K-8	-lesson plans -principal's observations -teacher reports	Middle and end of marking period
Students in grades 3-8 participate in the Accelerated Reader Program/Classroom teachers and computer coordinator	-students grades 3-5 required to pass a minimum of one test per quarter; students grades 6-8 required to pass a minimum of two tests per quarter -certificates of completion for students -Use the point system in clever, unique ways to motivate all students to	Middle and end of each marking period
If Accelerated Reader Program is truly being utilized, more books and test disks will be ordered to include grades 1 and 2/Computer Coordinator and Librarian	participate....	at semester break, 1996-97 school year

2.5. School-Improvemnt Plan, Excerpt B.

monthly meetings, use SIP goals to allocate monies and as a tool for principal evaluation, and implement many SIP objectives in ongoing committees. It is thus a product, record, and motor of deliberative problem-solving activities in each Chicago public school. The SIP's wide-open structure decisively illustrates that its purpose is not to assure compliance with particular instructions, but rather to stimulate ground-level actors to articulate their views about what most needs to be done and how best to do those things.

2.10. Communities of Inquiry in Chicago Policing

Policing reformers have operationalized the ideal of deliberative problem-solving twice in the course of developing community-policing institutions. The first was the Joint Community-Police Training (JCPT) program that took place from 1995 to 1996. The deliberative forums of monthly neighborhood beat meetings between residents and patrol officers, and the actions that those discussions produced constitute the second implementation of deliberative inquiry in community policing.

Though a training initiative in name, JCPT actually involved substantial community organization and problem-solving. Under this program, the city funded approximately one hundred field staff—some police but mostly "civilian" personnel—to mobilize residents around public-safety issues throughout the city. In each beat, designated organizers were charged with fostering resident participation by working with existing neighborhood-based organizations or by direct door-to-door canvassing of neighborhood residents. Trainers would then lead residents through a five-meeting, problem-solving curriculum over four months' time. At the end of this period (determined by funding constraints), the program's designers hoped that residents would be able to sustain problem-solving involvement without professional staffing or support.

JCPT embraced learning-by-doing as its pedagogical method, and the "doing" followed exactly the steps of the ideal deliberative problem-solving procedure described above. In the first session, trainers facilitated discussion among residents to select the most important crime issue in their neighborhoods and to analyze the causes of that problem (D1). Program designers stipulated that the situation had to possess three features in order to qualify as a problem: (1) it had to occur in a definable location; (2) there had to be identifiable offenders; and (3) victims had to be identifiable by category (e.g., motorists). These three aspects of problematic situations form the legs of what they called the "crime triangle."

In the second session, residents and patrol officers developed strategies to attack each of the three sides of the triangle (D2). Strategies often involved increasing patrol visibility, deployment of unmarked units, petitions, negotiations, and demonstrations. Often, however, they called upon participants to *leverage* resources not readily available to the group—various city services, an alderman's office, civic organizations. Strategies also included dividing the labor of implementation among group participants.

Between the second and third sessions, participants attempted to implement these strategies (D3), and in the third session participants discussed the successes of their efforts (D4) and devised new strategies if those chosen in the second session seemed not to be working (D5). The fourth meeting consisted of a wrap-up session to celebrate victories, solidify resident commitment to this problem-solving process through review of often surprising accomplishments, and set in place a resident leadership that would take responsibility for continuing the process absent staff support.

In addition to this short-lived organizing and training program, deliberative problem-solving has also been formally implemented at the core of

Chicago police operations. A general order to the patrol division—the rank and file of the police department—issued in April 1996 institutionalized the procedure through three complementary devices: beat meetings, beat teams, and a set of supervised instructions on problem-solving (Chicago Police Department 1996; Fung 1997c). Similar to JCPT, police and residents are to use these beat meetings to identify crime problems in the neighborhood, develop and implement strategies, evaluate results, and reiterate these problem-solving steps.

The 1996 general order directed police to form "beat teams" that consist of officers directly responsible for serving each beat—typically five patrol officers and their sergeant. These officers meet regularly in "beat-team meetings" to choose priority problems, develop strategies, and discuss the effectiveness of various strategies. Though orders instruct them to "give . . . special attention to the problems identified during beat community meetings" in the selection of priorities, police may override these resident recommendations because "beat community meetings may not be representative of the entire beat, and the problems they identify may not be representative of the problems on the beat." Community side participants can respond (deliberatively) to objectionable police decisions, however, at successive beat meetings.

The general order requires line-level police to document their problem-solving activities to enable monitoring and improvement of future effort through postfacto analysis. By capturing action on the written page, these forms show how authority has been extensively devolved to operational units and that those units follow deliberative problem-solving as laid out in section 2.8, above. Consider the "beat plan form" (figures 2.6, 2.7), which might more appropriately be labeled a "problem plan form" since a single beat typically has three or four such forms open at any given time—one for each open problem. The form leaves complete operational discretion to patrol officers, yet imposes the generative structure of cognition and action that I have described as deliberative problem-solving. In the space marked "D1," officers record the specific origins of this problem as a priority issue. In most cases, problems become priorities when they are raised at community beat meetings. In the spaces marked "D2," police in the beat team develop a series of strategies to address these problems through analysis of the problem, a guess about the time required to address it, and particular action items (strategies) together with the assignment and definition of tasks necessary to implement those strategies. Moving to the second side of this form, officers continuously monitor each other's implementation efforts and the effectiveness of those efforts in the space marked "D3/D4." Finally, in the space marked "D4," officers record the results of summary self-assessment after the problem has been "solved."

BEAT PLAN FORM
(Beat Priority Problem)
CHICAGO POLICE DEPARTMENT

1. BEAT:

2. PROBLEM REFERENCE NO. _____ _____ _____

3. DATE PLAN DEVELOPED:

4. CROSS REFERENCE NO. _____ _____ _____

5. BEAT PRIORITY PROBLEM AND LOCATION:

6. BRIEF DESCRIPTION OF THE BEAT PRIORITY PROBLEM

7. WHAT BROUGHT THIS PROBLEM TO YOUR ATTENTION?
(USE AS CRITERIA FOR MEASURING IMPACT OF PROBLEM-SOLVING)

CHECK ALL THAT APPLY:

☐ OFFICER OBSERVATION   ☐ BEAT COMMUNITY MEETING
☐ SUPERVISORS   ☐ OTHER COMMUNITY CONTACT
☐ OTHER UNITS   ☐ ELECTED OFFICIAL
☐ OTHER CITY AGENCY   ☐ OTHER _____

MANDATORY INFORMATION:

☐ # OF ARRESTS _____
☐ # OF CALLS FOR SERVICE _____
☐ # OF INCIDENTS / RD NOs _____
☐ ICAM (INCLUDE IN TRACKING FOLDER)

TIME SPAN USED: FROM: _____
TO: _____

8. PROBLEM OCCURS DURING:

☐ 1ST WATCH
☐ 2ND WATCH
☐ 3RD WATCH

SPECIFIC DAY(S):

SPECIFIC HOUR(S):

D1

9. ANALYSIS OF PROBLEM: DESCRIBE OFFENDER, VICTIM, AND LOCATION / ANSWER WHO, WHAT, WHERE, HOW AND WHY? (use additional paper if necessary)

List information - OFFENDER(S)

1.

2.

3.

4.

5.

List information - VICTIM(S)
(Who in the community is affected by this crime / disorder issue?)

1.

2.

3.

4.

5.

List information - LOCATION
(What about this location makes it conducive to the crime / disorder issue?)

1.

2.

3.

4.

5.

D2

10. DEVELOPMENT OF TARGETS / GOALS: (use box #7 to measure target / goals)

11. WHAT STRATEGIES WILL BE USED TO ADDRESS THE PROBLEM? (Continue on other side of form)

A. LAW ENFORCEMENT STRATEGY:

B. COMMUNITY STRATEGY:

RESPONSIBILITY ASSIGNED TO: (POLICE PERSONNEL)

RESPONSIBILITY ASSIGNED TO: (COMMUNITY CONTACT AND POLICE LIAISON)

D2/D3

2.6. Beat Plan Form, Side 1.

C. CITY SERVICE STRATEGY:

D. SPECIALIZED UNIT STRATEGY:

RESPONSIBILITY ASSIGNED TO: (CITY SERVICE CONTACT AND POLICE LIAISON)

RESPONSIBILITY ASSIGNED TO: (POLICE PERSONNEL)

E. ADDITIONAL STRATEGY:

F. ADDITIONAL STRATEGY:

RESPONSIBILITY ASSIGNED TO:

RESPONSIBILITY ASSIGNED TO:

12. PLAN PREPARED BY:	BEAT TEAM LEADER SIGNATURE	STAR NO.	DATE	PLAN APPROVED BY:	CAPS MANAGEMENT TEAM LEADER SIGNATURE	STAR NO.	DATE

13. ASSESSMENT OF PROGRESS TOWARD ADDRESSING THE PROBLEM (must be completed once a month and initialed by Beat Team Leader)

BEAT PRIORITY PROBLEM STRATEGIES (Police, City Service, Community Strategy)	ASSESSMENT OF PROGRESS	ASSESSMENT DATE	BEAT TEAM LEADER INITIALS

14. FINAL EVALUATION (To be used only when problem is officially closed)

A. WHAT IMPACT HAVE THE STRATEGIES HAD ON THE PROBLEM AND HOW DO YOU KNOW?
(Use measures such as officer observation, calls for service, crime analysis and beat community meetings)

PROBLEM HAS BEEN ☐ REDUCED ☐ ELIMINATED

B. WHICH STRATEGIES PROVED TO BE MOST EFFECTIVE AND WHY?

CLOSED BY:				CLOSURE APPROVED BY:			
BEAT TEAM LEADER SIGNATURE	STAR NO.	DATE		CAPS MANAGEMENT TEAM LEADER SIGNATURE		STAR NO.	DATE

2.7. Beat Plan Form, Side 2.

2.11. Conclusion

For most of this century, the CPD and CPS were organized like many other of Chicago's public agencies: in insular, hierarchical, and bureaucratic fashion. This institutional form resulted from the desire of Progressive reformers to close channels of undue political influence on city agencies and to increase their efficiency by imposing the best organizational techniques of the time. By the 1980s, however, the efficacy of the hierarchical bureaucratic form had come into question as these city agencies were asked to deal with increasingly diverse, complex, and seemingly intractable challenges to effective education and public safety. As in many other cities, these doubts fueled demands for public-sector reform. Unlike many of those cities, however, coalitions favoring school and police reform in Chicago included sophisticated and influential champions of citizen empowerment. Consequently, Chicago's agencies reformed themselves in ways that allow more resident and parent participation than perhaps any other large American city. The structures of these reforms are deeply practical and deliberative: they convene groups of users such as (parents and residents) and local officials (such as police officers and school staff) to establish visions, set priorities, and develop and implement problem-solving strategies. Rather than privileging decontextualized technique, this deliberative strategy of public action emphasizes local knowledge, cooperation with residents, and embedded ingenuity.

But participatory devolution as described above is insufficient to capture these benefits of civic engagement and public deliberation. Though the discussion thus far has emphasized the decentralizing moment of the Chicago reforms, that is only half of the story. It is the local-autonomy portion of the accountable autonomy idea. We turn now to the second part of this institutional design by considering some of the difficulties with decentralization, the institutional competencies of central administrative offices and external associations that are necessary to address these difficulties, and how actual reforms in the CPD and CPS began to develop those competencies.

3

Building Capacity and Accountability

THE previous chapter emphasized the decentralizing and participatory moment of the Chicago community-policing and school reforms. From the outset, however, even the harshest critics of bureaucratic malaise recognized the dangers inherent in decentralization, the difficulties of generating constructive citizen participation, and the need for external supports and checks to facilitate the problem-solving in the neighborhoods. Early experiences with the CPS and CPD reforms not only confirmed these worries, but also revealed further problems and pitfalls that led to the partial reinvention of central authority. Under the prior, hierarchical model of administration, the CPS and CPD central offices attempted to control the operational minutiae of local activity. Under these participatory reforms, however, they would develop mechanisms to support and monitor self-directed governance efforts within neighborhoods.

Old habits and commitments do not die easily, however. This shift in the role—the institutional competence—of central power has not been fully realized in either the CPS or CPD. The question of whether and how these agencies will address the shortcomings of participatory decentralization thus remains open. Some reformers, consistent with the prescription of accountable autonomy, see the need to reinvent central authority in ways that support local problem-solving efforts and hold them accountable. Others see irredeemable problems in local control and empowered citizen participation, and so favor reimposing central control: moving back to the hierarchical forms overturned by the 1994 and 1999 reforms. Overlaid with these concerns about efficacy are political aims of administrators and officials, on one hand, and community activists on the other. Officials have often resented the public criticisms that inevitably accompany popular mobilization and engagement and have themselves criticized the lack of professionalism and commitment of activist and community organizations. Conversely, community leaders are disposed to interpret centralized interventions and monitoring as encroachments upon local prerogative. An imaginative obstacle compounds these administrative and political ones: the dichotomy between centralization and decentralization dominates our notions of political structure and organizational design. This chapter nevertheless argues that a hybrid design, in which local autonomy requires centralized support and accountability and in which accomplishing broader aims requires street-level innovation and civic engagement, is more promising than either simple centralization or decentralization.

Political and programmatic obstacles have made the development of centralized institutional devices for accountable autonomy in the CPS and CPD slow and fitful. Nevertheless, both organizations have developed an array of centralized mechanisms that facilitate and bolster the integrity of local problem-solving efforts and quality of deliberations. For example, one study of the post-1988 CPS reforms found that:

> Most department heads cited changing relationships between the schools and the central office as the major impact of reform. Of the 21 departments questioned, 14 had developed new mission statements and had reorganized the structure and content of their school services in response to new needs under reform. Most described the changing relationship with schools as a shift in power, a reversal of the "old top-down system," where the central office is supportive rather than directive. Although there was general acknowledgement of the changed governance structure, evaluators also reported central office confusion and uncertainty about the level of initiative or leadership to take in relationships with schools. (Stewert and Hixson 1994)

Surveying the range of these mechanisms underscores the importance of robust, albeit reconfigured, centralized power *for the sake of local deliberative autonomy* and illuminates the variety of design challenges whose answers require rejecting the dichotomy between centralization and devolution. The political conflicts between proponents of local control and central authority highlight the practical difficulties of overcoming this dichotomy and establishing a stable hybrid form. Without such a hybrid form of democratic administration, however, the participatory reforms begun in the late 1980s and early 1990s in Chicago face daunting obstacles to sustained success.

3.1. Dilemmas of Devolution

As a matter of institutional design, the need for reconfigured central authority begins with the characteristic problems of strictly decentralized participatory problem-solving. If Chicago policing and education reforms had ended with the participatory, deliberative measures described in the previous chapter, they would have faced many additional pathologies and important opportunities to improve the fairness and effectiveness of these organizations would have been missed. The most important dilemmas of participatory devolution are: the difficulty of mobilizing citizens and conveying information about participatory opportunities and benefits; assuring that participants have the skills and knowledge necessary to deliberate and solve public problems effectively; assuring that participants have the commitment and determination to implement their decisions; domination and exclusion of some groups due to inequalities of power and voice between groups of citizens or between citizens and officials; the high variation and inequality of outcomes that inevitably accompanies decentralization; parochialism and consequent ineffectiveness in problem-solving; and the dependence of local actors on resources and organizations outside of their control. We shall consider these in turn.

The first problem concerns generating interest among citizens sufficient to bring about participation in municipal-governance opportunities. The main motivation for participation relies upon a trade of time for power and influence. Participatory devolution in Chicago created opportunities for citizens to exert real influence on two important public agencies. Potentially, this influence can improve very tangible aspects of local public life: safety in the streets and the quality of children's education. The price of obtaining these benefits, however, is personal commitment of time and energy through participation, deliberation, and, sometimes, action. The extent of participation depends upon whether public officials actually confer influence—whether they empower participants—and whether potential participants judge that benefits are worth the substantial temporal, psychic, and even material costs. Before they can make this calculation, however, they must become informed about these opportunities for engagement. In many Chicago neighborhoods, these information costs are nontrivial. At the most rudimentary level, residents must know the basic facts about these reforms: where and when meetings are held, how to run for election to LSC, and so forth. More importantly, they must believe that there is some benefit to participation: that meetings are not just talk shops or venting sessions. As we shall see, community organizing, outreach, and awareness efforts made by civic organizations and central-agency staff have been crucial in filling these information gaps and generating the interest that motivates participation.

Even if substantial numbers of residents participate in reforms like community policing and school governance, they may lack the skills to deliberate well and successfully grapple with the complex issues at hand. Participating in school-council governance and community policing requires considerably more knowledge and skill than voting or contributing to political campaigns. Residents, parents, community members, and street-level bureaucrats must possess the interpersonal competencies to be able to deliberate with one another and develop public-action strategies over time. They must also acquire substantive knowledge about, for instance, liquor and loitering laws, school budgeting, curriculum design, and analytic and problem-solving methodologies. While some of these skills might be acquired in the course of one's professional life and/or through participation in civic associations (Verba, Schlozman, and Brady 1995), others are so specialized that they can only be provided as part of the reform programs themselves.

The third dilemma of exclusion and domination stems from conflicts of interest and inequalities of power, status, and resources among participants. One danger, particularly pernicious in small groups, is the tendency of factions or individuals to dominate decision-making. When these groups make decisions through face-to-face discussion, as the communities of inquiry in Chicago community policing and school governance do, the possibilities for domination and exclusion may be amplified by education, aggressive communication styles, claims to expertise, and gender and racial differences refracted through cultural norms of argument and discourse (Mansbridge 1980; Sanders 1997). Ameliorating these pathologies of exclusion and domination often requires extralocal measures. As we shall see below, the CPS and CPD have developed checks and monitoring mechanisms to address these problems.

The inevitable variations in process and success between schools and police beats, a fourth consequence of the decentralization, creates both problems and opportunities. One difficulty is that differences in deliberative and problem-solving success, whether random or stemming from resource inequalities and circumstances, has real consequences for the quality of public services. LSC and beat groups that cannot deliberate well are likely to have less effective schools and more dangerous neighborhoods. Correctives must again come from outside the locality. Some helpful measures include redistributing resources to those in greater need. Others seek to identify less successful groups and provide additional guidance or intervention. One creative strategy, attempted by the CPS, would exploit this local variation by creating partnerships in which more successful schools—those that have developed effective governance, management, or pedagogical techniques—would receive support to transfer their innovations to less successful ones.

A fifth important dilemma of devolution, this one more specific to the context of municipal governance, is that local strategies for school improvement and public safety will often be quite limited without contributions, or at least cooperation, from external public and private actors. One common criticism of administrative differentiation is that agencies operate in parallel, isolated "stovepipes," but that coordination across these divisions is necessary to address many public problems. Many community-policing strategies, for example, require concerted action on the part of other city agencies—the transportation authority, liquor-licensing bodies, sanitation department, legal services, and parks department. Since actions at the neighborhood level lack the reach to alter the disposition or organization of these entities, only extralocal measures can secure this coordination and cooperation.

3.2. Training: Schools of Democracy in the Chicago Reforms

From the outset, advocates of police and school decentralization recognized that many citizens would find constructive engagement with professionals difficult. They therefore urged that training programs be developed and provided on a city-wide basis as a necessary part of the reform package. As it turned out, in both cases professionals would undergo exactly the same training as lay citizens, for the difficulties associated with exercising the power of deliberative problem-solving were new to both. Since there was no body of off-the shelf expertise or experts in deliberative local governance, training was necessarily a boot-strapping process.

The importance of training both staff and citizens has been emphasized throughout the course of community-policing reform: "From the start, the Chicago Police Department identified critical areas for change. . . . Other cities showed that community policing could not succeed without adequate training for officers. . . . An immense training effort, mounted using non-traditional teaching techniques, employed both civilians and trainers" (Chicago Community Policing Evaluation Consortium 1994, 11). That program consisted of twenty sessions of four hours each held over four weeks in 1993. Overall, 1,779 patrol officers, sergeants, and lieutenants received training in the problem-solving orientation of CAPS, leadership development, and "the decision making and interpersonal skills believed essential to CAPS' success . . . communications, problem solving, alliances, goal setting and ethics"(Chicago Community Policing Evaluation Consortium 1995, 22).

This training program expanded dramatically in 1994. Under a $2.9 million contract that spanned nineteen months, the city hired the Chicago Alliance on Neighborhood Safety (CANS), a community-based organization, to teach this curriculum to residents and officers. CANS dispatched teams consisting of community organizers, civilian trainers, and experienced police officers to each of the city's beats (Fung 1997e). Over the three or four months that they spent in each beat, the team would teach the method of deliberative problem-solving by leading residents and police officers through the practical-reasoning process described in the previous chapter. By the end of the period, residents had often learned the process by applying it themselves. In many cases, they could see progress on real-world problems, such as a neighborhood crack house or dangerous public park, that they had selected as part of the training exercise. This Joint Community-Police Training (JCPT) ran for two years. Over that time, organizers estimate that they trained some twelve thousand residents and several hundred police officers. As the community-policing program deepened within CPD and came to require the mastery of new perspectives, skills, and procedures, training and professional development at all levels became more elaborate. Between 1995 and 1998, in-service training programs were developed for sergeants—the front-line managers in police organizations. After 1999, the highest tiers of management—deputy superintendents, chiefs, and district commanders—received individualized courses of training to help them master the new community policing and accountability protocols.

School reformers also saw that LSC members might be initially bewildered by their new governance duties, and so developed their own series of training programs. During the first few years, groups within the CPS and nonprofit community organizations like the Chicago Association of Local School Councils and the Beverly Improvement Association provided training on an ad hoc basis to schools and LSC members who sought it out. In response to the perception that many LSCs were failing, the Illinois legislature passed a second major school-reform law, this one focused on school accountability, in 1995. One of its provisions was that all new LSC members were required to undergo three days, or eighteen hours, of training or else be removed from office. Training covered basic areas of school governance: principal selection and contract terms; school budgeting; LSC member responsibilities; teamwork; and school improvement planning. This program resembled community-policing efforts in that training was centrally coordinated by a group from the University of Illinois, but initially provided by experienced practitioners from community and school-reform organizations as well as school-system employees. As in the policing-training program, the board of education brought the program in-house in 1998 by banning outside, mostly community-based organizations from providing basic training (Scheid 1998). In 2000, community organizations won a substantial victory when the CPS agreed to allow external groups to provide required training for LSC members.

3.3. Mobilization

Just as the creation of opportunities for direct self-governance does not imply that citizens will possess capacities necessary to utilize them, neither does it mean that they will actually participate; some may not know and others may know but not care to join (Grinc 1994). In a second area of support, centralized efforts also attempted to boost awareness and partici-

TABLE 3.1
Public and Private Funding for LSC Mobilization ($ million)

Year	Private	Public/CPS	Total
1989	0.75	N/A	—
1991	0.75	1.2	1.95
1993	0.57	N/A	—
1996	0.25	1.4	1.65
1998	0.13	1.7	1.83
2000	0.42	1.3	1.72
2002	0.08	1.3	1.38

Source: McKersie (1996), Weisman (2000), and Catalyst Staff (May 2002).

pation in deliberative governance. Community-policing outreach has employed both mass-media and community-organizing techniques. In 1997 and 1999, the city spent $1.6 million annually on media efforts to advertise and educate residents about CAPS and its participation opportunities (Chicago Community Policing Evaluation Consortium 1999). Partially as a result of these television and radio spots, billboards, and a weekly cable television program called "CrimeWatch," approximately 79 percent of Chicago's adults knew about CAPS in 1998. These efforts have been supplemented by timed-tested community-organizing methods. First provided as part of the CANS training program, and then later managed from the mayor's office, the program has included as part of its staff between thirty and sixty community organizers that publicize beat meetings and partnership possibilities by visiting churches, neighborhood associations, and individual residences.

Rather than the continuous outreach exhibited in community policing, mobilization for school governance has focused on the biannual LSC elections. These efforts have been funded primarily through private sources as well as by the CPS. This money supports the production of public-service announcements in media outlets, materials distributed at schools and libraries, and community-organization efforts to recruit candidates to run for LCSs and mobilize voters for LSC elections. In the first year of elections, 1989, charitable foundations donated some $750,000 to candidate recruitment, but this sum steadily declined until the 2000 election year. CPS support follows the reverse pattern, rising steadily and then declining in 2000. Table 3.1 shows public and private levels of support for LSC election mobilization where figures are available. Though causality is of course difficult to establish, many associate downward trends in both the number of LSC candidates and voter turnout to this general decline in funding for outreach and mobilization.

3.4. Cognitive Templates for Deliberative Governance and Problem-Solving

In the Chicago reforms, centralized offices of the CPD and the CPS have performed the crucial, practical, and oft-ignored work of giving content to abstract notions like deliberation, problem-solving, and community engagement. In other words, they constitute "deliberation" and "participation" in the administrative realms of police and school governance by specifying who deliberates, the minima of when deliberation occurs, the cognitive methodology and boundaries of problem-solving, and the responsibilities of officials with regard to these deliberations. Since participatory deliberation was a new and dramatically different operational mode for both the CPS and CPD, and because street-level officials and residents of many neighborhoods lacked the capacity to develop their own procedures of deliberation, these templates had to be centrally supplied.

In developing training materials and organizing neighborhood meetings, police managers and community activists have advanced a rather limited definition of the kinds of issues that should count as community-policing problems. This specification excludes singular incidents, such as one rape or shooting, that lack an extended geographic or temporal span. It also excludes so-called root causes, for instance as poverty and unemployment. Bounding deliberation in these ways is not without its costs. Singular, highly visible incidents such as a neighborhood shooting or rape often draw public attention and create energy that might be channeled into community policing. Unless such incidents can be connected to underlying, repeated, patterns of behavior, however, it is unclear how residents can contribute to such incidents through problem-solving.

Some critics have charged that a deliberative focus on tangible problems to the exclusion of root-causes is unjustified because it distracts the attention of participants from fundamental issues for the sake of trivial ones. This criticism, however, misses the role and purpose of participatory deliberation in community policing and in accountable autonomy, generally. The institutional reforms aim not merely to create free spaces of deliberation, but to tie deliberation to public action, and public action to the solution of urgent problems of everyday life. When public institutions aim to create this *empowered* deliberation, the scope of deliberation must be bounded to the competencies of the institution that confers power and hosts deliberation. The institutional competence of the CPD revolves centrally around public safety and has recently expanded to include a multitude of factors that contribute to the decline of public safety: conditions in parks, cleanliness of streets, residential housing ordinances, and the like. It is appropriate that the scope of deliberations occurring under the

"The Crime Triangle is an important tool to use when we analyze a problem. We must gather information for all three sides to entirely understand the problem."

3.1. The Crime Triangle.

auspices of community policing expand and contract in concert with these institutional competencies. If, however, these deliberations expanded so far as to include issues that are linked to public safety but far outside the purview of the CPD—root-causes like the distribution of income and wealth or the absence of economic development—these deliberations would lose power. Talk would necessarily become disconnected from public action for the simple reason that strategies necessary to address these issues do not lie within the scope of what police, or agencies at one or two steps remove from the police, can do. Such expansion of deliberative scope would thus entail a contraction of empowerment. If community-policing deliberations were to become disempowered in this way, they would run the risk of becoming frustrating venting sessions. They would, thereby, become far less attractive as avenues of political participation to residents who wish to take action to improve neighborhood circumstances.

For these reasons, participants in community-policing meetings are directed to focus on chronic problems of crime and disorder that they have some ability to address. These problems are to be analyzed and broken down into three major elements of a "crime triangle": offender, victim, and location (Chicago Police Department 1996, 8–9; Skogan et al. 1999, 41–44). Figure 3.1 taken from CPD training materials, depicts this analytical tool.

Participants in beat meetings analyze these problems and develop solutions according to the deliberative procedures developed by community organizers and central CPD staff. This work occurs in both monthly community-policing beat meetings, which are attended by police officers and open to all neighborhood residents, and regular police-only staff meetings called "beat team meetings." Ideally, problem-solving follows the five-step procedure of practical deliberation in both of these venues.[1] CPD managers require police officers and sergeants to file "beat plans" that document their deliberations in order to help guide the group thought process through these steps and to construct a documentary trail.[2]

Compared to Chicago community policing, the efforts of the CPS offices of Accountability and School Improvement Planning to structure and guide deliberation are more ambitious but less-well implemented. Rather than focusing on individual problems, practical deliberation in school governance aims at improving the organization and operations of the entire school. The 1988 reforms established long-term site-based planning as one core activity of school governance. In particular, the state law required the staff, parents, and community members at each Chicago school to produce an SIP.[3] As a deliberative activity, developing the SIP compels those involved in school governance to agree upon a distinctive vision for their school, analyze the strengths and weaknesses of many aspects of school operation, and develop strategies for deploying discretionary resources and leveraging strengths to more fully realize school visions. Formally, school managers write the SIP and the LSC approves it and monitors its implementation. In practice, the SIP is a major document whose parts are composed by ad hoc committees of parents and staff who work through particular issues such as physical plant, curriculum, materials, discipline, and the like. In the ideal, each school's SIP is a living document, produced through continuous, reflective, and inclusive deliberation that guides other crucial school-level decisions.

As with community policing, this ordered and focused deliberation has not emerged spontaneously from autonomous LSC efforts. Rather, the responsibility translating this ideal of deliberation into school-level practice fell to CPS central-office staff. The Department of School Improvement Planning structured deliberation by requiring schools to submit SIPs that answer mandated questions and by providing a planning template.[4] Schools were not required to use this template for their SIP, but in practice nearly all of them followed it. The first draft template, in use until 1995, was perceived by most to be an incredibly cumbersome paperwork exercise that did little to guide substantive governance efforts; it ran more than one hundred pages for each school. Shortly thereafter, the CPS developed a much shorter, streamlined, and open template. For the 2001–2002 school year, the basic SIP template provided by CPS retained this same fundamental structure and is fourteen pages long. It required each school to lay out its vision, prioritized goals, budget allocations keyed to those goals, accomplishments and mission in each of those goals, strengths and weaknesses in areas such as reading, mathematics, and science, improvement strategies, and task allocations to implement those strategies (Chicago Public Schools 2000).

The central offices of both the CPS and CPD, then, advanced local deliberation in two respects. First, extralocal staff developed very practical and structured conceptions of deliberation and problem-solving for their particular issue-areas and promulgated tools to help local groups conduct their discussions according to these conceptions of deliberation. Second, central authorities required local groups to conduct active problem-solving according to these designs. Consistent with the logic of accountable autonomy, local groups enjoy wide discretion in setting priorities and developing strategies to achieve them. But autonomy is not license. They are therefore compelled to utilize their freedom actively and reasonably, and in particular to produce plans that document their deliberations and strategic thinking.

3.5. Bottom-Up, Top-Down Accountability

Beyond mechanisms to facilitate neighborhood-level governance processes, both the CPS and CPD have also developed accountability mechanisms to enhance the quality of local problem-solving, and to ensure that local school councils and beat groups follow through on their deliberative commitments. In hierarchical models, accountability runs top-down, with central supervisors specifying methods and ends, and monitoring subordinates to see that they comply. Under participatory devolution, accountability runs bottom-up. As we saw in the previous chapter, for instance, new avenues of engagement allow neighborhood residents, parents, and community members to monitor the activities of local officials—police officers and school staff—and to express their concerns about the performance or behavior of these public servants.

More distinctively, the CPS and CPD have both also developed mechanisms that one high-ranking police planner aptly described as "bottom-up, top-down" accountability. The general notion is that the hard work of setting priorities, developing problem-solving strategies, and implementing them should occur within LSCs and beat groups. But local groups may fail to develop effective solutions for lack of creativity or fail to implement them for want of will. Top-down, hierarchical accountability mechanisms can help to assure that they reflect and act with responsibility and commitment. Far from supplanting local prerogatives, this kind of oversight reinforces local autonomy by pressing neighborhood-level actors to "do what they say they will do." It is a contemporary implementation of Rousseau's cryptic aphorism that individuals under democratic institutions must occasionally be "forced to be free."[5]

The clearest examples of this kind of supervision come from management changes to the CPD in 2000 following internal frustration with the pace of reform since the initiation of CAPS. A department-wide review assessed the level of implementation of Chicago's new policing model in 1999. Based upon sporadic observations of twenty-five beats, interviews with police supervisors and officers, and anonymous surveys, the review identified wide variation in the degree and quality of problem-solving and community policing. One leader of the review reported that:

> We found all kinds of things: shouting matches between police and residents at beat meetings, beat facilitators charging for rooms. . . . One problem was that many officers did not have the skills to interact with community people—they had not been trained in this and had poor meeting skills. [More importantly,] there often wasn't much problem solving going on. Often, officers complained that watch commanders emphasized more traditional policing priorities at the expense of problem solving. (Anonymous subject, interview with author)

The final report was distributed to top police management, and they saw a clear need to develop hierarchical mechanisms of accountability to improve the quality of participation, deliberation, and problem-solving. Searching the nation's police departments for appropriate methods, officials visited New York City and considered adopting a version of the COMPSTAT performance-management approach (see chapter 1 of the present volume; Silverman 1999). They quickly rejected this model because they felt that it was "totally top-down" and could not incorporate the community-centered elements and bottom-up problem-solving that had become central strengths in Chicago.

Led by Deputy Superintendent Anthony Chiesa, a management team invented a hybrid approach to accountability that, according to an architect of the 2000 CPD round of reforms, would retain the bottom-up strengths but "fill the top-down gap." In the twenty-five police district offices, these reforms aimed to integrate community policing and problem-solving into ordinary police work by incorporating the problems and priorities identified through community meetings and problem-solving sessions directly into conventional channels of supervision and responsibility. The officers of each beat were to select particular neighborhood problems, often based upon community beat-meeting deliberations, as their explicit priorities for analysis and action. The priority problems and attendant strategies would be integrated into daily assignments, and monitored by police sergeants, watch commanders, and district commanders. Middle-ranking supervisors of police officers became responsible for pressing those under them to solve problems and implement strategies that emerge from deliberations with neighborhood residents and other officers. One of the tools used to manage this bottom-up, top-down operational process was each District's "CAPS Mission Board" (Chicago

3.2. CAPS Mission Board.

Community Policing Evaluation Consortium 2000, 152). The Seventh District board, as of 11 May 2001, is depicted in Figure 3.2.

Each row of the mission board lists and describes problems—usually drawn from community deliberations—that beat officers should address. At the beginning of each shift, officers note these priorities and the strategies developed to address them. At the end, they report back on steps taken on these mission priorities. As particular problems are solved over time, they are "closed," removed from the mission board, and other problems rise to fill their place.

The 2000 round of CAPS reforms also established mechanisms to align higher levels of supervision with the new problem-oriented focus of the Department. In regular "Headquarters Strategy and Accountability Meetings," the management and staff of individual districts met with the department's top management to review their performance and the quality of district-level planning. In these meetings, supervisors question district managers about their actions and problem-solving strategies in four core areas: (1) chronic crime and disorder; (2) emerging crime trends; (3) community concerns; and (4) rectifying management procedures and practices that impede this problem-solving. Similar to lower-level beat problem-solving activity, this new supervision technique did not aim to impose the dictates of supervisors upon subordinates, but rather to spur them to think creatively, develop effective strategies, and execute their own plans. As one police manager put it, "[unlike in New York], the goal is not to embarrass people, but to solve problems. . . . These meetings are geared to produce ideas."

In the CPS, bottom-up, top-down accountability relies upon performance rather than process measures. Initiated in 1995, its "probation" and "remediation" programs were an attempt to identify poorly performing schools and improve them through an array of interventions. Schools whose average student standardized test scores fell in the bottom 15 percent of all schools were placed on the "probation" list (Martinez 1996; Druffin 1998). A CPS department, the Office of Accountability, then inspected each school through site visits and personnel interviews to develop improvement strategies. Deliberative failures in the LSC were frequently one cause for the poor performance of the school, and in such cases the CPS center intervened with an array of methods.

A basic tension in this approach is that too forceful intervention from a central body can eliminate local autonomy and thus sacrifice the potential benefits of participatory devolution. For incorrigible cases, there may be no better alternative. If possible, however, the object of intervention should be to restore the integrity of deliberative mechanisms that regulate a community of inquiry.

To see how this works, consider the real case of a nonperforming LSC whose members had clustered into stable factions that opposed one another on almost every substantive issue.[6] The CPS Office of Accountability dispatched a team to review school operations and a facilitator to work with LSC members. Patricia Harvey, director of the Office of Accountability, explained that the object of these intervention efforts was to not to issue commands, but to refocus LSC members on the ultimate goal of school improvement and to create space in which they would be able to reconsider their conflicting positions in light of their deeper commitment to this common goal. When many in the LSC voiced their concern that the report of the review team mandated this or that action, Harvey responded that

the one page [report] is about a group of professionals coming in for a day with their point of view.

It [the report] is a snapshot, not a command. The command is that you sit down . . . and use it to come up with a concrete action plan. . . .

The content of the assessment [report] provides an x-ray reflection of the school's activities. What they [the reviewers] do is to write down what they see from an objective perspective. . . .

It is only when we step back that we see the whole picture. Only when you step back from your immediate, daily activities and refocus your attention can you see the other dimensions of the problem. We have all taken that test for looking at the picture of the old lady, and then you look again and it is a picture of a young woman. What makes us professional is that people who second-guess us actually help us out. None of us would go into surgery—a radical procedure—without a second guess. Unfortunately in education we have not done this enough. Teachers go into a classroom at twenty, close the door, and continue the same methods [whether they are working or not] for the next few decades. We are saying: let's plan for our kids [and] let's be confident enough to take another look at our plans and defend them—this brings the discussion to the next level.[7]

Dr. Frank Gardner, a former school-board president and former district superintendent, was the probation manager that CPS headquarters sent to Harper High School in Chicago. There, he facilitated meetings between various elements of the school staff in order to restore deliberative capacity. Principal Richard Parker comments that "when Dr. Gardner came in, he helped us clarify and define what we were going to do, but he also warned us that what we said we were going to do, *we would do*" (Williams 1997, 20; emphasis in original).

The degree to which facilitation and visioning techniques such as these can restore failures of deliberation is a matter of some speculation, probably more art than science. These examples merely illustrate how external interventions are often necessary to rectify breakdowns in local deliberation.

3.6. Enhancing Institutional Background Conditions for Problem-Solving

All problem-solving efforts, those of individuals as well as beat- and school-level communities of inquiry, depend for their success upon a background of receptive institutions. The efficacy of local deliberation in any particular area of public action depends upon the actions of many other parties: city agencies, elected officials, markets, laws, courts, civic organizations, and labor unions, to name just a few. A central body that derives its power and legitimacy from the accomplishments of its component groups can improve the disposition of institutions upon which these groups' local efforts depend, but which those within localities cannot affect.

Securing adequate funding is one of the most important services that the center can provide to its local groups. While extravagant funding does not automatically yield safe streets or effective schools, poor funding makes education and policing difficult indeed. In the case of public functions like education and policing, financing comes from taxes, which are themselves decided in the electoral and interest-group arenas. In this area, a centralized representative in agencies such as the CPS or CPD can act as one lobby among others to push for stabilization and expansion of its funding base. Reciprocally, those mobilized at the local level for neighborhood governance can also mobilize to support state-level financing for public agencies. For example, LSC members and associated organizations have become a reliable and active constituency for greater state financing for the CPS.

Beyond obvious goals like greater funding, some of the strategies of central support arise from the experimental discoveries of communities themselves. For example, early experiments in school-reform schemes of site-based management revealed that problem-solving requires precious and unbudgeted time. Typical of municipal contracts, the collective bargain between the Chicago Teachers' Union (CTU) and the Chicago Board of Education (CBE) specified strict work rules whose object was to minimize local discretion and maximize the amount of teacher classroom time. The contracts simply did not leave time for planning or problem-solving, and no single school could modify this collective-bargaining agreement that covered some 560 schools. The CTU and CBE negotiated a waiver system in which a voting majority of a school's teachers could exempt themselves from the time-structuring provisions of the collective bargain (Thomas and Griffin 1988). Many school faculties and LSCs have since utilized this waiver to implement a "time-banking" scheme that extends the length of the class day by ten or fifteen minutes for four days every week to create an extra hour of "banked" time each week for faculty-planning and problem-solving activities.

Since its inception, Chicago's community-policing program involved many other city agencies beyond the police. Early designers and supporters saw that enhancing public safety would require efforts not just from the police, but also from other public services. Largely made possible through the mayor's strong support, CAPS has developed effective procedures for interagency communication and coordination that put the services and resources of external bodies at the disposal of problem-solving groups at the beat level (Skogan and Hartnett 1997, 162–72). If a community-policing beat group identifies narcotics trafficking in a neighborhood park as a priority problem, for example, new interagency mechanisms put a range of public services at its disposal to solve this problem; it can request that illegally parked cars be towed, that street signs and lighting be improved, and that graffiti be removed. By creating the infrastructure for bottom-up orchestration of city resources to address explicitly identified public concerns, interagency-coordination reforms in Chicago amplify the powers that residents and police can deploy in their neighborhood-level deliberations.

A more focused instance in which a central authority has modified institutional background conditions for the sake of more effective problem-solving comes from efforts to eliminate drug houses. In many Chicago neighborhoods, there are houses used for narcotics trafficking and consumption. Due to the population density inherent in urban life, these criminal activities harm nearby residents through associated crimes like shootings, robbery, burglary, and battery; in the city, no fences can be high enough to make good neighbors out of crack dealers. It is unsurprising, therefore, that many local community-policing efforts have targeted their problem-solving energies upon drug houses. Often, absentee landlords own these drug houses. They collect the rent, but sometimes neglect the property's maintenance and ignore the negative externalities of tenants' behavior.

Dozens of groups have independently converged upon the following strategy for dealing with such situations. Residents try to persuade a landlord to clean up his property by, for example, evicting problem tenants, reporting criminal activity on the property to police, screening out potentially problematic would-be tenants, and maintaining or upgrading the property. If a landlord responds to these entreaties, resident groups may assist in various ways, and their partnership can be sufficient to eliminate the problem. If the landlord refuses to cooperate, then residents begin to build a legal case that can be used in housing court to seize the property and thereby remove the drug house. According to the Illinois nuisance-abatement law, a court may act against a drug house by "restraining all persons . . . from using the building for a period of one year" if it establishes that "nuisance was maintained with the intentional, knowing, reckless or negligent permission of the owner."[8] The nuisance in such cases is the trafficking of a controlled substance, and establishing negligence under this law requires three narcotics arrests on the property in question. To use this law, group residents worked with police to concentrate patrol, surveillance, and undercover action that would result in three arrests. Then, residents would press the case in housing court by testifying that narcotics activities did in fact severely burden neighborhood life. This strategy to persuade first, then prosecute, has shut down many of the city's drug houses.

Two changes in the institutional background made it easier for organized communities to utilize this approach. First, a 1996 city ordinance whittled away real estate property rights by enacting a stricter version of the Illinois nuisance-abatement law.[9] This ordinance shifted the burden of monitoring illegal activity to the property owner and created fines for allowing nuisances to occur: "any person who owns, manages or controls any premises and who encourages or permits illegal activity . . . shall be subject to a fine" for each day of the offense. Furthermore, whereas the Illinois law is triggered by illegal activity occurring inside particular premises, the Chicago law only requires a geographic nexus between the problem property and nuisance.[10] This provision is important because, as one officer put it, "your classic drug houses don't really exist any more because the dealers know that you can take the house away. Most of the action happens on the street in front of the house."

Second, the city's Law Department, known as Corporation Council, has created a Drug and Gang House Enforcement Section that helps community-policing groups utilize this law. They send staff lawyers to community beat meetings to provide legal expertise in the formulation and implementation of problem-solving strategies. If residents identify and prioritize a drug house, the lawyer will independently deploy the Law Department's resources to eliminate that drug house. According to the section's supervising attorney, the department uses the same strategy described above but backed by the power and resources of the city: persuade first and prosecute second. When corporation council targets a property, they first send city inspectors to document all code violations in addition to the nuisance. It then invites the landlord to a meeting to discuss the situation. The goal of this discussion is voluntary compliance and awareness as documented with a resolution letter signed by the property owner. If the landlord doesn't respond to the initial letter, rejects voluntary compliance, or doesn't show up to the meeting, city attorneys pursue measures in administrative court. They ask for fines and then for criminal-contempt charges that can result in up to 180 days of imprisonment. These two background measures, then, put substantial public authority and resources at the disposal of problem-solving communities in their efforts to eliminate drug houses by generalizing and strengthening a strategy that those communities themselves invented.

3.7. Networking Inquiry

As this anecdote about drug-house strategies suggests, neighborhood-level problem-solving groups dedicated to public priorities like safety and education may face similar challenges. In such cases, some communities may develop effective strategies while others fumble. Centralized, external mechanisms can address this situation by connecting similar groups together so they can share techniques and learn from one another via the pooling of information and experience. Following the metaphor of experimentation, each school and beat group's deliberative efforts can be viewed as sequential experiments in public problem-solving: the strategy is a hypothesis, implementation is the experiment, and evaluation analyzes its results. Networking communities together, then, vastly expands the quantity of trials—from 1 to 279 in the case of policing and to 560 with school governance.

Teachers' desires to communicate their experiences with one another surfaced in the course of a grant-development effort of the Traxton-Area Planning Association (TAPA).[11] TAPA is a Chicago civic organization that has for many years supported various educational initiatives in its community. One of its postreform projects was to develop a "teacher resource center" that would be a networking and professional-development hub for teachers at the community's high school and its seven feeder elementary schools. The resource center would provide common facilities for curriculum development and seminars on education. When asked how the idea to create a networking hub originated, one participant explained that "we conducted focus groups of teachers broken up by subject matter, and the idea kept popping up [in various focus groups]. It really came out that teachers need to talk to one another."

Beyond generic information-pooling through seminars and other such venues, formal arrangements for connecting communities might also utilize performance-based "benchmarking." So, just as the CPS "probation" list selects the bottom 15 percent of schools for special action, standardized tests and other measures might identify high-performing schools so that others can consider reproducing their strategies and techniques.

The CPS "Exemplary Schools Program," first piloted in the 1995–1996 school year, implemented just this strategy. Schools were invited to compete for recognition as an "exemplary school." To qualify for consideration, elementary schools had to demonstrate improvement in student standardized test scores and show that "student achievement on [standardized] . . . tests substantially exceeds *schools serving similar students*" (Children First 1995; emphasis in original). Beyond these minimal screens, schools were asked to explain their success in terms of instructional program, capacity to implement change in the school, LSC governance, collective faculty action, strategic planning, parental involvement, school discipline, and other measures. Selected schools (up to twenty-five) then received several thousand dollars each to create "learning sites" at their school to propagate these best practices to the staff and LSCs of other schools.

Two features of this program should not escape notice. First, designers did not prejudge a specific educational theory as best. Though the CPS did recommend a set of best educational practices, the application specifically stated that "schools will not be judged based upon the specific best practices in the *Self-Analysis Guide*, but on the overall coherence of their activities in these areas, in support of Quality Instruction and student achievement." Second, the ability to articulate the sources of one's success is itself a component of excellence: "Schools must be able to explain how their *Quality Instructional Program*, as well as their [other] practices . . . have made it possible for them to achieve exemplary results." The design of this program illustrates one way in which central authority in the public schools no longer claims to know best educational practice while nevertheless asserting a role in identifying and percolating best practices outward as they are revealed through street-level experiments.

Since local problem-solving became central to public-safety efforts, participants in community policing have also felt constrained by their own parochialism and the limitations of their experience and creativity. Community activists and police officers alike have taken pains to share lessons and best practices across beat boundaries on an informal basis, as opportunities present themselves. One police sergeant expressed it this way:

> The frustrating part is that I know what the model is, but the model isn't . . . being done right now. I don't really know what they're doing in [other] districts.
>
> There are other districts that are doing things completely differently than we are doing them here. I think it would be nice to have a forum, perhaps every six months.
>
> In [CAPS] training, they would take 25 sergeants, one from each district. So, now you're in there with someone from each of the other districts, so you can talk about what's going on in the other districts. I think that maybe once a year they should do this.
>
> Actually, it's been over a year since I've been to that training, and I really believe that now would be a great time to get us back down there, and get us back together, and kick it around a little bit.
>
> And so [the greatest frustration is] the isolation of being here and doing my thing here. I feel a great sense of accomplishment. I feel like I am doing the best I can do at this point with what I have to work with. I pretty much get by and I pretty much feel like I am doing a good job, but I think that there are more creative ways I could find to do things or other things that I could do that I haven't thought of [about which] it would be nice to get input from other people. Just to kick some of this stuff around with other people who are in the same boat. (Anonymous CPD officer, interview with author)

In 2001, program managers charged with improving the quality of beat problem-solving deliberations developed several mechanisms to document explanations and lessons from those who excel at deliberative problem-solving so that others could adopt and adapt their techniques. They developed a centralized data warehouse to collect beat-planning documents and individual neighborhood strategies. They have also developed a best-practices database that allows those who engage in community-policing problem-solving to locate strategies that have worked in other neighborhoods according to issue areas—gangs, narcotics, and prostitution—and actors implementing those strategies: police officers, residents, and other city services.

In a more full-throated police-accountability scheme, one might imagine using crime statistics to measure the performance of police officers in the way that student test scores are used to evaluate schools across the country. In considering this description of the CPD as accountable autonomy, one planner in the Office of Management Accountability at police headquarters reflected that "we are more committed than you realized to the 'autonomy' portion of this design. We are not like the schools. We will never develop rankings of the beats because the conditions of crime and contexts of problem-solving are so varied. We will never compare beat to beat and district to district" (Anonymous CPD manager, interview with author). For them, effective problem-solving requires local autonomy, sharing of best practices, and many kinds of centralized support and supervision. In their estimation, however, supervision that relied upon easily collected and quantified statistics would be misleading at best, and at worst impose counterproductive incentives and constraints on those street-level police officers, and residents, whose ingenuity determines the success or failure of the new policing.

3.8. Redistribution to the Least Capable

Left to their independent devices, some would surely flounder while others excelled at problem-solving due to their superior wealth, deliberative capacity, or brute luck. In decentralized environments, unequal capacities yield differential outcomes and some will receive better services than others (Weir 1994). A commitment to equity in the provision of services like education and policing requires centralized efforts to address such inequalities between communities. Much of the variance in problem-solving outcomes doubtless can be attributed to background conditions of social and economic inequality. Administrative agencies are often powerless to affect these socioeconomic conditions, however, and must frequently treat them as parameters rather than objects of institutional design. Much of the remaining variance in outcomes can be attributed to the differential problem-solving capacities between communities of inquiry. A supportive central apparatus can mitigate these differences by focusing its resources on developing the capacities of those who are least able.

Hypothetically, central staff could allocate some portion of resources toward remediation. They might rank the performance of local groups according to the best metrics available to identify "needy" communities. In the public schools, comparison of student standardized test scores across time and with other schools, attendance rates, graduation rates, active auditing of schools, parent and community surveys, and more subtle measures might compose such a metric. In neighborhood police beats, participation rates, quality of problems prioritized and solved, survey instruments, and comparative supervisor reports could all be employed to generate such rankings.

A redistributive center would then use its remediation resources to assist "needy" communities—sometimes through the direct injection of resources, but probably more often through the kinds of supportive measures described above. So, low participation and lack of deliberative capacities are two sources of failure that may be caused by background social and economic inequalities.[12] To offset these biases, a redistributive center might channel publicity and outreach resources to boost participation and focus training efforts in deliberation upon these least-able communities. According to William Julius Wilson's social-isolation hypothesis, the most disadvantaged underclass communities lack connections with powerful institutional actors in the political arena, the private economy, and other city agencies (Wilson 1987, 58–62). As was previously discussed, access to these resources in no small part determines the success of urban problem-solving efforts, and central authority can improve connections with such outside actors. It is therefore appropriate to channel these efforts toward those communities that lack such linkages. Networking-inquiry mechanisms aim to employ the discoveries of the most successful to teach the rest. A redistributive center might subsidize these kinds of peer-learning initiatives to link the best communities with the worst in order to bring experimental expertise where it is most desperately needed.

Unlike the other capacity and accountability functions discussed above, the CPS and CPD have not developed programs that explicitly perform this redistributive function of channeling resources to the communities most in need. Some of their programs do, however, implicitly redistribute administrative resources. The probation and remediation lists of the CPS, for example, provide training, managerial consultation, and occasionally additional funds to the worst-performing, and therefore neediest, schools. Within the unified Chicago school district, per-pupil funding levels are distributed to schools according to a formula that allocates more money to schools with higher proportions of students from low-income families; Chicago schools with more poor students, therefore, enjoy higher per-pupil funding levels than those with more wealthy ones. In community policing, the distribution of officers takes into account crime rates in the determination of beat boundaries; high-crime beats tend to be geographically smaller than low crime ones. Furthermore, the reorganization of the

CPD around the logic of local problem-solving creates pressure to channel police resources to the most crime-ridden communities. Common resources that are shared across beats—detectives, other special units, some city services, and a host of others—are now allocated in part according to the needs articulated through the development of problem-solving plans and schedules of priority problems. Those areas with the most urgent problems—as articulated in beat or district plans and as expressed in supervisory accountability meetings—now receive greater access to common departmental resources. Many managers regard this allocation scheme—according to problem-priority—as superior on grounds of both fairness and transparency to the logics of allocation by favoritism (flexible but unfair) or by rigid procedural rules (perhaps fair but not flexible).

3.9. Conflicts between Community and the Local State

This impressive array of institutional innovations in the CPS and CPD illustrates how both organizations have moved beyond simple participatory devolution to develop mechanisms that enhance both the capacity and accountability of local problem-solving groups. It would be misleading, however, to suggest that this reform path has been smooth, or that its progress is inexorable. Indeed, Chicago's community-policing and school reforms have been wrought with political conflict throughout. In both cases, city agencies and activist groups found themselves working together to design and implement the early stages of the participatory reforms. For a time, this alliance allowed a division of labor in which secondary associations and public agencies complemented one another (Cohen and Rogers 1992). Activist and community-based organizations deployed their expertise to build the capacities of residents and others to participate in local school-council and beat meetings and represent their perspectives at the city level. CPS and CPD reformers could receive and respond to this popular input.

For political and cultural reasons, however, these alliances were momentary and fragile. Part of the central mission of community organizations like CANS and PURE was to increase the voice and control of the city's citizens over the local state—police and schools, respectively. When those public agencies pursued a reform agenda that included participatory devolution, they built improbable alliances with activists. Public criticism and oppositional mobilization are also essential components of Chicago activism, however. Regarding community capacity, these organizations trained participants to monitor and criticize teachers, police officers, and other street-level bureaucrats for failing to be responsive, to do their jobs, or to live up to the promise of the reform programs. They also frequently criticized the police department and public schools for failing to respect popular voices, give neighborhoods their due, and advance participatory reform.

Chicago officialdom is famously intolerant of public criticism and independent political strength. Unwilling to be coopted and silenced, some of the leading community organizations supporting participatory reform soon alienated the city's officials and suffered their wrath. This conflict between the local state and community groups interacted with decisions about the course of institutional reform in the CPD and CPS.

Recall from chapter 2 that the most important community voice in police reform was CANS. It was arguably instrumental in shaping the participatory features that became the distinctive trademark of Chicago-style community policing. Following this work, CANS received the eighteen-month, $2.9 million-dollar contract described above to mobilize and train residents throughout the city to participate in CAPS.[13] This major source of funding allowed CANS to dramatically expand its staff and scope of operation by hiring dozens of organizers and trainers. In the course of organizing neighborhoods and training citizens not only to solve problems, but to hold local police and politicians accountable for contributing to neighborhood-safety efforts, CANS made enemies in city hall, the police department, among ward aldermen, and even with other community-based organizations.

In 1997, the city refused to renew CANS's organizing contract. Rather than subcontracting to an independent community group, the police department and the mayor's office would field its own organizers and trainers. Police officials argued that this functional integration was necessary to render mobilization and capacity-building efforts more uniform, efficient, and professional. Then–CPD Deputy Superintendent Chuck Ramsey said, "To bring community policing to the next level, we need to incorporate training into regular police department functions. We can't have third parties doing this." Others, however, argued that the decision to terminate funding for CANS was made from a desire to control the mobilization process and squelch criticism. Warren Friedman, executive director of CANS, traces the deterioration of city relations to the thin skins of city hall and the police department. "We got cut off because we were independent, and because we were critical when we saw wrong policy decisions. For instance, we had a tense meeting with the mayor's office and CPD after one report that criticized relations between youth and police." When asked whether the organization could have done anything to keep its city funding, longtime CANS supporter Alderman Joe Moore echoed Friedman's sentiment. "They could have become more of a lapdog of the administration, but they didn't want to do that," he said (interview with author).

Whatever the particular motives behind this decision, CANS suffered a severe blow from this loss of revenue. Subsequently, its reach diminished. Though it continued to agitate around police-responsibility and police-responsiveness issues, it was unable to regain its position as a major voice and force in Chicago community policing. Though local community organizations throughout the city continued to participate in various aspects of community policing, none rose to the stature and influence of CANS. Police reformers enjoyed a relatively free hand in devising and implementing many of the reforms described above because they were spared from the rigorous and vociferous, yet perhaps ultimately constructive, criticism that a stronger CANS might have offered.

In contrast to community policing, local school-governance reform grew out of a broad alliance that consisted of community groups, parent organizations, watchdog organizations, and business leaders.[14] Similar to CANS, these organizations would play important roles in the initial stages of school reform. They recruited candidates to turn out for local school-council elections, trained new LSC members in areas like budgeting, school-improvement planning, and the selection of principals. As with CANS, these groups also saw it as part of their mission to equip LSC members to be usefully critical of officials and public agencies: to point out shortcomings in the performance of principals and school staff, and to make demands upon the Board of Education and its administrators. Predictably, such criticism soured relations with school officials. In contrast to community policing, however, community-based school-reform groups were resilient. Compared to the solitary CANS, school-reform groups were more diverse, greater in number, and financially independent from the city. Groups like PURE and DFC were thus able to survive, if not thrive, while maintaining critical independence from CPS officials and helping many LSC members to be similarly independent.

In the face of this persistent external criticism, CPS reformers have pursued inconsistent institutional-reform strategies. On one hand, they have implemented various centralized measures to strengthen the local groups described above. CPS reformers may hope to make the best of school-based governance since the institution of LSC is entrenched in law and backed by robust political support. But precisely the opposite impulse— to diminish local autonomy and recentralize authority over schools—has been manifest in other CPS initiatives. This latter moment has assumed the form of a low-intensity conflict that is waged in battles over funding, administrative authority, and even the everyday details of running and governing schools.

One milestone in this conflict over the extent of local power was a 1995 law, backed both by Democratic Mayor Daley and Republican lawmakers, that granted the mayor substantial new powers over the Chicago schools: the ability to appoint a new, consolidated school board and relaxation of state-based oversight over the financial system.[15] In June 1995, Daley appointed two of his most aggressive senior staff members to head the CPS: his budget director, Paul Vallas, became the chief executive officer (the post was formerly called general superintendent) of the system and his chief of staff, Gery Chico, became chair of the new Chicago School Reform Board. As we have seen above, several of the main measures in this 1995 law actually used centralized methods to enhance local governance capacity and responsibility. Nevertheless, many local and national observers interpreted this law and subsequent personnel appointments as a retrenchment of centralized authority and therefore a reversal of the 1988 decentralizing reforms (Pearson and Kass 1995). One observer saw the Chicago shift as emblematic of a national trend toward recentralization in big-city school systems:

> If there is a moment when the re-centralization movement was energized, it occurred in the spring of 1995, when the Republican-controlled Illinois legislature decided to hand Chicago's Democratic mayor four years of unprecedented emergency authority to run the city's schools. At the time, speculation centered around the motive for the bill: Did Daley really want responsibility for a failing school system, or were Republican legislators simply trying to saddle him with an insurmountable task? (Mahtesian 1996)

A more clear assault on local school-council authority appeared in proposals put forward by the CPS to change the state-wide school-reform legislation in 1999. In what was to become Senate Bill 652, the CPS administration pressed state legislatures to shift substantial authority over principal selection from LSC to central offices. Under the proposed legislation, LSCs would be required to rehire any principal that received a "meets" or "exceeds expectations" performance rating from central administrators, and to dismiss principals who received less than a satisfactory central evaluation. In 1999, no Chicago principal whose contract was expiring received less than a satisfactory rating (Weissman and Ross 1999). Since the power to hire and fire principals is widely viewed as one of the most important prerogatives of LSC, many activists viewed this proposal as an attempt to reduce LSCs to advisory status. One director of a local school-governance support organization commented that "S.B. 652 clarified the threat of [CPS] central office initiatives for many people, and gave them a sense of what the LSCs might lose" (Interview with author). Many reform groups, including DFC, the Chicago School Leadership Cooperative (CSLC), and PURE lobbied against the measure and won the support of many Illinois legislators who favored local voice over school decisions. The resulting compromise legislation, passed in May

1999, retained principal-selection powers for LSCs. Dismissed principals gained the right to binding arbitration from a neutral party (appointed by the American Arbitration Association), and the board did not win the principal-selection authority that it initially sought.[16]

Beneath these visible campaigns and battles, the everyday governance of schools—selecting principals, writing SIPs, and monitoring them—has been marked by numerous skirmishes between community organizations and LSC members, on one side, and the CPS administration, on the other. Some complain that CPS officials frequently used technicalities to obstruct LSC oversight efforts and defend administrative prerogatives. For example, Chicago school-reform legislation charges LSCs with monitoring the implementation of SIPs. But CPS central administrators often attempted to prohibit LSC members from visiting classrooms and school grounds to conduct this activity. In a letter to a South Side LSC member, Chief Education Officer Cozette Buckney wrote:

> The principal of . . . has advised us of the proposed visitation of [school name] School classrooms during the day program currently being considered by the [school name] LSC for the ostensible purpose of monitoring implementation of [school name] School Improvement Plan. . . . However, neither classroom visitation nor teacher evaluation are within the powers and duties of local school councils as set fourth in the Illinois School Code. . . . Therefore, please be advised that no member of the [school name] LSC, whether individually or with other council members, will be allowed to conduct classroom visits during the instructional day.[17]

Another letter, from a Board of Education attorney to an LSC member of another school, reads: "This correspondence is to clarify the position of the Chicago Public Schools concerning your presence on school grounds. Specifically, it is our opinion that your legal rights to be present on school grounds extend only to attendance at Local School Council meetings."[18]

In other instances, central administrators have rejected LSC principal-selection decisions when filed just a few days beyond administrative deadlines. In a letter dated 1 June 1999, CPS Chief Executive Officer Paul Vallas wrote to an elementary school LSC chair:

> Thank you for submitting the names of three principal candidates for the [school name deleted] School to me. Please be advised that I will not be selecting any candidate for the Principalship of [school name deleted] School from the list you submitted to my office.
>
> I would also like to inform you that I will be appointing an interim principal effective July 1, 1999. According to Board rule, 4–22.3, the Chief Executive Officer has the authority to appoint an interim principal up to a period of one year due to the fact that the Local School Council did not submit the list of three names by May 1, 1999.[19]

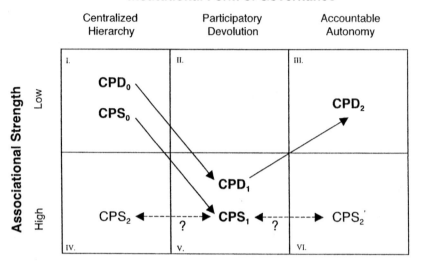

3.3. Association Strength and Institutional Change.

While the CPD has unambiguously pursued the path of accountable autonomy by developing centralized mechanisms to enhance local problem-solving capacity and autonomy, the CPS has equivocated between attempts to reinforce local governance and other efforts to retrench central authority at the expense of LSC autonomy. This difference becomes understandable in light of the absence of substantial community-based capacity for independent criticism in community policing, and the persistence of oppositional activist groups in public education. Whatever its problem-solving, administrative benefits for public officials, the participatory devolution of municipal organization creates favorable terrain on which oppositional community and neighborhood groups can mobilize. When groups utilize this terrain to organize resistance, as they have in Chicago public education, public officials may think twice about entrenching reforms that empower their critics. When these community-based forces are weak or absent, as in Chicago policing after the decline of CANS, defensive officials can operate with a freer hand.

Figure 3.3 charts these institutional choices and developments: Institutional configurations in the top row represent environments where the strength of independent community organizations and secondary associations are weak. In the bottom row, such groups are strong. The columns represent three alternative forms of governance institutions. Organizations in the left column (regions I and IV) are centralized and hierarchical, those in the center column (regions II and V) decentralized and participatory, and those in the right column (regions III and VI) exhibit the hybrid form of accountable autonomy.

To stylize and simplify, suppose that administrative reformers in both the police department and school system have two priorities. The first is to adopt organizational forms that are modern, efficient, and effective according to the currency of their disciplines. Their second priority is professional control and absence of external, independent criticism. The schematic narrative begins with the insular, hierarchical, pre-1990 forms of the CPS and CPD. These states are marked CPS_0 and CPD_0 and depicted as initial positions in region I. Due to the legitimation crises and reform ideas described in the previous chapter, both organizations formed practical and ideological alliances with community-based, participatory groups and adopted the major reforms of participatory devolution, shifting to the bottom center box. CPS_1 represents the organization after the LSC legislation of 1988 and CPD_1 marks police organization following the city-wide adoption of the CAPS—beat meetings, beat teams, and problem-solving—in 1995.

After this point, these two agencies evolve on divergent paths. As the community-organization partners in these endeavors mobilized residents, trained them to monitor and criticize public officials, and articulated demands and further criticisms, they threatened the second priority of administrators—their desire for professional autonomy and a free hand. The erstwhile alliance between community organizations and the local state fractured into tension, and sometimes combat, in both realms. In community policing, the main organization, CANS, declined due to its heavy reliance on funding from the city. With the potential for organized community opposition and criticism thus contained, police reformers were free to continue their participatory trajectory of reform by establishing robust management structures along the lines of the accountable-autonomy design. This end point is depicted in the low–associational strength, high–local autonomy region III as CPD_2.

Because community and civic organizations concerned with public education were more durable, CPS administrators faced a more difficult choice. They could not simultaneously satisfy both priorities of organizational effectiveness and professional autonomy. If they extended the devolutionary reforms by developing supports for LSCs, devolving funding and authority and the like, they risked strengthening the hand of threatening community-based organizations. These organizations could, and on occasion certainly would, act to limit and check professional discretion and organizational latitude. On the other hand, state law, political pressure, and the partial success of educational reform made it difficult to abandon the path of participation, devolution, and site-based management begun in 1988. In the latter half of the 1990s, the organization was unable to choose between these alternatives. Some measures, such as the probation and training supports discussed above, fit easily into the accountable-autonomy model. Others, such as the hostility of central administration toward many LSCs and the increasing reliance on high-stakes testing, move toward recentralization. These inconsistent, divergent trajectories are depicted as potential futures—CPS_2 (region IV) and CPS_2' (region VI). In 2002, it was unclear which institutional design—centralization or accountable autonomy—would ultimately prevail in the CPS.

The optimal space for accountable autonomy is clearly region VI. There, vigorous community organizations would mobilize residents, support them in their problem-solving activities, and hold public agencies accountable and render them responsive. These community organizations would operate in tandem, through a creative and critical tension, with public agencies that establish channels of public participation and harness that participation for local problem-solving. The Chicago reforms fall short of this ideal, however, because political and administrative leaders are unwilling to tolerate the kinds of criticism that are inevitably raised by capable community and activist organizations. Therefore, the CPS developments that approach region VI are tentative and unstable, while the CPD has developed accountable autonomy in the absence of strong civic voice (region III). Stable public institutions in region VI would require leaders to become less defensive and alter their notions of professionalism to include heavy, but healthy, doses of public criticism (Skolnick and Bayley 1986, 212). This change may require a simple change of leadership, or it may be merely wishful thinking in the face of political constraints and traditions.

The imperfect nature of these reforms should not obscure the extent of the change that has occurred since the late 1980s. Both the CPS and CPD have created profound opportunities and supports for ordinary city residents to exercise voice over their local state, and to contribute to the resolution of urgent pubic problems. With important limitations, they have nevertheless placed this deep democratization at the center of their administrative-reform programs. In the next three chapters, we examine the extent of participation, character of deliberation, and nature of public problem-solving as they have unfolded within the formal institutional structures elaborated above.

4

Challenges to Participation

THE preceding chapters offered accountable autonomy as a general institutional design that advances methods of direct and deliberative citizen participation to solve stubborn public problems. The CPD and CPS reconfigured many aspects of their formal organization along the lines of accountable autonomy in the late 1980s and 1990s. Though there are good reasons to suppose that these reforms will advance the aims of their architects—greater participation, deliberation, more equitable and effective policy outcomes—there is also a strong case that these innovative forms of governance and administration will disappoint both democrats and technocrats alike. These structures may demand too much from ordinary people; flesh-and-blood individuals may lack the motives, capabilities, or potentials that this flavor of participatory democracy requires. Multiple inequalities between individuals and neighborhoods in cities like Chicago may also upset the scheme. Furthermore, the theory may misunderstand the technology of policing or education by according too much credit to nonprofessionals, whether ordinary residents or parents of schoolchildren, or by overstating the importance of organizational learning, civic capacity, and local judgment.

4.1. Three Stages of Empirical Investigation

In order to assess whether the Chicago reforms in particular, and accountable autonomy generally, remain attractive despite such criticisms, it is necessary to move beyond conceptual argument and formal institutional evidence to consider the actual individuals—the residents, police officers, teachers, and parents—who inhabit these institutions and the processes that connect them. Do residents and parents find these channels of access sufficiently attractive that they participate, or do they stay at home? When they engage, do they deliberate, or does decision-making revolve around power, strategic bargaining, and attempts to dominate? Do they identify priorities and implement solutions, or are discussions meandering and ultimately pointless? We pursue answers to these questions in three stages. This chapter carries out the first two stages of investigation, while the third stage occupies the remainder of this volume.

The first stage constructs five critical social theoretic perspectives. Each of these predicts, in its own way, that the institutions of accountable autonomy will not operate in ways that advance democratic values or generate effective administrative outcomes. These perspectives, constructed from salient social theories, sharpen the criticisms against empowered participation.

Briefly, the first critical take operates from a *strong-rationality perspective*. This view holds that political actors will refuse to restrain the pursuit of their self-interest according to the norms of reasonable deliberation that accountable autonomy requires. In this and the following chapters, we shall examine actual cases to see whether residents and officials defy this strong rational description enough for the deliberative process to yield fair and effective outcomes. The *strong-egalitarian perspective* holds that social and material equality is a necessary condition of fair and effective deliberation. An important practical premise of accountable autonomy, by contrast, is that these participatory institutions can advance democratic values such as effectiveness and equal consideration (fairness) even under conditions of substantial material inequality and/or poverty. The *social-capital perspective* holds that participatory schemes like accountable autonomy require rich civic resources, dense networks of associations and norms. But proponents might contend to the contrary that these institutions will operate even in the absence of such social substrates, and that they may even contribute to the formation of social capital in areas that lack it. The *cultural-difference perspective* contends that directly democratic and deliberative schemes require a high degree of homogeneity, and consequently worries that participatory devolution will result in domination by culturally advantaged parties under heterogeneous conditions. But these institutions may be more robust and generate fair deliberation and cooperation across lines of difference. A fifth and final viewpoint, the *expertise perspective*, stresses the complex nature of modern problems. According to this widely held view, competent decision-making in areas like school governance and neighborhood safety require highly specialized training and knowledge that ordinary citizens lack and cannot be expected to acquire. Therefore, empowering these novices with public authority over such matters will be ineffective, and perhaps counterproductive. But reforms in both the CPS and CPD have attempted to construct institutions that link ordinary people to experts in a way that improves the efforts of each to achieve goals previously left to professionals.

The second stage of the empirical argument uses city-wide data on participation and opinion to examine the force of these critical perspectives. Each offers necessary conditions—convergence of interests, equality, wealth, cultural homogeneity, sufficient social capital—without which, they contend, accountable autonomy will not work. In their most pessimistic forms, these perspectives predict that individuals will not participate absent these conditions. By examining levels of participation and characteristics of participation in community policing and school governance across the city, we can assess these skeptical claims against the more sanguine expectation that, even without such favorable but rare background conditions, citizens will participate out of a desire to solve urgent problems. Both of the Chicago reform experiments are fortunate to have extensive research groups based at Northwestern University and the University of Chicago dedicated to their documentation and evaluation.[1] City-wide data gathered by these two research groups and others reveal substantial patterns of participation even in neighborhoods that lack conditions held to be necessary by skeptics.

These considerations clear the empirical underbrush, as it were, by showing that Chicago residents from many neighborhoods and circumstances participate in school-governance and community-policing reforms, and that therefore participation and deliberation do not require rare and demanding conditions, as some critics have claimed. Relatively robust participation is, however, necessary, but of itself insufficient for these participatory institutions to advance fairness, effectiveness, and the other core democratic values. These normative claims hinge upon details of actual deliberation—the character of individual pragmatic behavior, the problem-solving process, and the efforts of the supportive center— that these city-wide data cannot address. The third stage of empirical argument, then, uses case studies to explore these institutional processes at close range. Chapters 5 and 6 of this volume present ethnographically informed neighborhood-level case studies of accountable autonomy in action—three LSCs and three police beats—to further examine the character of pragmatic public action and participatory deliberation.

4.2. The Strong Rational-Choice Perspective

While the institutional design of accountable autonomy is compatible with, indeed utilizes, the insights of rational-choice theory, the common strong version of rational choice used to model individual behavior in political contexts precludes deliberation as such.[2] Participatory deliberation requires pragmatic citizens who are self-interested but uncertain about the appropriate strategies to advance their interests, competent but not omniscient, and rational but reasonable, while the strong theory of rational choice posits individuals who have complete preference orderings over outcomes and act single-mindedly to achieve their most desired available outcome. The strong theory of rational choice predicts that individuals know what they want and that they act, speak, and vote strategically in order to get that. According to this perspective, deliberative democratic settings will be no different from other social-choice situations, for instance ordinary voting; individuals will act strategically to maximize their interests according to fixed preference orderings (Austen-Smith 1993, 1994). Just as in other contexts, the rational-choice account predicts that deliberative institutions will function principally to aggregate the preexisting preferences of individuals into social choices (Downs 1957). Furthermore, since it takes strategies, interests, and preferences to be unproblematically formed and fixed *ex hypothesi*, the strict theory of rational-choice rejects the contention that pragmatic deliberation provides occasions for participants to discover more effective strategies, alter individual preferences and positions according to the demands of deliberative discussion, build practical or moral capacities, or solve common problems.

This rational-choice perspective predicts that accountable autonomy will fail to realize the democratic values of participation, deliberation, and fairness because it incorrectly characterizes the motives and behavior of individuals. In particular, the theory of rational choice predicts at least three failures of institutions that aim to be participatory and deliberative: overall participation rates will be low, participants will not constrain the pursuit of their preferences according to norms of reasonableness, and deliberation will fail to transform the participants' preferences.

First, the strong-rational perspective predicts low overall rates of public participation due to free-rider problems (Olsen 1965) and other incentive-incompatibilities.[3] Other attempts to engage residents in public safety programs vindicate this perspective. In one study, for example, Grinc (1994) writes that public-safety initiatives encounter "extreme difficulty in getting residents involved in community policing." In our examples of public education and policing, beat and school-governance groups generate public goods—better schools and safer neighborhoods—through the ingenuity and actions of individual citizens and public servants. Since a resident, parent, or teacher will often benefit from the outputs of these groups whether or not she contributes through participation, she will be tempted to "free-ride" by enjoying the benefits of safe neighborhoods and better schools without paying the costs of participation. In particular, an individual will contribute to a public good just in case the personal cost of the contribution is lower than the marginal personal benefit he derives from that good. Since the CPS and CPD reforms create quite small groups—a dozen individuals in the case of school governance and perhaps two dozen in the average community-policing group—it is somewhat less vulnerable to free-rider objections than endeavors encompassing large numbers of citizens. Nevertheless, adherents to strict versions of rational-choice theory are likely to predict that free-rider problems will afflict participatory democratic institutions with untenably low participation rates. Recent

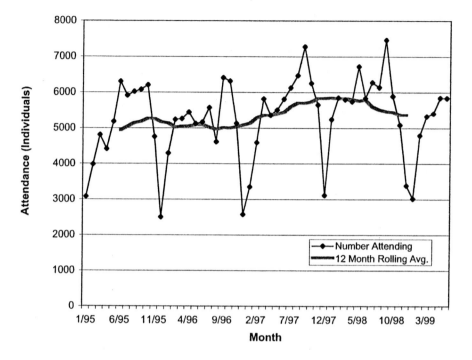

4.1. Beat-Meeting Attendance, 1995–1999.

experiences with both community policing and school governance in Chicago, however, have exhibited substantial levels of citizen participation.

Figure 4.1 depicts total resident attendance at community beat meetings in Chicago's 279 police beats between January 1995 and June 1999. At peak levels of attendance from April through August of 1995, upwards of six thousand Chicago residents attended community beat meetings every month. The average participation in any given beat meeting during this period was slightly more than twenty-one residents. Note that these figures include only formal beat meetings; residents often participate in numerous other face-to-face meetings such as subcommittees of beat groups, independent problem-solving meetings, ad hoc "call meetings," and rallies and demonstrations.

Similarly, participation statistics for LSC elections reveal moderate levels of public participation. Recall from the discussion of LSC structure that each elementary school LSC has eleven seats—the principal, two teachers, two community members, and six parents—and ten of them are selected through neighborhood elections. Elections have been held every

TABLE 4.1
LSC Election Statistics

	Year	Parent	Community	Teacher	Total
	1989	9,329	4,818	2,429	16,576
		(2.9)	(4.4)	(2.2)	(3.1)
	1991	4,739	1,858	1,545	8,142
		(1.5)	(1.7)	(1.4)	(1.5)
	1993	4,254	1,495	1,612	7,361
		(1.3)	(1.4)	(1.5)	(1.3)
Number of Candidates	1996	4,493	1,682	1,620	7,795
(candidates per seat)					
		(1.4)	(1.5)	(1.5)	(1.4)
	1998	4,073	1,540	1,480	7,093
		(1.2)	(1.4)	(1.3)	(1.2)
	2000	4,051	1,614	1,430	7,095
		(1.2)	(1.4)	(1.3)	(1.1)
	2002	4,200	1,675	1,480	7,355
		(1.3)	(1.5)	(1.3)	(1.3)
Number of Voters	1989	113,008	97,276	34,902	245,186
(parental turnout rate)					
		28.1%			
	1991	44,735	35,583	30,514	108,832
		10.3%			
	1993	33,701	23,544	27,435	84,680
		7.9%			
	1996	68,059	24,509	29,325	121,893
		16.0%			
	1998	52,752	15,991	25,867	94,610
		12.2%			
	2000	50,584	19,468	24,590	94,642
		11.8%			
	2002	N/A	N/A	N/A	N/A

Source: Chicago Public Schools and Catalyst Staff (April 2000; May 2000; May 2002).

two years since 1989, and table 4.1 presents aggregate statistics for these elections: This table counts only statistics relating to formal LSC elections; no aggregate data is available on the number of people who attend these LSC meetings (which are public events regulated under the Illinois Public Meetings law) as "members of the public," nor those who participate on LSC subcommittees. The table does suggest, however, that the supply of LSC seats roughly matches the demand to participate in school governance through this channel. In LSC elections between 1991 and 2000, between 30 percent and 50 percent of school elections went *un*contested and there were roughly 1.4 candidates for each open seat. Between 15 percent and 20 percent of the some 5,600 LSC seats in the city of Chicago stood vacant.[4]

These city-wide aggregate statistics show that free-rider effects have not driven participation in the new institutions of local school governance and community policing down to low and paralyzing levels. Actual participation levels are high enough—average attendance of between ten and twenty persons at community beat meetings and an average LSC size of nine persons—for these bodies to function as problem-solving and planning groups.

Nevertheless, overall participation rates are very low compared, for example, to the percentage of adults who vote in elections at any level. Do these governance institutions draw too few individuals into their ambit to be regarded as participatory *democratic* forms of governance? Several considerations weigh against this criticism. First, participation in an institution should be judged not just by its quantity, but also by its quality. Greater rates of participation could well pose obstacles to the quality of deliberative problem-solving in LSCs and community-policing groups. Neighborhood crises such as drive-by shootings or serial rapes, for example, often draw dozens of additional participants to community-policing meetings. When fifty or a hundred people attend, it becomes extremely difficult to conduct structured, much less sustained, inclusive, or effective, problem-solving deliberations. If there is a magic number for a group that is small enough so that all of its members can contribute seriously to an ongoing discussion, and yet large enough to offer diverse views and ample energies, it may not be so far from the actual numbers of people that actually participate in groups constituted by the Chicago reforms.

Second, judging the extent to which these rates of participation fall short of some participatory democratic ideal requires specifying a feasible ideal. One version of direct democracy holds that every citizen should participate in all important decisions. That ideal is plainly unfeasible in contemporary contexts. It demands too much in light of the plethora of areas of urgent public decision in contemporary life. Because there are many areas that could be opened to direct, participatory engagement—not just education and public safety, but also neighborhood planning, social services, environmental regulation, community development, the maintenance of parks other amenities, and the like—a more feasible ideal is that every citizen participate in some important arena of public life. On this account, not every resident of a neighborhood should be so concerned about public-safety issues that he or she attends community-policing meetings every month. It is enough that some participate in policing decisions, others participate in educational governance, and still others involve themselves in other dimensions of local urban public life.

Third, the democratic qualities of community-policing and school-governance groups depend not just upon the quantity and quality of participation inside the groups, but also upon connections between direct participants and other individuals. If direct participants roughly represent the interests and perspectives that exist outside of their groups, if groups are generally open to new participants who wish to join, and if participants are connected through networks of friendship or association to those who do not participate directly, then these bodies may generate fair decisions despite the relatively small number of direct participants. If, on the other hand, community-policing and school-governance groups operate as exclusionary cliques in which one, or only a few, interests dominate, then low participation rates may reinforce local oligarchic tendencies. Case materials in the following two chapters explore questions regarding the quality of participation and permeability of these governance processes.

Beyond participation, the rational-choice perspective is skeptical about the possibility of deliberation. When parties with disparate interests come together in a political situation in which they must agree to a single "social choice," the strict theory of rational choice predicts that each will advance his most important interests (maximize his expected value) to the extent that his bargaining power and the institutional rules of the game allow. The social choice, then, results from the aggregation of conflicting individual interests via negotiation and bargaining, voting, domination, or some other such mechanism. Jane Mansbridge (1980) has called the communication between such adversarial parties "competitive deliberation." Under the strict theory of rational choice, communication between parties may improve the quality of social choice by injecting information, but it does not alter the deeper interests or preferences of parties regarding the political questions at hand.[5]

Though a central justification for deliberation is that it may improve the quality of social choices by increasing available information, it departs from strong rationalism in two important respects. First, advocates of deliberation expect participants to regulate the pursuit of their interests according to the norms of fairness and public reason. In particular, parties should justify their proposals for group action with reasons that others can endorse and refrain from advancing interests and proposals that they cannot justify (Cohen 1989). To illustrate the difference symbolically, consider an agent A whose (decreasing) preference ordering over group actions is P_1, P_2, P_3, P_4}. Suppose further that his first choice P_1 is not justifiable to some other members of the group, but that A could, through force of numbers or power, induce the group to select P_1 as its social choice.

The strict theory of rational choice would expect that A advance P_1 as the group's social choice. Deliberative norms, on the other hand, demand and expect that A refrain from advancing P_1 and instead that he pursue $\{P_2 \ldots P_4\}$.

Beyond filtering unjustifiable preferences, deliberation also departs from the strict theory of rational choice in its predictions about the stability of individual preferences. Whereas strong rationality posits individuals who have stable preferences, advocates of deliberation argue that parties will transform their interests, preferences, allegiances, and identities as a result of discussion and action. For example, A may initially participate for instrumental reasons—because he wants to make his neighborhood safer or improve the quality of his children's school. After participating and benefiting, A may then develop an independent interest in the political institutions that invite engagement or in participation as an intrinsically rewarding activity.[6] In the bare terms above, participation in the process would in this case have altered A's preference ordering by introducing a new preference, P_5, for the stability and integrity of deliberative institutions or for his participation in them.[7]

In addition to acquiring interests in democratic processes, individuals may also develop their moral capacities through participation by making the preferences of agents themselves more justifiable. To continue our simple example above, deliberation might transform A's preference ordering from $\{P_1, P_2, P_3, P_4\}$ (before deliberation) to $\{P_2, P_1, P_3, P_4\}$ (after deliberation). Since P_2 is (ex hypothesi) intersubjectively justifiable while P_1 is not, the later preference ordering is superior to the first from the moral point of view. In this scenario, A develops other-regarding preferences or strengthens his solidarity with other participants as a result of deliberating with them.

Case studies in the next two chapters examine whether the strong theory of rationality or pragmatic deliberation better describes the behavior of actual participants in the arenas of school reform and of community policing in Chicago. All six cases allow us to examine whether individual preferences remain stable during the course of deliberative processes. In three of our six cases, residents face each other across lines of class and race that correspond with conflicting interests and preferences over outcomes. Actual processes of conflict and conflict resolution in these cases sometimes conform to strict rationality and sometimes follows deliberative courses. A close examination of the actual discussions and deliberations reveals, not surprisingly, that behavior depends upon such contingencies as the presence of facilitators capable of guiding deliberations and bridging conflict and upon whether the participants themselves understand and endorse norms of collective problem-solving and deliberation.

4.3. Strong Egalitarianism

The "strong egalitarian," our second imaginary critic, holds that background inequalities in society, especially those rooted in class, but also in race and gender, prevent the mechanisms of decentralized deliberative problem-solving from operating as the normative theory supposes. In particular, inequality will prevent these political institutions from generating fair or effective outputs. Even under the relatively undemanding institutions of representative democracy, political participation exhibits substantial upper-class participation biases.[8] Participatory devolution may exacerbate this problem if, as Jack Nagel writes, "the more intensive the form of participation, the greater the tendency of participants to over-represent high-status members of the population" (Nagel 1987, 58; Nagel 1992). Under conditions of severe inequality, for example, the least well-off may lack the basic resources—information, time, money, or skills—to participate in demanding deliberative institutions.[9] When unequal parties face one another in political arenas, furthermore, domination often results (Brest 1988; Cohen 1988; Forester 1999, 181–89).[10] Operationalizing this perspective in terms of institutional choice, the strong egalitarian holds that we ought not adopt deliberative or participatory prescriptions *without first* substantially equalizing the resources that citizens can deploy in the political process. Absent such redistribution, some institutional configuration—such as centralized command-and-control bureaucracy—is more likely to yield fair outcomes. The strong egalitarian's basic objection is that decentralizing schemes benefit those who are already well off while doing little or nothing for the worst off.

In order to avoid confusion, it is important to distinguish this strong egalitarianism from a weak egalitarian position. A weak egalitarian fully admits that increases in background equality would make deliberative processes more fair, more effective, and yield greater levels of participation. On this view, however, disadvantaged citizens will nevertheless overcome their resource poverty and participate when they believe that such participation will deliver goods such as improved education and public safety. According to this weak egalitarian account, greater need and demand for improved public goods offsets some of the obstacles to participation imposed by lack of resources. Though those who are less well-off will be able to use this kind of democracy to their advantage, they would participate more effectively and in greater numbers given additional resources. Indeed, one of the institutional functions of accountable autonomy's "supportive center" is to effect just this resource redistribution.[11] Consider the evidence for and against strong-egalitarian expectations on three questions: levels of participation across differently endowed neigh-

TABLE 4.2
Statistics for Beat-Meeting Attendance-Rate Variables

Variable	Mean	Standard Deviation
Black (%)	49.5	43.0
Hispanic (%)	17.4	23.7
College-educated (%)	16.4	16.3
Median Income ($)	24,055.3	9,727.3
Personal Crime Rate (per 1,000)	84.5	50.7
Homeowner (%)	38.1	22.5
Participation Rate (%)	35.4	17.5

borhoods; equality of participation within neighborhoods; and the dependence of problem-solving effectiveness upon neighborhood endowments.

First, the strong egalitarian expects that participation levels of advantaged neighborhoods will far exceed those of destitute areas. Wesley Skogan, an extremely close observer of community crime-prevention programs, has written in a survey of empirical studies that "the general lesson is that participation in anti-crime groups results from the same factors that stimulate general involvement in neighborhood affairs. Those factors are, above all, indicators of socio-economic status and class-linked attitudes concerning personal and political efficacy, extent of political information, and civic mindedness."[12] Yet city-wide evidence that compares neighborhood participation rates in Chicago's community-policing program weigh against strong-egalitarian predictions. Annual studies of Chicago's community-policing program from Skogan himself and his colleagues at the Institute for Policy Research at Northwestern University reveal that the pattern of participation in "Chicago reverses a common pattern across the country, one in which participation in civic affairs and even crime prevention is higher in better-educated, home-owning, and white neighborhoods" (Chicago Community Policing Evaluation Consortium 1996, 21).

To explore this trend, we use beat-meeting participation data reported in police department records of meetings in each of the city's 279 beats between January 1995 and May 1997.[13] Nine of these beats were eliminated due to insufficient demographic or attendance data, leaving 270 beats in our data sample. These records report 5,786 meetings, averaging 22 reported meetings per beat. For each beat, we constructed a statistic of beat-meeting participation per 10,000 residents by dividing (1) the average number of participants in the average meeting for that beat by (2) the number of adults living in that beat, and multiplying by (3) 10,000. This data set also contained demographic data for each beat that was constructed from tract-level 1990 census data. Table 4.2 shows summary statistics for beat meeting–participation rates (as the dependent variable)

TABLE 4.3
Beat-Meeting Attendance Rate—OLS Regression Results

Variable	Coefficient, B	SE	Beta
Black (%)	0.0275	0.0444	0.0630
Hispanic (%)	0.1012	0.0673	0.1285
College-educated (%)	−0.2174	0.1405	−0.1894
Median Income ($)	0.0004	0.0003	0.1824
Personal Crime Rate (per 1,000)*	0.038	0.0397	0.5512
Home-owner (%)	0.0804	0.1086	0.0967
R-Squared = 0.275			
N = 270			

* Statistically significant at the 1×10^{-6} level of confidence.

and a number of demographic variables: percentage of households who are black, percentage Hispanic, percent of adults with college degrees, median income, rate of personal crime in 1996, and percentage of households that own their homes.[14]

We refrain from developing a full model of the causes of participation in community-policing meetings here because our purpose is more limited. These data explore the degree to which commonly accepted conditions of political participation, in particular socioeconomic advantage, work to exclude the less advantaged. Following completely standard expectations and models about political participation, then, we treat the percentage of a neighborhood's population that is black or Hispanic as a proxy for racial disadvantage, the percentage of college-educated adults in a neighborhood and its median income to be proxies for advantages in deliberative skills and resources, respectively. The percentage of households in a neighborhood that own the homes in which they live we take to measure both economic advantage and neighborhood stability; previous studies have found home-ownership rates to be prime predictors of neighborhood engagement in public-safety programs and other forms of self-help.[15] The personal-crime rate in a neighborhood is a proxy for the potential "demand" for police action. Demand is a crucial variable in this model that does not correspond directly with common predictors of participation in other studies of political engagement.

Table 4.3 gives the OLS multiple-regression results for these six independent variables as predictors of participation. The only statistically significant factor in this regression—and the one with the most substantial coefficient—is personal-crime rate.[16] According to this model, an increase of 40 crimes per 1,000 residents (mean personal-crime rate in Chicago was 84 crimes per 1000 residents in 1996) corresponds to an increase in beat-meeting attendance of 8 persons per 10,000 adults, or some 4 persons per meeting in a medium-sized beat. The same predicted increase requires, according to this regression, an increase in neighborhood mean household income of $20,000 (almost doubling the mean neighborhood median household income of $24,000). Interestingly, the effect of the college-educated variable on beat-meeting attendance is small, but in the *opposite* of the expected direction; the regression model finds that the controlled effect of increasing the number of college graduates in a neighborhood weakly reduces beat-meeting attendance. A decrease of 8 monthly participants per 10,000 adult residents corresponds with a 38 percent increase in college graduates, tripling the mean percentage of college graduates in the beats (16 percent).

While this finding is unsurprising in itself—people who live in high-crime areas show up to community-policing meetings in greater numbers—it does weigh against the strong egalitarian contention that disadvantaged individuals (many of whom live in high-crime areas) lack the resources to participate in decentralized democratic institutions. On the other hand, it confirms a design principle of the original CPS reforms and of accountable autonomy, generally. Even the least well-off participate when doing so confers powers upon them to address urgent issues such as neighborhood security.

Though participation patterns in LSC elections have been less well documented and the trends themselves more equivocal, the data also weigh against the strong egalitarian expectation that those in less well-off areas will exhibit substantially lower levels of participation. In their study of the 1991 Chicago LSC elections, DFC analyzed the number of candidates standing for election to parent seats on LSCs according to student-body characteristics of race, income, and ethnicity. An average of nine parental candidates stood for election at any given school, and the study found no substantial relationship between levels of parental candidacy and (1) percentage of Hispanic students, or (2) percentage of African-American students (Designs for Change 1991, 7).[17] The study found a slight *positive correlation* between the percentage of low-income students at a given school and the number of parental candidates standing for election in 1991. Authors of that study did not report full regression results, and so the correlation may have been statistically insignificant.

Data from the 1996 Chicago LSC elections confirms this pattern of participation.[18] Consider in more detail the relationships between school-level variables such as school size, percentage of students from low-income families at a particular school,[19] student mobility,[20] percentage of African-American students, and percentage of Hispanic students and two indicators of LSC participation: the number of parental candidates standing for election at each school[21] and the parent turnout at each school

TABLE 4.4
Descriptive Statistics for 1996 School Elections

Variable	Average	Standard Deviation
Parent Candidates	8.28	2.75
Parents Voting (%)	19.7	12.3
School Size (# of Students)	661	283
Low-Income (%)	84.3	18.2
Mobility Rate (%)	29.2	15.7
Black (%)	58.4	42.5
Hispanic (%)	27.2	33.5

election.[22] Table 4.4 gives descriptive statistics (at the school level) for these four independent and two dependent variables for the 465 elementary schools for which data were available.[23]

So, the average school had 8.3 parents standing in the 1996 LSC elections, and thus two of the parental seats were contested. Twenty percent of its parents turned out to vote for these candidates. Demographically, the average school had 661 students, 84 percent of which could be classified as "Low-Income," 58.4 percent of the students were African-American, and 27.2 percent were Hispanic. Using these data from the 1996 elections, we did not find the slight positive relationship between the number of parents standing for election at a school and the percentage of low-income students at that school; instead, we found no discernible relationship between these two variables at all. Figure 4.2 groups schools according to percentage of low-income students, and then charts average number of parental candidates in the 1996 LSC election for that group of schools.[24] The error bars range to a 95-percent confidence interval for the population mean in each of the groups.

This lack of correlation between the number of parental candidates and obvious SES school-level characteristics was verified by regressing the number of parental candidates against school size, percentage low-income students, mobility rate, percentage of African-American students, and percentage of Hispanic students. The results of this multiple regression—coefficients (B), standard errors, and standardized coefficients $(Beta)$—are shown in the left half of table 4.5. It should be noted that these variables explain very little—approximately 7.5 percent (R^2) of the observed variation in number of parent candidates. Of the five independent variables, only school size bears a statistically significant relationship with number of parental candidates. This 1996 data therefore verifies the finding of the 1991 Designs for Change study that there is no statistically significant relationship between the number of parents that stand for candidacy at a school and race or ethnicity. Beyond this, note that the magnitude of the coefficients on the statistically insignificant variables is

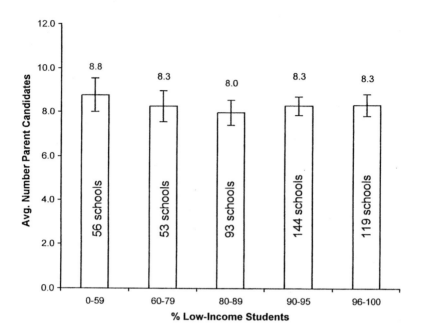

4.2. Number of Parent Candidates versus Percent Low-Income Students.

quite low—a 50-percent decrease (almost three standard deviations) in low-income students would generate an increment of only 0.25 additional parental candidates. To the extent that the number of candidates standing for election at a school measures the willingness to participate in deliberative activities around school improvement, the 1996 LSC election statistics reject the strong-egalitarian expectation that better-off neighborhoods and better-off schools will enjoy advantageous participatory reserves of candidates willing to serve.

The right-hand side of table 4.5 reports the correlation between these same demographic variables and a second measure of participation: turnout rate of parents in the 1996 LSC elections. Turnout rate for each school is defined as the number of parents voting divided by the number of parents eligible to vote at that school's election. We omitted school size from this regression. As with the first regression, these variables account for only a small fraction—6.4 percent—of the observed variance in parent-turnout rates. Unlike the previous model, however, all explanatory variables are statistically significant; the poverty, race, and ethnicity variables are statistically significant at the 0.01 level of confidence for a two-tailed t-test, and student mobility is significant at the 0.05 level. The magnitude

TABLE 4.5
Predictors of Participation in 1996 LSC Elections—OLS Regression Results

Variable:	Parental Candidates			Parent Voting Turnout Rate		
	B	SE B	Beta	B	SE B	Beta
School Size	0.002**	0.0005	0.246	—	—	—
Low-Income (%)	−0.005	0.010	−0.035	−0.183**	0.048	−0.272
Mobility Rate	−0.006	0.009	−0.037	−0.092*	0.041	−0.117
Black (%)	−0.007	0.008	−0.107	0.113**	0.037	0.390
Hispanic (%)	−0.003	0.010	−0.039	0.122**	0.045	0.334
	R-Squared: 0.075			R-Squared: 0.064		
	N: 465			N: 465		

* Coefficient is statistically significant at the .05 level of confidence.
** Coefficient is statistically significant at the .01 level of confidence.

of the coefficient on low-income is small, but in the expected direction; as the percentage of low-income students at a school increases, parent turnout rate declines *slightly*. According to the regression results, an increase of 25 percent in the portion of low-income students at a school corresponds to a decrease of 4.5 percent in the fraction of parents turning out to vote in an LSC election (see figure 4.3). Similarly, increases in student mobility (and thus decreases in school stability) produce small declines in parental-turnout rates. Interestingly, the coefficients on race and ethnicity variables are also small, but in the *opposite* of the expected directions. Whereas previous studies have found that African-Americans and Hispanics are somewhat less likely to vote than others, higher proportions of black and Hispanic students in a school correlated with slightly higher parental turnout rates in the 1996 LSC elections.[25]

Demographic predictors of parental turnout in LSC elections provide limited support for strong-egalitarian expectations about the correlation between socioeconomic status and participation, but the correlation is not strong enough to distinguish it from weak-egalitarian explanations in this regard. These data, however, do not bear out the strong-egalitarian expectation that the most disadvantaged neighborhoods will exhibit very low levels of participation. First, the presence or absence of candidates better indicates neighborhood participatory capacity than voter turnout because those who serve on the LSC, not voters, must invest the time and mental energy required for LSC membership. On this candidate dimension, better off-neighborhoods cannot be statistically distinguished from the worst-off neighborhoods. On the dimension of voter turnout, we interpret the small magnitude of the relationship between school poverty turnout to support the weak-egalitarian expectation that participation will be higher given more resources, but that even the worst-off neighbor-

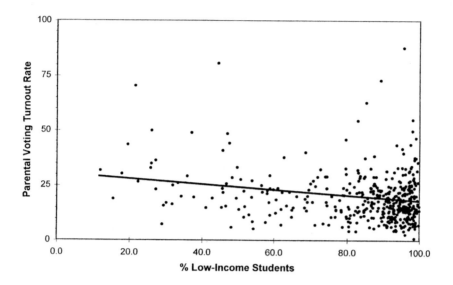

4.3. School Parental Voting Turnout Rate versus Percent
Low-Income Students.

hoods will still find local democratic processes useful and will not be excluded from them.

These patterns of participation for both community-policing and local
school-governance institutions, considered across all of Chicago's neighborhoods, diverge sharply from strong-egalitarian expectations. These
data are fully consistent, however, with a more optimistic weak-egalitarian prediction that disadvantaged citizens will overcome quite substantial
barriers to participate in institutions that credibly promise to reward such
activity with concrete improvements to the public goods upon which
those citizens rely. Individuals in socioeconomically disadvantaged areas
enjoy substantive, not just formal, access to these participatory institutions, and levels of participation across a range of neighborhood settings
are robust.

The second strong-egalitarian prediction is that participation biases
will manifest themselves within neighborhoods. A weak-egalitarian theory, compatible with participatory deliberation, anticipates this same
trend of bias. Presume that two factors explain participation: the demand
for participation—captured in crime rate or school quality—and the resources that an individual uses to participate. Examining participation
within a neighborhood holds the first factor constant (since neighbors
face largely the same school quality and threat of crime) and so intraneigh-

borhood variations in participation will be explained principally by differences in the resources available to residents. But even if they are substantially underrepresented compared to their better-off neighbors, can the rate of participation from worst-off individuals nevertheless be high enough to generate decisions that benefit them? This depends upon the extent to which decision-making abides by the norms of fair deliberation.

Community policing–participation data do indeed reveal an upper-class intrabeat participation bias. For example, home ownership is a very strong predictor of participation in community-policing beat meetings. A survey conducted by researchers at Northwestern University of 2,610 beat participants in 165 representative beats revealed that the proportion of home-owners in beat meetings was far larger than their presence in the general population of the beats from which they came (Chicago Community Policing Evaluation Consortium 1996).

Representation within LSCs is also skewed toward the more well-off. The Consortium on Chicago School Research conducted a survey of all LSC members in Chicago between May 1995 and February 1996 (Ryan et al. 1997). Using a probability sample, the survey found that the educational level of LSC members in aggregate exceeded that of adults in Chicago. So, for instance 13 percent of LSC members in the probability sample lacked a high school diploma, while 34 percent of the adults in Chicago had no high school diploma. Furthermore, this city-wide educational bias was reproduced when examining the LSCs of individual schools. The report found that, "even in schools with virtually all low-income students, the educational level of LSC members is almost equal to that of the general Chicago population" (Ryan 1997, 7). Treating educational level as a proxy for advantage, then, better-off members of a neighborhood are disproportionately well represented in LSCs.

Within beats and LSCs, patterns of participation are consistent with expectations of both weak- and strong-egalitarian theories: the presence of less well-off residents (renters and the better educated) is *low but still substantial* in most beats and LSCs. In order to distinguish between the two views, we would have to know whether disadvantaged persons generally participate in community-policing beat meetings at rates sufficient to assert and justify their priorities and solutions in deliberative processes. This question itself turns on the character of discussion in these meetings—in less deliberative processes, minorities must rely more on the strength of numbers than on the power of persuasion—and so further examination of the strong-egalitarian criticisms in this regard must await the case-level evidence presented in the following chapters.

Yet a third criticism from the strong-egalitarian perspective concerns the quality of participation and its results rather than its magnitude. Many factors other than the sheer quantity of participation determine the integrity of deliberative problem-solving. These considerations—including the cognitive and deliberative skills of participants, their technical expertise in areas such as budgeting, policing, and education, the resources that each of them can contribute to group actions, organizational connections to leverage resources, and participants' dispositions to cooperate with one another—may be positively correlated to other dimensions of advantage like income and education. The strong egalitarian therefore expects that wealthy participants in better-off neighborhoods will generate positive outcomes much more easily and frequently than those in disadvantaged neighborhoods.

Because accountable autonomy relies upon distinctive processes of deliberation and participation, it is difficult to use existing data sets and secondary analyses to examine this third strong-egalitarian critique. Four prior studies of the Chicago experiments, however, do incorporate measures of procedural success similar to that of accountable autonomy. Two of these studies equivocally confirm the strong-egalitarian hypothesis that better-off residents will use accountable-autonomy institutions more effectively than impoverished ones, and two of the prior studies reject this prediction.

In 1993, researchers at the Consortium on Chicago School Research released a report examining the effectiveness of the approximately five hundred LSCs at Chicago elementary schools (Bryk et al. 1993). They constructed a dichotomous scheme of LSC problem-solving success. Unsuccessful LSCs pursued "unfocussed initiatives" that lacked coherent planning, implemented "add-on" programs with little innovation or relation to one another, and failed to focus on core teaching activities. Successful LSCs, on the other hand, conducted "systemic restructuring activities" that exhibited a "shared, unified, coherent school vision," sustained debate on school programs and goals, implemented changes to classroom practice, and focused staff-development programs (Bryk et al. 1993, 15). The study found no relationship between economic advantage and LSC success:

> the average percentage of low income students in the schools in these two groups ["unfocussed initiatives" and "systemic approach"] were virtually identical. That is, systemic approaches to school improvement are evident in the poorest schools as well as in relatively more advantaged ones. In general, the opportunities provided by PA 85–1418 [the law creating LSC governance] for school improvement have been equitably accessed by schools across the system. (Bryk et al. 1993, 19).

A 1997 report from the Consortium on Chicago School Research (Ryan et al. 1997, 33–37), based on a city-wide survey, compared characteristics of a group of thirty LSCs deemed to be most productive against another group of thirty deemed to be least productive. "Productivity" was defined as the ability of an LSC to execute its legally mandated functions of school-improvement planning, principal-selection, and school budgeting.

Three findings of this report are worth noting; two of them reject the strong- and weak-egalitarian hypotheses, while the third supports the egalitarian contention. Unfortunately, authors of this report do not provide quantitative descriptions of these findings, and so our interpretations of the data must remain tentative. The study found first that "parents and community representatives on the most productive councils have a slightly *lower* educational level than members on the least productive councils. About 60 percent of the members on the most productive councils are likely to have at least some college as compared to nearly 70 percent of the members of the least productive councils."[26] The consortium's second notable finding is that "when we focus on the most productive councils, they are located all across the city in virtually every neighborhood. This finding on LSCs extends results from our earlier reports that the opportunities created by the 1988 Reform Act have been broadly seized across the various neighborhoods of the city" (Ryan et al. 1997, 34). The third finding, this one by contrast confirming the weak- and strong-egalitarian expectations, is that "the 30 least productive councils . . . are more likely to be located in neighborhoods with high concentrations of poverty" (Ryan et al. 1997, 34).

The other two reports examine problem-solving success in the context of community policing. The Institute for Policy Research at Northwestern University surveyed the efforts of 354 civilian participants of the JCPT Program (see chapter 5) in late 1995 (Chicago Community Policing Evaluation Consortium 1996, 53–60). Respondents reported that their groups discussed a total of 693 problems, and they attempted to solve 63 percent of these. The study found that

> there were differences in demographic groups in terms of the likelihood of trying to solve problems. . . . The longer people had lived in their current neighborhood, the more likely they were to try to solve problems. There were no important differences across levels of education or between home renter and owners. . . . *Those living in households with an annual income of less then $10,000 tried to solve problems half of the time, while those in households with an annual income of $40,000 or more tried to solve problems three-fourths of the time.* Half of the Hispanics attempted to solve the problems they listed, while about two-thirds of whites and blacks tried to solve the problems they listed. (Chicago Community Policing Evaluation Consortium 1996, 55; emphasis mine)

This finding provides only weak support for the strong-egalitarian expectation of upper-class problem-solving bias. The support is weak first because the differences in problem-solving propensity correlate with only one of three measures of class advantage—income, but not education or home-ownership. Second, the bias within neighborhoods is consistent with weak egalitarianism, as well as with the strong version. Those in the

TABLE 4.6
Beat Problem-Solving Success versus Median Family Income

Problem-solving Success:	Median Family Income Quartile of Neighborhood (relative to Chicago)		
	0–25% (poor)	25–75% (middle)	75–100% (wealthy)
Failing or Struggling	1	4	1
Reasonable	2	1	2
Excellent	3	0	1

least-advantaged category still attempted to solve many problems that would have gone unaddressed in the absence of community-policing institutions. It is fully consistent with the weak-egalitarian view that this group of participants would have tried to solve even more problems—50 percent more—if each of them had the private resources associated with a $30,000 increase in annual income.

Finally, a more recent study from the Institute for Policy Research examined the problem-solving efforts of fifteen Chicago police beats in some detail (Chicago Community Policing Evaluation Consortium 1997, 95–132; Skogan et al. 1999). Using case study methods that examined the level of police and community involvement and efficacy, the report categorized these beats according to four levels of success: excellent, reasonable, struggling, and failing. The cross-tabulation presented in table 4.6 summarizes the results of this study and shows the number of beats in each category according to three grades of median family income (according to the family's quartile ranking within the city of Chicago) in the neighborhood:

The strong egalitarian predicts that neighborhood efforts will cluster in the upper left-hand corner (poor neighborhoods, failed efforts) and bottom right-hand corner (wealthy neighborhoods, successful problem-solving) of this cross-tabulation. The limited cases examined by the Institute for Policy Research show no such clustering; poor neighborhoods seem to exhibit slightly better problem-solving programs than those neighborhoods with median incomes in the upper three quartiles. Three of the four programs ranked as excellent come from poor neighborhoods, and only one of the six failures is in the poorest of beats. This study, then, disconfirms the strong-egalitarian expectation that successful problem-solving will be associated positively and strongly with neighborhood advantage.

4.4. Social Capital

In addition to these rational-choice and strong-egalitarian perspectives, neo-Tocquevillean social theories offer a third critique of accountable autonomy. Robert Putnam (1993, 1994, 1995, 1996, 2000) has developed the most prominent and articulated contemporary version of this view. In his study of Italian regional governments, Putnam argued that the performance of democratic political institutions depends in large measure on social capital—the extent to which citizens participate in horizontal networks of associations and other social relationships.[27] On this view, the mechanism that connects social capital with democratic performance is what he calls "generalized reciprocity." Membership in associations of all kinds can foster adherence to a principle of generalized reciprocity in their members: "I'll do for you now, without expecting anything immediately in return and perhaps even without even knowing you, confident that down the road you or someone else will return the favor" (Putnam 2000, 134). Generalized reciprocity contributes to democratic governance in two ways. First, citizens will comply with the requirements of democratic government more often, make sure that others comply, and so help solve pervasive free-rider problems: "people who trust their fellow citizens . . . serve more readily on juries, . . . comply more fully with their tax obligations, . . . are less likely to lie, cheat, or steal, and are more likely to respect the rights of others" (Putnam 2000, 136–37). Second, generalized reciprocity enables citizens—in part because they can overcome free-rider problems—to demand accountability from governments and to sanction them when they fail to perform (Putnam 1993, 182; Levi 1996).

Because face-to-face institutions might depend even more heavily on social capital and generalized reciprocity than conventional representative political institutions and because many urban neighborhoods lack just those stocks of social capital, this perspective would seem to regard empowered particpation reforms as especially foolhardy under contemporary urban conditions. This attribution may be too quick, however. Proponents of the social-capital thesis have generally argued that (1) greater stocks of social capital (2) increase the quality of democratic governance (3) given some fixed set of democratic political institutions. Since accountable-autonomy reforms themselves transform the political institutions, the expectations of social-capital theorists are less clear than they may seem.

As with egalitarians, whose concerns revolve around conventional forms of capital, social-capital critiques of accountable autonomy can be parsed usefully into strong and weak versions. The strong view sees abundant stocks of social capital as essential for participatory forms of governance like those found in the Chicago schools and police to operate fairly or effectively. Absent robust habits of association, such reforms may actually be counterproductive since they reduce rule-driven, bureaucratic forms of accountability and depend more heavily upon the engagement and cooperation of ordinary citizens and street level officials compared to traditional administrative forms. Analogous to the strong-egalitarian perspective, this view predicts that those areas rich in social capital will be able to take advantage of opportunities for civic engagement. At best, areas low in social capital will lack the wherewithal to seize these democratic opportunities, and at worst the reforms will increase corruption and local domination.

Analogous to the weak-egalitarian perspective, a more forgiving view expects that social capital will be helpful to the extent that it aids in the acquisition of those skills and dispositions necessary for participatory and deliberative problem-solving, but that the presence of social capital is neither a necessary nor sufficient condition for these institutions to perform well. On this view, even areas with low social capital may be better off under accountable-autonomy forms than under hierarchical administrative ones because the benefits of participation accrue even to relatively isolated individuals. The quality of deliberation and participation may indeed be greater in high–social-capital areas than in low ones, but accountable autonomy may nevertheless be a worthwhile course of reform even for the latter kind of neighborhoods. These simple theoretical implications of the social capital hypothesis for accountable autonomy might be refined in many directions, but the basic dichotomy serves our purposes here. Unfortunately, little of the secondary analysis and available data on the Chicago school-reform and community-policing experiments bears upon the relationship between stocks of social capital and institutional performance. A more elaborate formulation of the social-capital theory would therefore outstrip available data on these matters.

Only one recent Institute for Policy Research (IPR) study of community policing has investigated the effects of social capital on CAPS (Chicago Community Policing Evaluation Consortium 1997). For each of the fifteen beats under investigation, the researchers constructed a measure of community capacity that included (1) neighborhood levels of informal social control,[28] (2) involvement in neighborhood organizations, (3) ability to extract resources from outside organizations and bring them to bear on neighborhood problems ("downtown connections"), and (4) political capacity.[29] This index of community capacity provides, then, a rough measure of social capital.[30] The study found, strikingly, that

> there is no direct association between community capacity and CAPS implementation. In earlier sections of the report, measure after measure pointed to advantages shared by the same set of communities. The benefits of informal social control, organizational involvement, political mobilization, and downtown connections all seems to accrue to the same fortunate areas. They were also the most homogenous, stable, home-owning and affluent beats. However, it is *not* the case that better-off places with a home-grown capability for handling problems are also the beats where community policing is working best. Only [one beat] scored near the top on both dimensions. . . . To the contrary, four of the

most highly rated beats [in terms of community policing] are to be found among
those with relatively little community capacity.[31] (Chicago Community Policing
Evaluation Consortium 1997; emphasis in original)

A similar study of social capital and school-governance performance
yielded very similar findings (Ryan 1997). Researchers from the Consortium on Chicago School Research surveyed LSC members about their
organizational memberships to measure levels of "social capital" on various LSCs. Fully expecting to find correlations between social capital and
school-council performance, researchers were quite surprised to find no
significant relationships between these two variables. Data on this point
are far from conclusive, but they allay first-order concerns that the lack
of social-capital poses a decisive obstacle to institutions that demand extensive citizen participation.

A more practical, and perhaps urgent, point at which accountable-autonomy engages social-capital investigations concerns how bereft urban
neighborhoods might increase their social capital. Reversing the causal
arrow that runs from social capital to the performance of democratic
institutions, portions of the next two chapters explore the extent to which
accountable-autonomy institutions provide incentives for individuals to
form associations and engage with one another in ways that build social
capital.

4.5. Unity and the Politics of Difference

Historians and theorists of direct democracy, republicanism, and commu-
nitarianism have often favored polities that are homogenous with respect
to race, gender, history, and culture. The Athenian Assembly in the fifth
century, B.C., was hardly an inclusive forum. According to a law passed
by Pericles, the Assembly admitted only male citizens—whose status was
conferred by both parents being Athenian citizens—and thus excluded
women, slaves, and free immigrants.[32] Both Rousseau (1987) and Montesquieu (1989) saw homogeneity as a precondition for the success of democratic institutions. Those who lament the supposed passing of shared commitments and civic identities might be skeptical of participatory
institutions like those established by the Chicago reforms because diversity, not unity, prevails in many neighborhoods there.

Worse still, imposing such strong democratic forms upon social conditions of diversity and difference may amplify the inequalities and possibilities of subjugation. Many feminist and cultural theorists—always cogni-
zant of the needs of minorities—contend that deliberative forms of
democracy can allow dominant parties to silence others by privileging

certain ways of communicating, perspectives, and interests (Mansbridge 1980; Young 1990, 1996; Fraser 1992; Phillips 1993, 1996). While conventional pluralist politics—characterized by Jane Mansbridge as "adversarial democracy"—encourage diversity and disagreement, more deliberative or discursive alternatives seem to presume similarities and strive toward consensus in suffocating ways. First, critics such as Iris Marion Young (1996), Nancy Fraser (1992), and Lynn Sanders (1997) contend that deliberative modes entrench one culturally advantaged mode of communication—assertive, reason-giving argument—as the universal mode. As a consequence, such institutions devalue other important communicative acts such as storytelling, rhetoric, and expressions of need. Deliberative institutions thus favor specific styles of communication that are typically possessed by culturally privileged—usually male, usually white—members of American society. Young, for example, argues that:

> [The view of] Deliberative theorists . . . fails to notice that the social power that can prevent people from being equal speakers derives . . . from an internalized sense of the right one has to speak or not to speak, and from the devaluation of some people's style of speech and the elevation of others. The model of deliberative democracy . . . tends to assume that deliberation is culturally neutral and universal.
>
> Deliberation is competition. Parties to dispute aim to win the argument, not to reach mutual understanding. Restricting practices of democratic discussion to moves in a contest where some win and others lose privileges those who like contests and know the rules of the game. Speech that is assertive and confrontational is here more valued than speech that is tentative, exploratory, or conciliatory. (Young 1996, 122–23)

A second criticism, powerfully documented by Jane Mansbridge and seconded by many others, is that discursive modes of democracy aim at, and often presume, false agreement upon a common good. In plural contexts, where interests conflict and no such good is common, striving toward consensus can "stimulate conformity to the majority against one's own real interests . . . assemblies designed to produce feelings of community can thus backfire and intimidate the less self-reliant. . . . those who have no trouble speaking in public defend their interests; it does not give the average citizen comparable protection" (Mansbridge 1980, 274).

These two criticisms target general formulations of deliberative democracy, and it should be noted that the specific features of deliberation in accountable autonomy that depart from the accounts of theorists such as Habermas (1989) and Cohen (1989) somewhat deflect the force of these criticisms. With its highly decentered architecture, the Chicago reforms have created multiple spatially and functionally dispersed sites of participatory deliberation and action. This proliferation of public spheres makes it more likely that many of them will be composed primarily of, and thus controlled by, those excluded from more centralized political processes. Distributing control in this way addresses the first criticism by creating formal public spaces for many styles of discourse, in which a single culturally privileged mode need not dominate. It addresses the second objection by providing opportunities to advance diverse ends by creating many sites. Decentralizing the public sphere in this way conforms partially with Nancy Fraser's prescription for "subaltern counterpublics that are ... parallel discursive arenas where members of subordinated social groups invent and circulate counter discourses" (Fraser 1996, 123).

The pragmatic dimension of deliberation in accountable autonomy mitigates some exclusionary tendencies of other varieties of deliberative democracy. Participants deliberate principally about the priority of common problems and how to solve those problems. Each step of this problem-solving process is open to just the kinds of culturally subordinated communication validated by Young and Fraser—indeed it blurs the distinction between "affective" and "rational" modes of thought and speech.[33] For example, the identification and prioritization of common problems usually involves the expression of concrete needs, often through narrative, rather than the articulation and defense of abstract positions and values. Beyond this, the aim of each participant in the process is to discover effective solutions to the problems; since listening carefully and considering alternatives is often a better approach in this endeavor than trying to "win the argument," pragmatic deliberation is likely to be less of a blood sport than has been feared by some critics. Finally, local problem-solving demands a much thinner consensus than other forms of deliberation; it establishes tentative agreements about effective solutions rather than an enduring consensus on values or goods, and these agreements are always open to reconsideration and revision.

Given these institutional differences between accountable autonomy and the models of deliberative democracy criticized by theorists of difference, it is not clear what empirical outcomes such critics would expect from the kinds of reforms implemented in Chicago. A stalwart difference critic might maintain that the similarities to other versions of deliberation are more salient than the differences, and thus that the same exclusions will infect accountable autonomy. In terms of aggregate participation patterns, this might then translate to an expectation that women and people of color will participate in these institutions less than men, and in particular white men.[34]

The available empirical evidence on participation in community policing diverges surprisingly from the expectations of difference critics on this point. In its 1996 report, the Institute for Policy Research surveyed 2,740 participants in the city-wide JCPT Program.[35] They divided participants into seven categories according to neighborhood, race, ethnicity, and class demographics. In every neighborhood demographic category, substantially more women participated than men. Beyond this, there was no clear ethnic or racial bias in any demographic category (Chicago Community Policing Evaluation Consortium 1996, 48).

This pattern of female gender bias in community-policing participation is repeated by patterns of beat-meeting attendance. Between 1995 and 1996, researchers from Northwestern University studied monthly community-policing meetings in 139 of the city's 279 beats. Over that period, they observed 2,190 meetings, averaging 16 meetings per beat. Using this data, a measure of gender bias can be constructed for each beat by subtracting (1) the percentage of adults in living in a beat who were women from (2) the percentage of participants in that beat who were women (over all of the beat's observed meetings). Thus, a gender-bias result greater than zero indicates that women were overrepresented in a beat's meetings, and under zero indicates that they were underrepresented. Figure 4.4 charts the frequency of gender-bias levels for all of the 139 observed beats:

The average gender bias over these 139 beats was 5.9 percent. Using a two-tailed t-test, the hypothesis that the means of a sample consisting of the percentage of adults living in each of the 139 beats who are women and a sample consisting of the percentages of participants in meetings in each of the 139 beats who are female can be rejected at the 0.01 level of confidence. The results of a t-test comparing the means of these two samples are shown in table 4.7:

Similarly, survey data from LSC members also reveals substantial positive female gender bias in participation: approximately 70 percent of LSC members are female.[36] Regarding race and ethnicity, studies show that African-American and Hispanics participate actively in LSC governance. According to the 1997 survey conducted by the Consortium on Chicago School Research discussed above, 42 percent of LSC members are African-American (38 percent of Chicago's population is African-American), 14 percent of members are Hispanic (compared to 20 percent of Chicago's population), and 40 percent are white (38 percent of Chicagoans are non-Hispanic white). The authors of that report conclude that "the racial ethnic composition of individual councils tends to resemble the race and ethnicity of the students in the schools (Ryan et al. 1997, 11).

Some data from integrated settings, however, bears out predictions of theorists of difference regarding representation. In mixed-ethnicity schools where the student body averages 50 percent white, for example, an average of 85 percent of the LSC members are white (Ryan et al. 1997, 10–11). While the data on participation in community policing in table 4.5 indicates fair representation, other data indicate that when Hispanics consti-

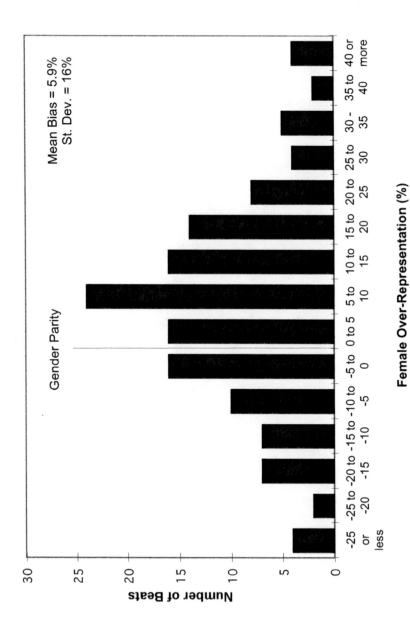

4.4. Gender Bias in Beat-Meeting Attendance.

TABLE 4.7
T-Test for Statistical Significance of Gender Bias

	Percentage of Females	
	Meetings	Beat Population
Mean	58.2	52.3
Variance	267.2	7.2
Observations	139	139
Pearson Correlation	0.11	—
Hypothesized Mean Difference	0	—
t Stat	4.3	—
P(T<=t) one-tail	1.6E-05	—
t Critical one-tail	1.7	—
P(T<=t) two-tail	3.3E-05	—
t Critical two-tail	1.98	—

tute only a minority of a neighborhood's population, they tend to be underrepresented at community-policing beat meetings. The Institute for Policy Research's 1996 report found that "Hispanics did not start turning out in large numbers [to beat meetings] until they made up about half of the population of the beat. Then their attendance rate grew quickly" (Chicago Community Policing Evaluation Consortium 1996; 35).

On the dimensions of presence and representation, then, available data on aggregate participation in Chicago community-policing and school-reform programs offer mixed support for the skeptical predictions of theorists of difference. While these organized sites of deliberation by no means exclude women as measured by attendance—indeed they constitute numerical majorities—minority members participate less in integrated contexts. Even there, however, "underrepresentation" more accurately describes the statistical profile than "exclusion." Furthermore, the numerous decentralized sites of political participation offered by the reforms of school governance and community policing create opportunities for the public engagement of people of color that simply did not exist before the reforms. In the words of school-reform observers, "the institution of Local School Councils . . . has allowed approximately 1,800 African-American parents and community residents to serve as elected officials and to gain the skills associated with this experience. They represent an overwhelming percentage of the minority elected public officials in Illinois" (Ryan et al. 1997, 11).

But presence does not entail respect; simply showing up doesn't mean that others will listen or that one's concerns will be heeded. Even if patterns of presence differ from those predicted by a theorist of differences, she may still argue that these measures are too crude to detect exclusions that occur despite substantial representation of women and people of color. Her second objection might be that within such meetings, members of disadvantaged groups will suffer systemic domination. Such individuals may be less likely to speak up than more articulate, aggressive, and culturally advantaged participants. Their modes of communication may be systematically ignored because they do not conform to styles of argument and reason-giving privileged by "deliberative" expectations. Unfortunately, existing studies of school governance and community policing have not amassed evidence that can establish whether this more subtle mode of cultural domination prevails. The case studies that follow are thus attentive to such mechanisms of silencing and domination.

4.6. Expertise

A fifth family of perspectives focuses on problems of competence rather than rationality or fairness. This view's principal concern is that ordinary citizens will lack the specialized knowledge, skills, and habits of thought necessary to make effective decisions in complex administrative areas like education and policing. Ignorance, harmful enough under representative systems of government, cripples even more intensely when ordinary citizens are given real voice over technical operations. One version of this objection comes from efficiencies generated by specialization and divisions of labor; professionals, by virtue of their training, experience, and constant exposure, will be better positioned than lay persons to make problem-solving decisions.[37] In another version of this objection, Joseph Schumpeter (1942, 262) argued that political arenas often stupefy otherwise competent individuals. James Wilson combined both of these objections when he argued against local democratic control of city police, writing that "it is hard enough to run a good police department when it is subject to second-rate politicians in city hall; it would be much harder if it were subject to fourth-rate politicians in the wards and neighborhoods" (1968, 286). This theory of expertise, then, supposes that the demands of specialization limit the number qualified to make or supervise technical decisions to a small minority.[38]

While no one can deny the importance of competence, accountable autonomy offers three responses to this critique. First, the Chicago reforms reduce the complexity and cognitive burdens of problem-solving by devolving authority along both spatial and functional dimensions. Second, they provide explicitly for policy- and skill-specific participant training; they do not presume that the knowledge and talents that participants acquire outside their processes sufficiently equip them to participate effectively, and so resources for training and technical assistance are important features of institutional design. In our concrete example of school governance, Illinois state law requires LSC members to undergo mandatory training in school-financing, strategic-planning, and principal-selection. Several initiatives within the context of Chicago community policing have created teams of trainers that circulate among neighborhoods to provide problem-solving instruction. Finally, because some of the skills and talents required for effective public problem-solving do not fall easily into disciplinary or professional categories, professional habits can inhibit constructive innovation by constraining thought and action to the bounds of professional orthodoxy. From this perspective, the diversity of views, talents, and experiences that nonprofessional participants bring can strengthen, rather than dilute, problem-solving efforts.

Along these lines, police supervisors and independent policy evaluators view officers who use only "traditional police approaches"—expert solutions like increased patrol and surveillance—as failures in community policing and those who devise innovative solutions as successful. Explicitly, police managers have begun to look unfavorably toward those who do not manage to transcend the canonical expert procedures and methods instilled by its own instructional apparatus.[39] Engaged citizens, then, might help generate these imaginative solutions. Insofar as the general skill of problem-solving contributes to effective public action, optimism about the value of citizen participation is buttressed by the supposed expert's lack of confidence in his or her own abilities. In a 1994 survey of Chicago police officers, only 16 percent felt very qualified to identify neighborhood problems, and only one in ten felt qualified to develop or evaluate solutions (Skogan and Hartnett 1997, 77–78).

These two sets of arguments, then, offer different predictions about how citizens and officials will act, and interact, in participatory contexts. The defender of conventional expertise predicts either that citizen voices will make no substantial contribution to problem-solving or, worse, that popular participation will degrade the quality of decisions because citizens will make uninformed and unrealistic demands.[40] Proponents of appropriately structured participation, on the other hand, expect that ordinary citizens can overcome the barriers of ignorance through training and the experience of participation itself, and that those who do so will make important contributions in both devising and implementing problem-solving strategies. Unfortunately, very few of the secondary analyses of Chicago's reforms have developed data necessary to examine this hypothesis on the city-wide level. Perhaps the most obvious operational prediction of this expert perspective is that local units (schools, police beats) with the least popular participation will operate most effectively. When citizens don't show up, they cannot waste the valuable time of experts, nor can they obstruct problem-solving with unfeasible proposals. Unfortunately, the axioms of Chicago school and police observers eliminated this possibility from their perspectives. Increased community participation has been treated as part of the definition of success rather than a possible cause of failure in all of the secondary studies on Chicago school reform and community policing that have examined this question.

We therefore turn to less direct attitudinal evidence to test the expert perspective. If lay-participants typically obstruct organizational progress, then we would expect experts themselves—teachers, principals, and police officers—to voice this objection to popular participation.[41] In June of 1992, the Consortium on Chicago School Research administered a survey on school governance to all elementary and high school principals in the city.[42] The results of that survey do not bear out the prediction of expertise theory that lay-participants add little value. When asked whether the LSC "contributes to academic improvements," 58 percent of principals agreed or strongly agreed, while 20 percent disagreed or strongly disagreed. When asked whether the LSC participated in developing the SIP, 77 percent agreed or strongly agreed, while 13 percent disagreed or strongly disagreed. When asked whether the "LSC pressures me to spend money in ways that I think are inappropriate," 87 percent of responding principals disagreed or strongly disagreed.

Surveys of police opinions about the value of resident contributions to problem-solving map less crisply onto these predictions from expertise. The surveys that have been administered to police officers ask about their attitudes and prospective opinions rather than concrete problem-solving experiences, and so these data do not directly gauge whether police officers' opinions about the value of citizen participation more closely match the predictions of the expertise perspective. Overall, surveys of Chicago police reveal that they, like police in other large cities, are quite pessimistic about the attitudes of civilians. In a 1993 survey, half of responding police officers agreed that "most people do not respect the police," and two-thirds agreed that "citizens don't understand the problems of the police" (Skogan and Hartnett 1997, 78). Despite this dim view of police-resident relations, police officers were relatively sanguine about the potential contribution of residents to problem-solving where crime and public-safety issues were concerned: 53 percent of police officers agreed that "citizens know more about what goes on in their area than officers who patrol there" and 74 percent agreed that "police officers should work with citizens to try and solve the problems in their beat." Beyond this, police officers in 1993—before the implementation of Chicago community-policing institutions—worried that citizen involvement would jeopardize police autonomy. More than 60 percent of police respondents thought that community-policing reforms would create "greater demand on police resources," while more than 70 percent thought that they would result in "more unreasonable demands on police by community groups" (Skogan and Hartnett 1997, 84). This same survey was administered to police officers again in 1995, after two years' experience with the reforms, and substantially fewer officers thought that community policing would reduce their autonomy or create unreasonable demands (Skogan and Hartnett 1997, 107).

This chapter drew upon a large body of city-wide empirical evidence to investigate the most damning first-order criticisms of empowered participation. These objections were constructed in the form of five critical perspectives—strong rational-choice, strong-egalitarian, social-capital, cultural difference, and expertise. Since the claims of these perspectives are based upon deeply held, but nevertheless speculative, suppositions about the behavior of citizens and officials, only empirical evidence can settle the debate. We therefore investigated each perspective's critical claims about political participation under accountable autonomy using available secondary and city-wide empirical evidence. Surprisingly, these data validated few of the empirical expectations raised by these perspectives and thus have cleared the way against common and important first-order objections to appropriately designed direct, pragmatic, and democratic institutions for empowered participation.

These data, however, leave empowered participation as something of a residual theory. As a general matter, the level and character of participation in Chicago's neighborhoods irrespective of local conditions is high enough to conduct deliberative problem-solving in community policing and school governance. These data could not, however, reveal the extent and fashion in which such activity occurs. We must turn to more fine-grained types of evidence to probe the subtle operation of these processes themselves. The next two chapters thus examine experiences of participatory deliberation in six neighborhood-level cases.

5

Deliberation and Poverty

5.1. Deliberation in Contexts of Poverty and Social Conflict

Though far from conclusive, the city-wide data presented in the preceding chapter provide some empirical ground for optimism about the potential of the Chicago community-policing and school-governance reforms. Several years of experience with this novel form of urban governance show that it meets many of the challenges raised by five first-blush objections to participatory democracy—strong versions of rational-choice theory and egalitarianism, social-capital theory, a theory of difference, and an elite-technocratic perspective. These data, however, addressed only the roughest inputs (e.g., neighborhood wealth and racial characteristics) and outputs (e.g., participation rates and other characteristics of engagement, participants' satisfaction with processes or outcomes). We could not use them to assess more fine-grained claims for and against public participation, deliberation, and civic problem-solving.

To gain purchase and resolution on the empirical reality of deliberative problem-solving, this chapter and the next recount experiences of participation and local governance as they unfolded in three police beats and three schools. These neighborhood-level investigations do not definitively establish the conditions and mechanisms of decentralized deliberative governance—six cases cannot bear such a heavy burden of proof. Rather, they serve three more modest purposes. First, they illuminate how processes such as deliberative problem-solving and centralized support and mobilization that were described formally and conceptually in chapters 2 and 3 actually operate in practice.

Second, these case studies probe the effects of two especially important background conditions: poverty and social conflict. This chapter focuses on poverty and the next upon conflict. As discussed above, the absence of resources and agreement are thought to be especially unfavorable for participatory and deliberative forms of democratic decision-making. Nevertheless, participatory-democratic reforms are often undertaken precisely to benefit individuals who live under such circumstances. Though data from the previous chapter show that the Chicago reforms draw substantial levels of *participation* even in poor and heterogeneous neighborhoods, those data could not address whether the character of decision-making in those neighborhoods was more or less likely to be *deliberative*, *fair*, or *effective*. For example, though residents of poor neighborhoods participated at least as frequently as those from wealthier ones, available quantitative data could not determine the relative capacity of unequal groups to utilize these new democratic institutions. Though more women participated than men, men may have dominated proceedings despite their numerical weakness. Though heterogeneous neighborhoods drew diverse participants, we could not determine whether members of different groups deliberated constructively with one another. Similarly, though both educational and policing professionals responded that lay-participants played important and complementary roles, those data could not reveal whether professionals set agendas and performed the "heavy lifting" of developing and implementing strategies, or whether citizens contributed substantially to public decisions and actions.

Finally, these six case studies aim to fill a gap that has separated theoretical treatments of deliberative democracy from empirical research. Most academic work on deliberation has focused on the theoretical conditions, justifications, and hoped-for outcomes of deliberation at the cost of ignoring how people actually deliberate. Given the substantial interest in deliberation, prior research offers surprisingly few accounts of how deliberation actually occurs on the ground (Mansbridge 1980; Nagel 1992; Gastil 1993; Fishkin 1995; Forester 1999, 194; Pelletier 1999; Weeks 2000). These case studies help to fill this relative silence by documenting and probing actual deliberations structured according to the rules of accountable autonomy.

The following cases examine three sets of questions that relate the *institutions* of accountable autonomy to its *democratic performance*, understood as the realization of core public values such the effectiveness and fairness of public action through the participation and deliberation of citizens and street-level officials. These three general questions are:

1. How well does accountable autonomy establish deliberative and participatory decision processes and generate fair and effective outcomes in light of initial neighborhood conditions such as poverty, inequality, and social conflict?

2. Given a set of initial conditions and prior institutions (hierarchical and insular school and police organizations) in a neighborhood, do these institutions perform better than the hierarchical bureaucracies that preceded them?

3. Finally, do *city-wide* institutional reforms such as Chicago school reform and community policing set into motion the *ground-level* micromechanisms of fairness and effectiveness postulated in the preceding chapters?

Each of these questions can be rendered as an extended hypothesis regarding the sources of success and failure in accountable autonomy. The first hypothesis asserts that democratic performance depends upon the existence of favorable neighborhood-level "initial conditions," and that the relative democratic performance of different neighborhoods governed under these deliberative-democratic institutions will therefore be a function of those underlying circumstances. Along these lines, one frequent criticism of institutional forms like accountable autonomy is that they yield positive outcomes only under certain narrow conditions—the presence of wealth, education, homogeneity—and that therefore their benefits will accrue only to those who are already well-off.[1] Recall that chapter 4 presented substantial, but not conclusive, data against these hypotheses about the importance of wealth and uniform interests. To further probe these claims, the case studies will attempt to gauge the relative democratic performance of accountable autonomy under various sets of "initial conditions." In particular, we compare the (intercase) *relative performance* of participatory deliberation in neighborhoods that enjoy very favorable conditions to that of neighborhoods characterized by levels of blight and social conflict that are frequently considered unfavorable to participatory democracy.

The second hypothesis compares the democratic performance of these institutions against the hierarchically organized school and police system that preceded it in each of the cases. Do these reforms improve the local operations of the school and police departments compared to the previous traditional bureaucratic structures? To shed light on this question of democratic performance under different governance regimes, we will attempt to make rough (intra-case) assessments of whether postreform institutions, compared to the prior hierarchical administrative structures, advanced the central democratic values of deliberation, civic engagement, public accountability, and fair and effective public action.

The third hypothesis contends that democratic success can be attributed to its deliberative procedures and mechanisms rather than to favorable "initial conditions." The reforms and formal institutions of the CPS and CPD described in the previous chapters are designed in part to set various kinds of mechanisms into action. In chapter 1, these mechanisms were described as directed discretion, cross-functional coordination, institutional learning, civic trust, and reasonable deliberation. If community-policing or school-governance groups fail to follow the deliberative problem-solving procedure prescribed in chapter 2, then they will be less likely to produce fair and effective outcomes. According to this hypothesis, democratic success is driven primarily by the extent of implementation. The case studies examine actual processes of deliberation and problem-solving to gauge whether dimensions of institutional success can be attributed to these mechanisms rather than other unanticipated and untheorized factors such as luck, dedicated community activists or professionals, or conventional local politics.

5.2. Initial Conditions: Six Cases in Three Neighborhoods

The following cases examine problem-solving deliberations in three elementary (K–8) LSCs and three community-policing groups between February 1996 and August 1997. These schools and beats were located in three South-Side neighborhoods, with one school and one policing group in each. For ease of reference, each neighborhood bears an alias: "Central," "Southtown," and "Traxton."[2] Continuing this anonymity, I shall refer to each of the three police beats by its neighborhood alias and "beat," and each school by its neighborhood alias and the suffix "elementary." So, the case study school in Traxton is denominated as "Traxton Elementary," the policing case study in Central as "Central Beat," and so on. Central is located in the heart of Chicago's South Side and its physical and demographic characteristics resemble those of many central-city neighborhoods. The two sides of "Traxton" are separated by a set of railroad tracks; the residents on one side are quite well-to-do, while those on the other are impoverished by comparison. "Southtown" lies on the far southern edge of the city, and its long-time residents are African-Americans and whites of primarily Polish descent, but a sizable number of Hispanics have moved into the area in recent years. The approximate areas of the three neighborhoods are indicated on the this map of Chicago (fig. 5.1):

Selected demographic characteristics of each neighborhood appear in table 5.1.[3]

The neighborhood-level examination of accountable autonomy begins by constructing rough "prior expectations" about the likelihood of *institutional success*—fair and effective problem-solving generated by participatory deliberation—under various neighborhood-level *initial conditions*. The exploration of each case examines how deliberative processes and institutions operate given its starting point in the space of initial conditions. Initial conditions are just those variables that social scientists typically deploy as independent variables in regressions or as background conditions to deeper ethnographic or case studies: racial composition, wealth, education, social capital, prior histories, and so on. A full understanding of participatory deliberation would require examining the phenomena in a wide range of such initial conditions. Fair and effective problem-solving might strictly require certain favorable conditions, or there could be a more probabilistic relationship between effective problem-solving and the socioeconomic and cultural circumstances in which it occurs. The practical and scholarly interest in accountable autonomy would then rest in part upon the frequency with which those initial conditions existed.

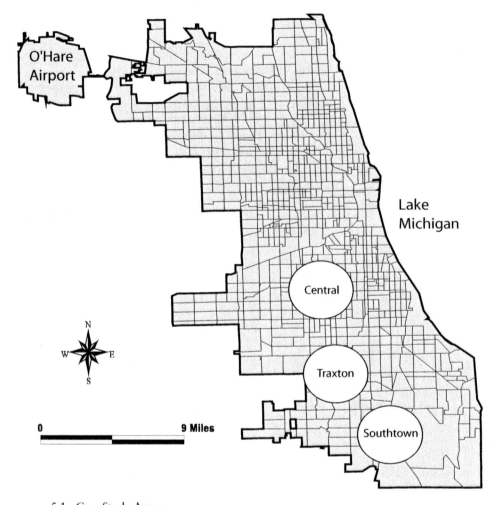

5.1. Case Study Areas.

Though we would like to examine the many dimensions potentially salient to the success of accountable autonomy, these case studies purchase depth at the expense of breadth. Limitations imposed by a small-N study of six cases require judiciousness in the selection of initial conditions. To economize, we selected two dimensions of initial conditions that are politically and theoretically salient because they pose the greatest challenges for participatory democracy: *wealth and poverty of resources*, on one hand, and the *similarity or dispersion of interests*, on the other. Expectations about the relationship between these two dimensions of initial conditions and the performance of institutions like accountable auton-

TABLE 5.1
Selected Characteristics of Case Study Neighborhoods

Neighborhood	Population	Black (%)	White, Non-Hispanic (%)	Hispanic (%)	Income less than $15,000/yr %	Median Household Income ($)
Central	6,297	99.4	0.4	0.3	50.2	15,192
Traxton	9,306	66.6	33.1	0.3	16.7	37,335
Southtown	7,769	78.3	2.5	19.1	54.4	14,074
All Chicago	2.78 million	39.0	38.1	19.2	29.7	30,707

Source: 1990 Census data.

omy are straightforward and have been stated many times in the literature on political participation and collective action. Those who possess an abundance of resources are more likely to succeed in deliberation and problem-solving than those who are relatively impoverished. Public and private resources like time, skill, and money are often thought to be necessary for effective deliberation. Furthermore, they also provide the wherewithal to implement problem-solving strategies that result from deliberation. On the second dimension of interest dispersion or social conflict, deliberation is a mode of collective decision and action. As reasoned discussion about group goals, it is commonly thought that situations in which parties have conflicting or dispersed aims will likely degenerate into adversarial contests, while in situations where parties share interests that are largely common deliberation will progress more easily.

The analysis below treats median family income as a proxy for the level of neighborhood resources. There are many other important and relevant kinds of local resources—the abundance of public goods, nonmaterial individual resources such as time and education, and social capital—that we shall explore as they arise in the case material. Because it is more difficult to translate these additional factors into comparable metrics across cases and because these kinds of resources frequently correlate with private income, we use income as a proxy measure for resource level. We divide this dimension of neighborhood income-resources into three qualitative bands: those which are relatively wealthy, situations of medium wealth, and poor neighborhoods.[4] Other things being equal, the Chicago reforms should deliver the greatest benefit to neighborhoods in the top level (see figure 5.2).

The degree of interest dispersion is the second dimension of initial conditions considered. At this point, it is important to highlight a few methodological choices about how interests are treated. The interests that parties have are the *revealed* interests that they advance (or fail to advance) in discursive processes. These interests were ascribed interpretively, through field observations and interviews; there is an inevitable amount of controversial interpretation in any such exercise. While parties' class, race, geographic (e.g., east side or west side of neighborhood), and structural (public official, citizen, et cetera) positions and self-identities (activist, Black Muslim, police officer, principal) figure importantly in the constitution of their interests, there is no one-to-one mapping from the positions and identities of parties onto their interests. Beyond the loose relationship between structural position and interest, I also take the interests of parties to be plastic. One central feature of successful deliberation is that parties transform their interests in the course of goal-directed, reason-governed discussion. In this discussion of the initial condition of the cases, then, we attempt to specify the content of parties' interests and the level of disper-

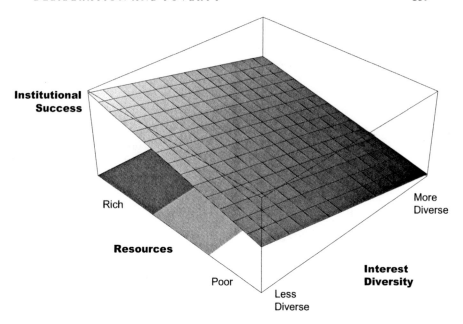

5.2 Hypothesized Institutional Success versus Initial Conditions.

sion in those interests at the beginning of the observation period. We fully expect that these interests and levels of disagreement will change during the case study period and after it; one aim of the examination is to establish the relationship between deliberative processes and the transformation of parties' interests (Mansbridge 1980; Forester 1999).

Imagine interest dispersion and resource level in an X-Y plane that forms the domain of a function whose range, a unidimensional measure of performance, is plotted on the Z-axis. Our prior expectations, or hypotheses, about the effects of abundance and agreement upon institutional performance in neighborhoods, then, describe a surface similar to the one depicted in figure 5.2: For a given neighborhood, we can plot its position in resources and diversity in the X-Y plane. At a given level of neighborhood resources, we expect that deliberative decision processes will generate more fair and effective outcomes when the parties in that neighborhood share many interests in common (low interest diversity) than when their interests conflict intensely. Thus the plane slopes downward (indicating lower institutional performance) as diversity of interests increases. At a given level of interest diversity, furthermore, the plane slopes downward because we expect that wealthier neighborhoods will be better able to effectively solve problems and deliberate than less wealthy ones.

5.3. Initial Conditions of the Six Cases.

Thus interpreting the two dimensions of resource level and interest dispersion, figure 5.3 depicts the six cases in this two-dimensional space of initial conditions: Traxton Elementary is located in the wealthy part of the Traxton neighborhood (with its median household income of over $60,000, this section ranked in the top ten census tracts in the city of Chicago) and draws most of its student body and parent participation from that area, and so it is accordingly classified as wealthy. Traxton Beat, on the other hand, encompasses both the wealthy area served by Traxton Elementary and a poorer adjacent region. Averaging these different median income levels, we place Traxton in the middle region of the resource scale. While conflict was certainly not absent in the deliberations of Traxton Elementary participants, participants shared similar aspirations for their school. In Traxton Beat, interests and perspectives divided predictably along class lines, and so we characterize its level of interest dispersion as "more diverse." Residents had different views about which problems the police should treat as priorities, the proper role of officers, and police-civilian relationships differed between better-off and less well-off residents.

The administrative boundaries for school and policing in Central lie in a poor African-American neighborhood whose median household income of $15,000 places it in the bottom quintile of Chicago's census tracts. Therefore, both Central Elementary and Central Beat fall in the "poor" region of our resource-level chart. Participants in the governance of Central Elementary inherited long histories of multi-faceted conflict—factions of the community had fought each other for years prior to the observation period, and the professional staff of the school were divided one against another and in tenuous alliances with community factions—and so the school-governance case is classified along the "more diverse" side of the interest-dispersion spectrum. The professional and citizen participants in Central's community-policing effort, by contrast, lacked this history of animosity; they had little in the way of prior interactions with one another, and came to the community-policing project with a similar general objective: the safety of the neighborhood. So the case of Central Beat is classified as having "less dispersed" interests.

Finally, Southtown is a neighborhood composed mostly of African-American and Hispanic residents. In terms of income, residents who live in the policing and school boundaries of Southtown are quite poor; median household income falls in the bottom quintile of Chicago's census tracts, so both Southtown Beat and Elementary fall in the "poor" region of the resource space. Southtown Beat served Hispanic and African-American residents who had a history of racial animosity that occasionally flared into violence. Because they came to the community-policing effort literally speaking different languages, living in different parts of the neighborhood, having few habits of cooperation, and asserting different priorities, this case is characterized as having participants with "dispersed" interests. By contrast, Southtown Elementary served African-American children and their families almost exclusively, and parents who participated in the process of school governance shared many of the same goals and educational perspectives as other parents and school staff. Because of this initial agreement, Southtown Elementary is located in the left-hand region—less "dispersion" of interests—of figure 5.3.

Given these prior expectations about the advantages of homogeneous interests and wealth, five of the six are "hard cases" in the sense that they occur under unfavorable background conditions. Only the participants of local governance in Traxton Elementary enjoy the advantages of wealth and aligned interests. The other five cases face one or both challenges of unfavorable material-resource conditions or conflicting interests. The material inequality and racial diversity of Traxton Beat holds theoretical interest because it stresses the moral capacities of the participants; we expect domination by wealthy parties to result, but deliberative norms require otherwise. Four of the six cases occur in conditions of severe resource-scarcity. We focus the lion's share of our attention on the low end of the socioeconomic ladder for two reasons. First, one of the most common challenges to deliberative, decentralized democratic proposals is that the worst-off suffer under these regimes. It is important to know in some detail, therefore, how the institutions of accountable autonomy operate under conditions of destitution. Second, from the practical and scholarly perspectives, the import effects of any such proposal are the benefits that it yields for the least advantaged in society; if it does not work for them, it cannot advance our democratic aspirations very far. In particular, we want to know whether accountable autonomy advances core democratic values more effectively than our received political institutions, even under highly unfavorable conditions.

5.3. Southtown Elementary Becomes Harambee Academy

The demographic profile of Southtown Elementary is typical for low-income, African-American schools in Chicago.[5] In 1996, 697 students were enrolled in the 9 grades (K–8) at Southtown. Two of those students were Hispanic, and the rest were African-American. Approximately 88 percent of them came from low-income families—that is, families who received public aid, had children that were in institutions for neglected or delinquent children, supported in foster homes with public funds, or eligible to receive free or reduced-price lunches. The figure for Southtown Elementary is only slightly higher than that for Chicago as a whole, where 83.2 percent of elementary school students qualify as "low-income." Educational efforts were hampered by the school's unusually high mobility rate—defined as the percentage of students who enroll or leave during the academic year—of 52.4 percent in 1996.[6]

Despite these difficult—but by no means extraordinary—inner-city conditions, Southtown Elementary maintained a respectable atmosphere and level of academic performance. Its chronic truancy rate—defined as the number of students absent for 10 percent or more of the prior 180 school days—was 0.5 percent, compared with a Chicago-wide average of 4.7 percent. Average class-size for most grades at Southtown Elementary was comparable to other Chicago elementary schools in 1996: the average kindergarten class at Southtown had 26.3 children; Southtown's average first-grade class had 19.8 students while the Chicago average was 23.6; 19.1 students were in the average third-grade class at Southtown while Chicago schools as a whole averaged 22.2 students; sixth-grade figures were 21.6 students per class at Southtown and 23.0 for Chicago; and there were 25.6 eighth graders in the average Southtown class, but only 23.5 students in eighth-grade classes system-wide.

Test scores at Southtown Elementary indicated that school administrators were competent, but not stellar. Slightly lower than the system-wide average, student scores roughly tracked the more difficult demographic conditions of the students that attended Southtown compared to Chicago as a whole. According to the standardized tests of the Illinois Goals Assessment Program (IGAP), 1996 Southtown student reading and writing scores as measured in the third, sixth, and eighth grades roughly matched the CPS average. IGAP Math, Science, and Social Science scores, however, fell substantially behind city-wide averages in all tested grades (Chicago Public Schools 1996). The Iowa Test of Basic Skills (ITBS) is the other major standardized test used in CPS. According to 1997 ITBS tests, only 18 percent of Southtown Elementary students met or exceeded national norms for reading and 20 percent met or exceeded national norms for mathematics.[7] These percentages placed Southtown Elementary in the fourth (second lowest) quintile of public elementary schools in Chicago. In the system as a whole, 30.3 percent of elementary school students exceeded national ITBS norms in reading and 35.9 percent beat the national norms in math.

This statistical profile describes the terrain against which parent, community, and professional participants in LSC governance attempted to use the powers granted them by the 1988 school-reform law to improve educational outcomes at their school and tailor other aspects of its operation to their needs. During the 1996–1997 school year, the Southtown community was fortunate to have a principal—call him Jerry Bradford—who was a strong and competent administrator that embodied the African-American culture and perspective of others in the school community. He was a role model who enjoyed broad and deep support and trust from his staff.

This unity of perception and interest between the school staff, community, and its principal resulted in a governance dynamic that utilized opportunities for participatory school improvement, but did so in ways that fell short of equal participation between professionals and citizens. Principal Bradford and his staff took the lead in formulating school proposals and developing strategies to implement them, and then sought the approval and sometimes active contribution of lay participants to execute those strategies. Though these proposals were innovative and remain quite promising, lay participants served primarily as monitors and supporters rather than as fully equal innovators. In an environment of mutual trust and agreement on ends, it is understandable that the difficult intellectual work of developing school-governance proposals would be left to paid professionals. Systematically generating that trust and agreement would be a substantial achievement for any institutional reform. Nevertheless, the relative deficit in lay-participation disappoints the most demanding expectations for parental engagement.

5.3.1. Innovative Responses to Local Conditions

Perhaps the most impressive aspect of the school professionals—the principal, teachers who serve on the LSC, and others in the school staff—who have taken the mantle of school governance at Southtown Elementary was their capacity to select controversial educational strategies that seem well suited to Southtown's context. Despite vehement disagreement among educational scholars and practitioners about the merit of those strategies, the Southtown team implemented them persistently and always with an eye to adaptation and correction. Two such strategies stand out: transforming the school from its standardized generic environment to one that revolved around Afrocentric themes and the adoption and implementation of Direct-Instruction pedagogical methods.

In 1995, Principal Bradford constructed a fairly radical proposal with his staff and several of the more-involved parents and community members. Under the 1988 school-reform law, each school was directed to develop for itself a distinctive vision, mission, and philosophy, which in turn would be supported by all manner of school programs. What if they took this latitude seriously by changing the generic "Southtown Elementary" into an Afrocentric environment? Specific modifications of school programs, pedagogical methods, and curriculum entailed by this shift would have to be worked out, but the general hope was that such a transformation would make the school more engaging and learning-conducive for the uniformly African-American student body. Parents, community members, and school professionals alike immediately found the idea attractive. One community LSC member put it this way:

> For centuries, the white man has [been putting us down]. Why pledge allegiance to the white man's America, and why educate our children in the schools designed by and for them? Once he [Principal Bradford] put the idea before us, it just got approved. [Two of the new teachers], one in kindergarten and one in first grade, are both very good and they are both white. They have no problem at all with the Afrocentric curriculum. We are not talking about teaching Ebonics instead of English or anything crazy like that, but it does help [build] respect.[8]

In 1996, the school officially changed its name from Southtown Elementary to Harambee Academy to reflect a new Afrocentric focus.[9] In seeking CPS approval for the name change and justifying it, Southtown-Harambee's 1997 SIP explained that:

> [Harambee Academy], formerly known as [Southtown Elementary School] is a Pre/Kdgn–8th grade service center located . . . on Chicago's South Side.
> The name change reflects the school's present Black population as well as a

new direction in the search for Academic excellence.

[Harambee] was one of three great African Empires of the 15th through 16th century, located in northwest Africa. Because of its enduring legacy and glorious past, the school will implement an Afrocentric curriculum in 1997. In conjunction with the Afrocentric curriculum, which we believe will enhance reading scores, various other activities will be implemented.

The principal and LSC have transformed the school atmosphere to convey pride in the scholarly accomplishments of ancient Africa and to build African-American identity, generally. For example, art and décor in the school celebrate ancient and modern African and African-American accomplishments, many of the school materials have been selected for their Afrocentric relevance. In one LSC meeting, the council changed the name of their athletic teams to the "Harambee Scholars" and changed their mascot from a scorpion to a mortarboard and scroll to reflect the general notion, in line with their vision of Afrocentric education, that athletics is not an end in itself, but rather part of a well-rounded education. In time, this cultural transformation of the school may elevate indicators of school productivity, such as student test scores, or graduates' future educational or employment performance.

In a second, less exotic but perhaps more controversial reform, the principal and staff at Harambee decided to employ Direct-Instruction (DI) methods to teach reading at the lower grade levels in 1994. Of the educational theorists who have an opinion on such matters, "behavioralists" generally support DI methods of rote learning, practice, and memorization, while other cognitive psychologists support so called "progressive, whole-language" institutional approaches that use situated learning techniques whose lessons derive from engaging activities. Many major educational associations oppose DI on the grounds that it is class-biased—typically deployed in low-income environments. Barbara Bowman of the Erikson Institute for Advanced Study in Child Development opposed DI because it is premised on the view that "they're poor, so they can't learn the same way middle-class kids learn." Karen Smith, associate director of the National Council of English Teachers, writes that "it goes against everything we think"; and Larry Schweinart of the High Scope/Perry Research Project in Ypsilanti, Michigan, has commented that DI is "extremely authoritarian." In typical command-and-control fashion, the California State Board of Education eliminated the most prominent DI program from its approved list of reading programs on the grounds that its stories had no literary merit.[10]

Despite these objections, Harambee adopted DI methods to teach reading in 1994 to its younger grades and then expanded the program to encompass the upper grades in 1996. School staff explicitly adopted DI curriculum because they felt that their students, given high mobility and low levels of educational preparedness, would respond more readily to DI than to progressive, whole-language strategies. Given the prior discussion of Afrocentric transformation and substantial efforts to develop black pride and self-respect, it is unlikely that school staff adopted DI out of colonial, classist, or racist assumptions, as some educational experts fear. Rather, school staff claim that they adopted DI as a promising strategy for reading improvement in light of local constraints. Though these programs are unlikely to generate immediate benefits, reading test scores have risen since adoption of the program, and school staff attribute this rise to the adoption of DI. As with Afrocentric transformation, it is unclear whether adoption of DI methods will generate the desired educational outcomes. But one central aim of participatory devolution is to accommodate just this kind of uncertainty by devolving authority to make such decisions to the ground-level actors who are most familiar with local conditions and best situated to evaluate program outcomes.

5.3.2. Civic Engagement and Resource Acquisition

Partially as a result of its thrifty school administration, Harambee Academy is thankfully free from the worst symptoms of severe resource-deprivation that can be found in many accounts of inner-city schools (Kozol 1991). The physical structure itself is well maintained, almost immaculate. While there is no great surplus of books and other teaching materials, neither is there a severe shortage. So, for example, the school had sufficient resources to implement the two major changes—to Afrocentrism and to Direct Instruction—described above. Despite this adequate, if not abundant, funding, Principal Bradford and others on the LSCs have developed a systematic capacity to acquire substantial new resources from the central administration of CPS. More and more, CPS allocates discretionary funds—for new educational programs, physical plant, capital equipment, and the like—through contests akin to foundation grants or other requests-for-proposals. Whereas prior to the 1988 reforms, these monies were allocated on bureaucratic criteria such as centrally determined need or queue position, school personnel must increasingly win funds by demonstrating their ability to use additional monies effectively and imaginatively, all the while showing strict need. The dangers in such a scheme are as evident as its advantages. CPS administration gains some confidence that its grants will not simply be wasted through incompetence or graft, but the most needy schools may never develop the organizational capacities necessary to acquire additional funds under these arrangements. Harambee personnel used this resource-allocation regime to their advantage by developing the expertise to assemble persuasive and innovative plans, by engaging the help of willing community members with specific expertise in, for example, architecture and computer networks, and by nurturing connections with key CPS personnel. In 1995, they persuaded CPS to build a new permanent addition to the school structure, and in 1997 they acquired some $250,000 in additional capital monies from the central administration to install a school-wide computer network with workstations in every classroom and full Internet connectivity.

Though Harambee Academy was not particularly overcrowded, Principal Bradford and others expanded the scope of school activities by adding a pre-kindergarten program and additional classroom space. Since the central administration of CPS allocated building-expansion funds principally on the basis of overcrowding, the Harambee group in charge of school expansion developed alternative justifications and a particularly persuasive proposal to receive necessary funding. They developed two complementary arguments for the addition. First, existing district pre-kindergarten facilities were located far away from the students' homes, and the long walk subjected children to the dangers of crime and inclement winter weather. Beyond this, a properly designed addition to the school would allow safer and more efficient use of school space by creating a new school office that would monitor entry and exit points and monitor hall traffic so as to reduce truancy and time out of class. The group then worked with independent and school-board architects to design a suitable addition. The group rejected the board architect's original plans because, according to one member of the group, they themselves had seen additions at other Chicago schools with "much nicer structures—two stories, ADA [Americans with Disabilities Act] compliant, atriums, secure labs, and the rest." After several rounds of dialogue between these members of the local school community and professional architects, parties agreed on a design that met their needs. The LSC tapped one of its members who had substantial "downtown connections" to bring this set of plans to the school board. He reported that "I knew who I had to talk to, and the rest of the LSC just let me deal with it. . . . It took only 30–60 days to put the deal together, and the addition itself was built between Fall 1995 and Spring 1996." After it was completed, the addition operated as envisioned, and school staff and parents expressed satisfaction with the modifications.

Harambee staff also felt that improving the school required substantial additional technological capabilities. They accepted the wisdom that children in the K–8 grades must become familiar and comfortable with computer hardware and software if they are to compete effectively later both educationally and occupationally. Responding to this particular need would require substantial investment for workstations and desktop computers, network hardware, system software, instructional software, maintenance, and staff training. In the 1996–1997 school year, school staff formed a "Technology Team" of eight teaching staff. In an effort that paralleled the structural addition, the team worked with local technology professionals to develop a comprehensive, quite persuasive Technology Plan. This plan provided for: five computers in each of twenty classrooms; an additional computer lab of thirty computers; a network connecting all of these to one another in a Local Area Network (LAN) and to the Chicago Public Schools–Wide Area Network (WAN); evaluation of educational software by site visits to Chicago schools with exemplary technology programs; training for all teachers; and incorporation of all technology into existing instructional programs.[11] The total projected cost of implementing the Technology Plan was estimated at $228,000. Impressed with both the school's need and the thoughtfulness of the proposal, CPS awarded Harambee the necessary funds in 1997.

5.3.3. Studied Trust: Lay Participation as Monitoring, not Direct Innovation

These innovations at Harambee Academy were made possible by the decentralizing reforms and incentives of the 1988 school-reform legislation. The devolution of decision authority to individual schools enabled the LSC to adopt an Afrocentric flavor for its school and to choose Direct Instruction pedagogical methods. At the same time, it created the incentives for them to acquire additional resources by developing persuasive, competent programs. These experiences are consistent with the institutional-innovation and civic-engagement components of accountable autonomy (see chapter 1). In a departure from egalitarian accounts of deliberation, however, these innovations were developed by professional staff—largely following the lead of Principal Bradford—for the most part without the creative input of nonprofessional members of the LSC or in the wider school community. So for example, the Technology Plan discussed above was developed primarily by a Technology Team consisting exclusively of school administrators and teachers. The Harambee 1996–1997 SIP lists Principal Bradford, his assistant principal, the school's reading and math coordinators, six teachers, but no parents or community members under the heading of "Individuals who helped to develop the SIP."[12] Nonprofessionals did not participate as equals with professionals, then, in the sense that professionals, not community members or parents, designed the important innovations at Harambee. Parents and community members, however, did importantly support these major initiatives and other school operations, generally.

The first reason for the relative passivity of nonprofessionals is that they saw themselves as supporters and monitors, not as developers, of educational innovations. One Harambee LSC member offered this remarkably lucid argument for why the LSC should act as a monitor, not creator, of curriculums:

> I don't think that the LSC should touch textbook decisions or curriculum change. Suppose that you are a fourth-grade teacher, and I as an LSC member say that you can teach best with [Textbook X] but you say that you can teach best with [Textbook Y], and I override you. Then suppose that that fourth-grade class goes down. There is nothing that I can do to hold you accountable once I have overridden you. The best I can do, as an LSC member, is to say to the principal or the teacher, "You got what you want, now you better deliver." I have been a schoolhouse volunteer for decades, but what do I know about curriculums?

Second and complementarily, nonprofessionals might not have felt the need to take a more active role because an effective monitoring mechanism gave them confidence that school staff were acting effectively in the best interest of the school as a whole. School governance operated with a high level of transparency. Large decisions affecting the likes of the school budget, allocation of discretionary monies, the SIP, and the Technology Plan were all submitted for group discussion in the LSC, as were small decisions the name of the athletic team, its colors, and the disposition of unused computers. In addition, indicators of school performance, such as test scores, staff development, and attendance rates, were regularly discussed at LSC meetings. Parents and community members did have the wherewithal to question school staff on these and other issues. Consider the following exchange about the possible negative effect of standardized-testing practices on school instruction, and then about disadvantaged students:

> FEMALE PARENT: I understand that the IGAP [Illinois Goals Assessment Program] tests kids in grades 3, 6, and 9. I understand that there are board reasons to focus on grades 3, 6, and 8, but I think that if we put a little more attention earlier, we could nip this problem in the bud [while kids are still young].
> LSC COMMUNITY MEMBER: We do focus on many other grades. We just started a Direct Instruction reading program for our preschool kids. We fought hard against the [CPS] board to be able to do this.
> LSC TEACHER: Though the IGAP does test in grades 3, 6, and 9, we have strong learning objectives for every grade, and they all fit together.
> FEMALE PARENT: But there are no after-school programs. What is there to do to address children with special needs and problems?

PRINCIPAL BRADFORD: We don't have after-school learning for kids because of safety issues, but what we have done is split up the academically depressed classrooms and put those kids with special needs and problems in smaller classes. They gave us two extra psychologists—we have acquired additional staff for many kids since September because they need the service. Our special-education group is enlarging, and they told us to slow down, but we responded that these kids need these services. There is movement, even if it is small, to help the children at these lower grades. You should come and check these programs out by talking to Ms. _____ [Instructor] and our new psychologist.

The school professionals at Harambee Academy seem to have ably advanced the general interests of the school community. Assured by this monitoring mechanism of observing the actions of school staff and inferring benevolent motives, parents and community members felt less need to act positively because they developed a studied trust of professionals.

A less sanguine explanation, shared in particular by the strong-egalitarian and expertise perspectives is that nonprofessionals lacked the capacity to participate as equals with educational professionals. Because of the lack of skills and knowledge that often accompanies poverty or because of the nature of specialization, lay participants in Harambee Academy governance might have lacked the power or confidence to oppose the principal and his staff *even if monitoring had revealed conflicts of interest*. The events of this case did not offer evidence sufficient to adjudicate between this less-sanguine explanation and the benevolent account of studied trust; all of the proposed innovations enjoyed a consensus of support from school professionals, parents, and community alike. The next chapter, however, examines several episodes in which residents do not acquiesce silently in conflicts with professionals.

5.3.4. Participation and Institutional Performance at Harambee Academy

Despite these deficits, opportunities for local autonomy and citizen participation improved the quality of school governance and educational effectiveness at Harambee Academy in several ways, among them the elevation, albeit modest, of standardized test scores. Both reading and math scores have risen at Harambee over the last two years, but only slightly and no more than in the CPS as a whole. Though test scores do not offer evidence of particularly effective governance at Harambee, we expect these measures to respond rather slowly to changes in school programs

(Bryk et al. 1998), and so they are a highly imperfect instrument with which to measure the effectiveness of school governance. The primary evidence for the effectiveness of Harambee's governance group consists in its ability to formulate and implement bold initiatives in the school's educational programs and in resource acquisition. That it was able to select, implement, and evaluate the results of a Direct-Instructional program and to design and install a sophisticated computer network, and to integrate associated instructional materials, for example, reveal a systemic innovative capacity that promises, though it cannot assure, improved educational outcomes. The development of this systematic capacity leads us to rank Harambee rather highly on the scale of effectiveness, and certainly more highly than Southtown School as governed by the command-and-control regulations that preceded the 1988 school reforms.

More straightforwardly, the shift to Afrocentrism at Harambee shows how Harambee personnel made use of the space opened by decentralizing school reform. In their own understanding, LSC empowerment provided the opportunity for those involved with Harambee to break out of the generic school atmosphere established many years ago by white administrators and to set a new tone of Afrocentrism tailored to its demographics and the urgent concerns of students, parents, community members, and staff.

While the institutions of accountable autonomy thus made Harambee Academy more effective through local autonomy and participation, it was somewhat less successful in engendering equal deliberation between parents and community residents, on one side, and school staff, on the other. School staff used the latitude created by the 1988 school reforms to create deliberative problem-solving groups—the SIP committee, the Technology Team, and the school-expansion group—composed almost exclusively of school staff. The reforms brought a kind of deliberative workplace democracy to Harambee. School professionals engaged problem-solving and agenda-setting deliberation that was not available to them prior to the LSC reforms. This deliberation for the most part excluded nonprofessionals, however, and so relegated them to the less-direct role of monitoring and implementation.

5.4. Central Beat: Nonsystematic Problem-Solving

Located in the south-central part of the city, the six-by-eight–block area of Central Beat is quite similar to Southtown in many respects. Central lies in the heart of Chicago's South Side, and fits with many stereotypes about the rough inner city. The neighborhood's population is exclusively

African-American, most of the residents are quite poor—some 42 percent of the population lives below the poverty line—and about 58 percent of the families are headed by females. The 1990 census figures show that roughly one-quarter of the civilian population was unemployed. Like Southtown, Central sits firmly in the poorest quintile of Chicago neighborhoods. We therefore classify it with respect to the material-resource dimension of initial conditions as "poor."[13]

Also, as was the case with Southtown School/Harambee Academy, there were no deep and active interest cleavages in the community-policing process. The neighborhood of Central Beat was racially homogeneous and there were no clear geographic barriers. Two divisions that surfaced in community-policing meetings, however, ought to be noted. The first, roughly correlated to economic advantage, was home-ownership. The most consistent participants at beat meetings owned their houses, had lived in this neighborhood for some time, and were comparatively well-off (though still quite poor by the city's standards). One or two dedicated participants in community-policing hailed from the very poorest blocks of the neighborhood, but their voices were less articulate and less frequently heard. A second implicit cleavage was the conflict between predominantly "law-abiding citizens" and those connected with narcotics use and trafficking. In the most violent episodes of this conflict, community activists in Central's community policing activities were threatened and their houses firebombed. Though these divisions of interest were significant, active community-policing participants nevertheless shared enough explicit agreement on the goals and tasks of policing that we classify the case here as having a "low dispersion" of interests on that measure of initial condition.

Central faced a very high crime rate and other urban-decay problems. In 1996, the beat had an annual personal crime rate of 126 crimes per 1,000 residents. This figure is approximately 50 percent greater than that for the city overall and places Central Beat in the most violent quintile of Chicago police beats. Nine homicides occurred in the very small area of Central Beat in 1995 and 1996. All of the victims were between eighteen and forty years of age, and all but one died by gunshot. The ninth was stabbed to death.[14] In addition to this violent crime, police and residents cited narcotics trafficking, burglaries, and gang activity—principally by the Gangster Disciples—as urgent neighborhood concerns. In addition to these strictly criminal problems, residents also complained about the large number of abandoned buildings and vacant lots in the area.

Though Central Beat resembles Southtown Elementary in its initial conditions of poverty and unified interests, and the challenges in both cases are quite severe, participatory problem-solving processes exhibited very different strengths and weaknesses. Whereas nonprofessional participation was for the most part limited to monitoring in Southtown Elementary, ordinary residents played a much greater role in the identification and solution of problems in Central Beat. Whereas the problem-solving innovations and efforts in Southtown Elementary were systematic, Central Beat's deliberations were haphazard.

5.4.1. Cross-Functional Coordination in Two Hot Spots

Between November 1996 and December 1997, the community-policing group engaged in two sustained problem-solving efforts. As is quite common with Chicago community-policing targets, both issues were initially raised by neighbors complaining of crime and social disorder in nearby buildings. Furthermore, both problem-solving efforts exemplified two mechanisms of accountable autonomy: civic engagement and cross-functional coordination between police, other city agencies, and community activity.[15]

The first problem was brought to the attention of beat-meeting participants by Maria Wilson, a long-time resident and home-owner. Though her block was one of the cleanest and most well-kept in the beat—there was only one abandoned house—the house adjacent to hers had been owned by an absentee landlord named Denvers for the past fifteen years. According to Wilson, Denvers had rented the building to a seemingly endless series of problem-tenants, mostly poor women receiving public assistance, who caused various kinds of criminal and social disturbances. Over a decade and half, Wilson's complaints included the exploitation of poor tenants by Denvers, several fires that occurred in the building, unsanitary conditions, occasional fights, and appliances hurled through the air. More seriously, the alleys around the house sometimes served as an open-air drug market. She reflected upon these various events:

> [Denvers] talks to these ADC [recipients of Aid to Families with Dependent Children] women like they are dogs [and he is extorting money from them through scams like inflated gas prices]. . . . Since I have been around, there have been five fires in that building. Two on the second floor, two on the first floor, and one in the basement. . . . I got inspectors to come down to check out water in the basement. They found that there was no gas and rats. One time they found a rat in bed with a baby down there. . . . Once, there was a guy who played his radio out a second-floor window. One time a scale flew out his window and broke mine. I took him to court. I am not used to this kind of thing. . . . A while back, there were two women who moved into the second floor, and they put up garbage bags over the windows. That is a gang thing you know. This was around Christmas. . . . [Starting] at nine A.M. in the summers, the men

would come out and drink on the porch. They have so many kids, one woman had four and the other five. . . . There is traffic all night long, buying drugs, and it is heavy in the summer. They got so bold that they would stand in the alley and [there was] traffic both ways, dealing. Over the past few months, there have been five or six different sets of people. Two on the first floor. One in the basement [was] selling [narcotics], and some troublemakers on the second floor. (Interview with author)

These events motivated Mrs. Wilson to join the Central Beat's community-policing efforts in June 1996. She raised these issues before the group and they designated the property as a priority problem and employed a number of strategies over the next ten months to address it. First, police and residents increased communication between them to make patrols more effective. To further direct police efforts, residents organized a phone tree and block watch to monitor activities around the problem house and call for police when they saw suspicious activity. This intensified surveillance resulted in several Possession of a Controlled Substance (PCS) arrests around the problem building. Second, instantiating the mechanism of *cross-functional coordination*, residents deployed city lawyers to act against Denvers under the city Nuisance Abatement law and city building inspectors to enforce housing codes.[16] The inspectors issued numerous citations and lawyers brought Denvers to building court. Residents formed themselves into a court-advocacy committee to show to the judge that the Denvers property was a blight on the neighborhood. Wilson reports that in court advocacy, "When they call the address [for a court hearing], everyone [in the advocacy group] stands up and this makes a huge difference. The judge asks us to introduce ourselves and say something about why we are there."

These sustained efforts brought Denvers to housing court several times. The judge ordered him to make repairs to the building and held him responsible for the criminal activity in it. When Denvers failed to make the repairs and control the problems, the judge issued a series of escalating fines, and then finally imprisoned him for several weeks. These punitive measures produced results. Several months later, Wilson reported that Denvers had installed new electrical and gas systems in the house, evicted the previous tenants, and begun renting to more peaceful neighbors.

After cutting their teeth on the relatively manageable problem of the Denvers house, residents targeted drug activity on a much more troubled block on the south side of the beat as their second priority problem. According to the testimony of residents and police, nearly all of the residents who lived on this block were involved in narcotics or gang activity. Police records documenting multiple arrests for PCS offenses confirm these allegations. Mrs. Ann Rivers, another long-time resident of Central and community-policing activist, was the exception to this alleged pattern.[17] Like Mrs. Wilson, Rivers had felt victimized by sometimes-violent criminal activity for years:

> I have lived in this house for twenty years. Many years ago, I used to see an ice cream truck parked across the street for hours at a time, and lines of people coming to buy from it. I didn't know what it was until my husband explained that they were dealing drugs out of it. I couldn't let my kids hang out there, because they would just get bullied [by the older gang members]. When he was young, my son got cut up real bad, on his face and arms because he wouldn't join [the gang]. My daughter got beat up, too. [Despite all this] they never joined. On my block, I have seen stabbings and shootings. We have gotten shot at, and I figure it is a kind of warning. A couple of years ago, they [the neighbors] had put gasoline all around our house and were going to light it up. For some reason, they left for a while, maybe to get a lighter, and my husband came home and saw the gas. He called the police and they responded before they were able to light the gas up. Last year, they [the neighbors] threw a firebomb through our window.[18] This is what made us really get involved [in community policing]. (Interview with author)

Following the firebombing incident, Mrs. Rivers and her husband became regular participants in Central Beat's community-policing activities. In its regular meetings, police and residents agreed that Rivers's block should receive sustained attention. As their initial strategy, police beat officers intensified patrol around the area. Tactical police officers also executed several search warrants at locations they perceived to be key centers of drug activity.[19] During these searches, they seized substantial quantities of crack cocaine and firearms, and they made several arrests. Community-policing participants from Central and several surrounding beats have organized "take-back-the-streets" marches that always pass through Mrs. Rivers's block. After five months, drug and gang activity persisted on her block, but Mrs. Rivers felt certain that it had become much less violent.

Significantly, Mrs. Rivers had transformed herself from a shy victim of ambient crime into a committed and outspoken activist in the course of participating in Chicago community policing. Rivers had not been previously involved in any neighborhood groups or other associations. For the first few month of our acquaintance, she was so shy that she refused to be interviewed. When I finally spoke with her, I asked her why she had avoided me for so long. She said that: "It took me a while to get the confidence to speak [to you]. I have learned from [other community-policing activists] how to speak up. I used to be afraid of everything, because I didn't know what to do in many situations, but I am not afraid any more. . . . I feel like I am giving back to the community now [through her community-policing work]." By the end of the observation period, Mrs. Rivers had become one of the most active community-policing partici-pants in Central Beat. The rest of the group elected her to the leadership position of beat facilitator, and she joined several other area community organizations.[20]

5.4.2. Nonsystematic Directed Discretion: Laissez-Faire Discussion and Police Response

Beyond these two sustained efforts, attentively championed by Mrs. Wil-son and Mrs. Rivers, police and citizens for the most part fell into a more haphazard mode of selecting issues and responding to them: citizens raised problems as they came to mind—such as drug dealing on a particular cor-ner, burglaries, or traffic problems—and police used familiar methods to address those problems.[21] More systematic participatory deliberation would have improved Central Beat's problem-solving efforts in three ways.

First, individual problems would have benefited from more sustained at-tention. For example, residents frequently raised complaints about narcot-ics activity at various addresses throughout the beat, and police responded by temporarily deploying uniformed and plainclothes officers to make drug arrests at those locations. In this haphazard mode, problems were quickly dropped, often before they were effectively addressed. With more sustained deliberative problem-solving processes, participants might have moved be-yond short-term deployment of police for drug arrests to more enduring measures that addressed the factors that made those spots attractive to illicit activity: the configuration of physical space (lights, traffic, abandoned houses), nearby drug houses, and traffic access points.

Second, sustained deliberation might have resulted in more imaginative community-policing strategies that utilized the energies of citizens and city agencies beyond the police department. Whereas the two sustained problem-solving efforts led by Mrs. Wilson and Mrs. Rivers exploited an array of innovative strategies, police responded to most problems raised in Central Beat—drugs, burglaries, traffic, et cetera—with their familiar techniques: intensified patrol, citation, and occasionally plainclothes sur-veillance. Had these problems been the subject of more sustained discus-sion, rather than simply noted by police, the group might have developed more innovative strategies to deal with them.

Third, and critically, more structured and sustained deliberation might have led the group to self-consciously prioritize problems and allocate their problem-solving energies according to a schedule of urgency. In the first-come, first-served, town-meeting style of discussion that prevailed in

Central Beat, problems received an implicit prioritization based upon the order and force with which they were raised. Since the beat exhibited little in the way of economic or other salient division, laissez-faire discussion did not generate systematically biased outcomes. The problems that were targeted, however, reflected chance contingencies, for instance as whether residents from particular blocks attended meetings. Without doubt, the properties next to the houses of Mrs. Wilson and Mrs. Rivers were severe problems and deserved collective attention. Beyond these problems, however, beat discussions and subsequent police responses focused on burglaries and narcotics activity in the central portion of the beats, as well as traffic and illegal truck-garaging in the beat's southwest area. According to narcotics and homicide reports and the testimony of individual police officers, however, the west side of the beat, in particular Haywood Street (see figure 5.3), had a number of drug-house "hot spots" that were foci for violent crime. Because no one raised these issues in open discussion at beat meetings, they did not receive attention from the community-policing group. Because structured problem-solving deliberation would have involved an explicit discussion of questions of urgency, perhaps including police testimony and the use of readily available crime maps, it might well have directed attention toward these neglected regions of the beat.

What explains the failure of Central-Beat participants to be more disciplined in their problem-solving deliberations? A strong-egalitarian critic might argue that structured deliberation demands greater capacities of participation, analysis, and persistence than haphazard discussion. These capacities often correlate with income and access to other resources. Since Central residents are poor, they lacked these resources and therefore perhaps also the skills necessary for structured deliberation. According to the strong egalitarian, Central Beat is only one instance of the quite insurmountable obstacles that deliberative problem-solving will encounter in poorer communities.

Two observations, however, suggest that poverty and its associated deprivations did not condemn the residents and officers of Central beat to haphazard, nonsystematic deliberation. First, Mrs. Wilson and Mrs. Rivers possessed and exercised just those capacities thought to be necessary for structured deliberation: they led the group in the development of innovative and effective strategies that abated two rather serious and persistent public-safety problems. Their actions weigh against the thesis that poor neighborhoods lack citizens who are capable of structured deliberation. The second observation explains why these two individuals' limited deliberative problem-solving did not translate to a broader group practice of structured deliberation. Though structured deliberative problem-solving is an explicit part of the institutional design of community policing, neither the CPD nor other authorities had devoted substantial energy to propagating the practice down to the beat level. Unlike Traxton Beat, discussed in chapter 6, there were no agents from city agencies or community-based organizations to supply the methods and templates of structured deliberative problem-solving to meeting participants in Central Beat. In other words, the well-developed methodologies and process of community problem-solving discussed in chapters 2 and 3 had not spread to the local actors in Central Beat.

Structured deliberation is unlikely to arise without conscious understanding and effort, and no one from either the community or the police department rose to the task. With greater effort to impart and implement structured deliberation—perhaps in the form of face-to-face training of community participants or police or wider distribution of instructional materials—Central might have moved from haphazard discussion to structured deliberation. Whether these efforts would have been able to overcome the skill deficits that accompany poverty remains open to speculation. As with Southtown/Harambee, the experience of Central Beat cannot reveal whether a more serious effort to confer the skills of deliberative problem-solving would have allowed participants to engage in sustained joing community-policing despite the obstacle of poverty.

5.4.3. Impacts of Accountable Autonomy in Central Beat

Despite this haphazardness, the Chicago community-policing reforms set in place structures for local participation and deliberation that residents used to improve public-safety outcomes in Central Beat. Though group actions to advance public safety would have been more effective still with structured deliberation, even the mode of laissez-faire problem-selection and -response was more effective than policing in the prior insular bureaucratic mode and fairly effective on its own terms. Recall that the main methods of police action prior to community-policing reform were preventative patrol and emergency response (see chapter 2). For years this practice failed to address narcotics hot spots around the residences of Mrs. Wilson and Mrs. Rivers. Community-policing reforms created opportunities for these women and other residents to direct police power, increase the efficacy of their own self-organization, and leverage the powers of other city agencies to successfully address their concerns. Even the mode of laissez-faire discussion and police response generated more effective results than traditional policing by facilitating interaction between residents and police and generating flows of information and action—limited as it was to using traditional police strategies—where it otherwise would not have occurred.

Though the area is by no means safe and narcotics trafficking is still common, residents exercised, and felt that they exercised, more control over the shape and level of safety in their neighborhood. Over a relatively short period, residents addressed two serious "hot spots" and directed police activity in more limited fashion on other problems. One participant described their enhanced autonomy this way: "I know that things will get better on my block. Things move quicker now, and I have already seen some arrests. I have already seen that since I have gotten involved [in community policing] others are joining in as well—two more on my block alone. I don't want to be a police [officer], but I do want to be a part of the family [of the community]."

Similarly, the mechanism of studied trust generated mutual sentiments of solidarity between police and the residents that have gotten involved.[22] Mrs. Wilson put it this way: "I know that sometimes you have to push the police. [Their attitude is] "If you don't care, I don't. If you don't know, then I don't." You have to keep at them. [But] they [the police] really work with us and we really appreciate it. I don't know what we would do without them." As we shall see in the discussion of Southtown Beat in the next chapter, many police officers remain skeptical about the motives, knowledge, and commitment of residents. In Central Beat, however, police respect the dedication of residents and value their local knowledge. In several discussions with police officers, I asked whether they thought that residents exaggerated their claims about crimes around their blocks to solicit greater police response. Invariably, the officers responded that residents usually know crime situations better than police, that often police surveillance revealed that resident complaints were accurate, and that they were glad to have this kind of help.

5.5. Traxton School: Wealth and Embedded Agreement

The third ground-level examination of accountable autonomy moves from the quite troubled neighborhoods of Central and Southtown to the relatively advantaged Traxton area. Traxton Elementary operates in an environment that is both wealthy and socially unified, and so offers a stark contrast to the previous two cases and those that follow in the next chapter. It is a small elementary school; its total 1996 enrollment of 310 students (Chicago Public Schools 1996) was less than half that of either Harambee Academy or Central Elementary. Approximately 80 percent of these students were drawn from the wealthier, west side of Traxton (see figure 6.1) and adjacent well-off areas, and 20 percent of the students were bussed in from other Chicago neighborhoods. In 1996, less than 20 percent of the students came from low-income families. By this measure,

Traxton's student body ranked easily in the top 5 percent of Chicago's most wealthy schools. Beyond this, the student body was quite stable. Traxton's mobility rate between 1990 and 1998 ranged between 4 percent and 8 percent, compared to a city-wide rate of between 30 percent and 35 percent. Traxton school, like the neighborhood itself, was racially integrated. In 1996, 57 percent of the students were black, 37 percent were white, and the remainder were evenly divided between Hispanics and Asians. Black students were overrepresented at Traxton compared to the racial profile of the adult population due to two factors: more black children than white were bussed to the school and many white parents who live in the neighborhood sent their children to private schools. Because both the residents of Traxton's neighborhood and the families of its students were well-off by Chicago's urban standards, we classify this case as being "more wealthy" on the material-resource dimension of initial conditions (see figure 5.3).

With respect to interest dispersion, those involved in the governance of Traxton Elementary exhibited strong agreement on many fundamental issues of school improvement. Disagreements usually concerned strategic choices and were always discussed in an open, cordial, and deliberative manner. Racial differences never crystallized into a salient political fissure; racially diverse governance was inclusive and school policies seemed to advance the interests of all of its students. Relations between the nonprofessionals on the LSC more generally were quite cooperative throughout. Traxton Elementary's principal, Molly Sorenson, no doubt deserved much of the credit for this coherent style of school governance. She had worked at Traxton School, first as teacher and then as its principal, since the early 1960s. Over that long period, she developed excellent relationships with active parents and community members, school staff, and local political notables. Though many individuals in each of these communities were quite active in school affairs, they all trusted and respected Principal Sorenson. She felt that Traxton's LSC treated her as the school's leader: "They are very helpful . . . they ask me what I need to do a better job, and they say, "We feel like you are the chairman of the board, and call us in when you need us." As with the chairman of a corporate board, however, trust and faith in Sorenson were predicated on good performance. One long-time school activist seconded, but qualified, the principal's characterization of her role:

> With education and curriculum, there is nothing to complain about because we are one of the top schools in the city. We on the LSC handle other kinds of problems, the [Chicago] Board [of Education], physical plant, et cetera. We also handle problems [raised when] other parents complain about particular

programs or school policies. But the curriculum is great. [Sorenson and her staff] see every child for her own needs, whether she is learning-disabled, gifted, or whatever.

These deep agreements and reservoirs of good will led to the classification of Traxton Elementary as a case of "low" dispersion of interests with respect to that initial condition.

As one might expect from all of these advantages both inside and outside the school, the students of Traxton perform extremely well compared to other Chicago elementary pupils. In the 1995–1996 school year, none of its students were chronically truant and its drop-out rate was zero. On ITBS standardized exams, all grades consistently tested at one or two grades *above* their chronological level; the average third-grader at Traxton in 1995 tested at 4.4 median grade equivalents in math, the average sixth-grader at 7.9 grade equivalents in reading. Seventy-five percent of Traxton's students met or exceeded national testing norms for reading and 76.7 percent for math. These ITBS test scores easily placed Traxton in the best-testing 5 percent of Chicago elementary schools.

Given these initial conditions and excellent track record, Traxton Elementary presents something of an "easy" case for accountable autonomy. If participatory deliberation is at all promising, then it should perform well under these favorable conditions of wealth and consensus. The processes of participatory school governance in Traxton during the 1996–1997 school year largely confirmed these optimistic expectations. A close examination of Traxton Elementary clarifies the operation of accountable autonomy by illuminating how the mechanisms that generate fairness and effectiveness—deliberation, civic engagement, directed discretion, studied trust, cross-functional coordination, and institutionalized innovation—operated over that period.

5.5.1. Leveraging Civic Engagement into School Improvement

Deep consensus in Traxton Elementary's LSC gave rise to a distinct species of the general five-step deliberative problem-solving process described in chapter 2. The agenda-setting process, problem-identification and -prioritization, was typically quite compressed because LSC members quickly agreed on the urgency of various problems once they were raised. Subsequently, a simple and implicit division of labor determined whether responsibility for developing and implementing strategies would fall to Principal Sorenson and her staff or whether parents and community members would take the lead. If the problem concerned narrowly academic issues such as test scores, curriculum, pedagogy, or school discipline, school professionals would develop strategies, implement them, and report back to the larger group on progress. If, on the other hand, the problem dealt with issues that fell outside of this narrow professional expertise, responsibility for strategy development and implementation typically fell to parents and community members. In the 1995–1996 school year, priority problems that fell into later category included classroom overcrowding, inadequate heating, aging and dangerous wiring, technology issues, the need to improve grounds, and the desire to establish information-pooling and collaborative networks with nearby schools. Each of these problems was arguably as important to the quality of education as more traditional concerns like textbook selection or pedagogical method. For each of them, the parent and/or community members of the LSC and others in the nonprofessional school community developed plans to fund and implement solutions.

Many of Traxton's nonacademic priority problems, and therefore much of the energies of its LSC, concerned the poor quality of the physical environment. Traxton's school building was among the oldest in the city. One CPS study assessed it as one of the half-dozen school buildings that would be cheaper to rebuild from the ground up than to repair and update. CPS administrators did not, however, offer to fund a new building for Traxton Elementary. Physical-plant problems were compounded by the unpredictable bureaucratic environment of the CPS. In order to improve services and save funds, the CPS privatized building and grounds maintenance by subcontracting to a private company that would provide these services to the entire school system. Unfortunately, this company proved quite unresponsive to requests from Traxton staff and its LSC. Despite its enviable connections to the CPS hierarchy, Traxton was unable to secure substantial capital-improvement funds from that source. Finally, Traxton Elementary was too poor to fund these improvements from its own discretionary sources. Despite—or more precisely, because of—the wealth of the families of Traxton-School students, Traxton's per pupil budget is substantially smaller than those of other schools in Chicago. The CPS system determines school budgets by allocating a fixed amount per pupil, and then supplementing this amount from state and federal sources according to the percentage of low-income students at the school. As a result of this formula, Traxton School's per-pupil budget was approximately $4,500 compared to a figure of approximately $5,500 for Central Elementary and Harambee Academy. All of these factors confound the seemingly straightforward problem of building improvement.

The grounds around the school itself constituted another problem. Years ago, the entire area had been paved with asphalt, which the harsh Chicago weather had broken eventually up. By 1990, according to one

LSC member, the area around the school was "a horrible mess. When my kids were there it was called Lake [Traxton] because the asphalt would not drain. We tried to get the [CPS] board to do something for a while, but finally realized that we had to act on our own." After designating the issue as a priority, the LSC formed a grounds committee to solve the problem. They developed a plan in 1993 to transform the dilapidated asphalt area into a grassed playground. They identified a local architect to develop the plans on a pro bono basis, and then raised funds from parents and local foundations totaling $50,000 to implement the plan. Contractors removed the asphalt in 1993 and the final landscaping was completed in 1996.

Traxton's LSC addressed two other problems through persistent diplomacy rather than raw fundraising ability. The school building and its grounds had fallen into disrepair because the private contractor, chosen and mandated by CPS, performed substandard work and failed to respond to repeated work requests from school staff. Principal Sorenson raised this issue at the November 1996 LSC meeting, others quickly agreed that it was a priority, and one LSC parent volunteered to resolve the issue. After negotiations with both the contractor's personnel and their manager failed, the Traxton parent finally reached a CPS official. After a series of extended discussions, the contractor was finally persuaded to assign a more capable grounds crew to Traxton.

More critically, a building inspection in 1996 revealed that the fire-alarm system had failed, and that the design did not comply with building regulations. Combined with the school's antiquated electrical system, LSC members felt that the building constituted a fire hazard. The school lacked discretionary funds to update either of these systems and LSC members felt that the matter was too urgent to await time-consuming fundraising; the school petitioned CPS. Using its authority as the official school-governance body, the LSC wrote a harshly worded letter to Paul Vallas, then chief executive officer of CPS. One fundamental plank of Vallas's management philosophy had been to hold schools accountable for responsible performance, and Traxton School hoped to hold Vallas reciprocally accountable. In part, that letter read:[23]

Dear Mr. Vallas,

This letter is to inform you of what we, the [Traxton] Local School Council, consider to be serious structural and safety hazards existing in our building. We are also requesting your assistance in resolving these issues as quickly as possible.

The present fire alarm system is dangerously inadequate. . . . this is a building code violation which has been consistently ignored by the Compliance Board. We are outraged that the only steps taken to alleviate this problem is to repeatedly request that this issue be continued to a later meeting date. . . . This system must be replaced *immediately.*

The electrical system of [Traxton] is, at best, antiquated. . . . all circuits are full, necessitating installation of new panels and increased riser ampacity [*sic*]. . . . All wiring is substandard and the system is so obsolete it is no longer manufactured, nor are proper parts available. . . . This system has met code requirements due to a "Grandfather Clause.". . .

[This] Negligence cannot be tolerated if we are to follow through on the delivery of instruction as outlined in our School Improvement Plan.

This letter was copied to the mayor, the alderman, and several other highly placed school officials. Furthermore, it was backed by the implicit, credible, and well-understood threat of mobilizing substantial political opposition from the various neighborhood and civic associations in Traxton.[24] By the next LSC meeting, CPS CEO Paul Vallas had spoken to several of the LSC members and one of them reported to the group that "Vallas wants to give us whatever we need to repair this building because of that letter." Not long afterwards, they received the necessary funding and support for a new fire-alarm system from CPS capital-improvement coffers.

In addition to these physical improvements, parents and community members contributed to two capital-intensive additions that integrate more directly into the school's educational program: a technology lab and a multicenter facility for area teachers to share classroom methods, materials, and other kinds of information. By early 1996, the LSC had decided that improving the sophistication of the school's computer equipment and integrating that technology into the pedagogy of more traditional subjects was a top priority. As at Harambee, they formed an ad hoc "Technology Team," again composed of school staff and nonprofessionals, to develop and implement a strategy to meet this need. They began work in 1996 by examining the computer labs of top schools around the city. One lab, located at a technically oriented junior high school, stood above the others, and so the committee designed a proposal for a technology lab around the hardware and educational software of this preferred model. Both the larger LSC and the school staff voted to approve the plan. In May, they began to lobby the Board of Education for funds to implement the program. In June, the board announced that they would devote $125,000 to the program. By October 1996, computers, network hardware, and educational and applications software had been purchased and installed. By 1997, the school network included three computers in every classroom and a central cluster with a dozen workstations. The most technologically literate teachers began incorporating this new capacity into their classes immediately, while others began training to gain the new teaching skills.

Principal Sorenson and two or three others on the LSC systematically tracked grant opportunities from local and national foundations that might bring them additional resources to expand and deepen their educational program. In 1996, a major foundation devoted to educational goals offered grants to Chicago schools who proposed innovative partnerships with outside agencies. Traxton School, in conjunction with a local civic organization, the Traxton Area Planning Association, responded to this opportunity.[25] Using focus groups composed of their own teachers and those from nearby schools, the joint committee determined that teachers felt quite isolated from one another, and that one of their major needs was to share techniques and ideas. One LSC member who worked on the grant recalls that "we conducted focus groups of teachers organized according to the subjects that they taught. The same thing kept popping up in group after group. It really came out that teachers felt like they needed to talk to one another." Out of this finding, the grant committee developed a proposal, eventually funded, to establish a small resource center with minimal capabilities—a fax machine, photocopier, and space for meetings and seminars, in which teachers from area schools could communicate with one another.

Taken on its own merits, these achievements may seem remarkable only to those in the hierarchical school bureaucracy whose routines could not accomplish them. It is fortunate, one might say, that a school should enjoy such energetic—and astute—staff, parents, and community members. A surfeit of volunteer spirit or associational enthusiasm might account for one or two of these projects. What one overlooks in considering them one at a time, however, is the systemic collective process—distinct from both the logics of random volunteerism and command-and-control administration—that led to the selection of these particular projects and motivated those on the LSC and others to follow through on every single one of them. That process is just the deliberative problem-solving procedure of selecting the school's top problems in a consensus fashion that establishes group priorities, and then, as a matter of public responsibility and common commitment, developing and implementing the strategies that promise to address those priorities.

5.5.2. Vigilant Monitoring and Systematic Adjustment

Though the governance of Traxton Elementary exhibited extraordinary teamwork, its politics was not without heated conflict. Both this teamwork and conflict, however, were grounded in the same deep commitment to improving the educational environment. One expression of that commitment was the energetic cooperation that led to the implementation of novel programs and remedies described in the previous section. In a second manifestation of this commitment, however, parents and residents exercised great vigilance in monitoring the school's daily performance by listening to the students there, tracking performance-indicators like standardized test scores, and by participating in more general discussions about educational reform. This watchfulness occasionally revealed short-comings in the school's programs or educational practices—an absence of such discoveries would probably indicate dereliction—which in turn gave rise to sometimes vigorous conflict and criticism. Those who issued criticisms, therefore, almost always tempered them in the understanding that school improvement inevitably involves making choices that hind-sight reveals to be poor, and they made them with the confidence that flaws, once pointed out, would be earnestly corrected. Those who re-ceived criticisms, usually the school staff or Principal Sorenson, under-stood that it came not with recrimination, but rather as valuable feedback on the degree of program success. This process of monitoring—error de-tection, then criticism, then correction—was a more robust form of the mechanism that was at work in Harambee Academy. Even in the highly cooperative environment of Traxton Elementary, then, relations were not characterized by simple blind trust, but by the more practical and reflec-tive policy of "trust, but verify."

Sometimes inquiring criticisms reflected incomplete knowledge of school activities and were easily resolved. At one LSC meeting, for exam-ple, a parent in the audience complained that "I just want to say that I am proud of our school, but I am pretty worried that we are getting overcrowded. The building has always been full, but one class in the fifth grade is up to forty students now. I also know that some people have been working on trying to get a building addition, but we need to do something in the meantime to deal with this overcrowding." Principal Sorenson re-sponded first by recounting efforts to expand available classroom space and second by explaining several instructional responses to the problem of overcrowding. On the former, several LSC members had been working with an architect, again on a pro bono basis, to design a school addition and had been exploring funding avenues with the Board of Education. Unfortunately, however, near-term prospects for funding this addition seemed dim. As an additional measure, Sorenson had requested from the board several mobile classroom units that could temporarily relieve stu-dent crowding. The board rejected this request, as well. Unable to obtain relief from these external sources, school staff then responded by modi-fying developing programs to insure that the most needy students did not get left behind in large classes. The program, called "pull-out" in reading and math, surveyed teachers of large classes to identify those students most in need of additional attention and then pulled those students out for small-group instruction. "I do these surveys all the time to make sure that no one falls through the cracks. . . . In the biggest classes, we have to make sure that no one is falling behind. . . . Because of this pull-out program, fifth-grade classes are very seldom full." She then provided (from memory) a breakdown of the size of every class according to grade and teacher. Impressed with this extended explanation, the parent who launched the initial query responded that "it's good to have this break-down, because we didn't know [what was being done about crowding]; it looks like we came to the right place."

Other criticisms identified real operational flaws and induced corrective adjustments. The discovery of problems in a Spanish program illustrates this feedback loop. In response to strong desires from parents to initiate a foreign-language program, school staff hired a part time Spanish teacher and adopted a well-regarded set of instructional materials in 1993. After two years' experience with the program, students showed only limited interest in the program and parents based upon their children's com-ments, began to express some doubt about the quality of instruction. In response to these complaints, the LSC moved to restructure the language program by establishing a regime in which concerned parents and school staff could together design a new effort and more closely monitor its im-plementation. They began by surveying concerned parents about weak-nesses in the existing program and holding several open meetings to dis-cuss the issue. In the 1996–1997 school year, This communication resulted in changes, including selection of new language materials, a new instructor, and shifting the class to an early-morning slot that would allow those most interested to attend. They also established midyear and end-of-year public-evaluation points for the new program. Parents reported greater satisfaction, but reserved their judgment pending the scheduled evaluations.

The issue of school uniforms caused a protracted debate among Trax-ton parents. Unlike many other Chicago schools where discipline and se-curity are paramount concerns, a substantial fraction of parents of Trax-ton students opposed a mandatory uniform policy.[26] In typically democratic fashion, consideration of whether to adopt such a policy began in 1995 with a survey of parents. Most of those who responded favored such a policy and voiced common reasons for doing so—it would make the school more orderly and decrease fashion competition among students. The minority who opposed the policy offered equally common and speculative justifications—that such a policy would impose a stulti-fying sense of conformity and cramp an important dimension of students' self-expression. Since factions were not likely to reach a consensus posi-tion on this issue, the LSC was faced with the difficult choice of siding with one or the other. They settled the issue through a vote in which the LSC approved a uniform policy that would become effective at the start of the 1996–1997 school year. That summer, a letter was sent from the LSC to parents informing them that they should purchase uniforms for their children because they would be "strongly encouraged" to wear them in the upcoming school year. This wording turned out to be problematic because the LSC had adopted a "mandatory" uniform policy. Principal Sorenson, who favored the policy, was now charged with enforcing it. But parents were given the impression that compliance was optional.

When many students habitually failed to wear their uniforms in the winter of 1996, Sorenson favored stricter enforcement. As representatives and functional intermediaries between parents and school staff, however, some on the LSC—though they favored the policy, generally—saw that this strict and surprising enforcement would poison relations with parents who objected to the policy. Therefore maintaining procedural integrity by adhering to the letter's word was more important than immediate enforcement. In the following exchange, Sorenson was persuaded by this argument and changed her approach:

> SORENSON: A lot of the kids are getting pressure from their friends not to wear the uniforms. According to the [CPS] board, if the LSC passes it, it is a rule. For discipline, it is like any other school policy. [We write] a letter to parents for no uniform. Three letters means detention. This is a school policy, and I need the LSC support on this issue. I get stuff back from parents saying that I should not send any more notes. My letter said: "I hope that in the spirit of unity, you will change your mind about this. But if you don't, then [we will enforce it]."
>
> LSC PARENT 1: The first letter was encouraging, but not forceful enough. It was not clear at the beginning that it was a hard-and-fast rule.
>
> SORENSON: The word "optional" was a mistake.
>
> LSC PARENT 2: It should be a harder rule, but you can't change on people in midstream. Maybe next year we should phase it in.
>
> LSC COMMUNITY MEMBER: We should make it clear that next year uniforms will be mandatory.
>
> LSC PARENT 3: It does seem unfair that punitive measures should kick in midstream.
>
> LSC PARENT 2: My suggestion is that we announce that it is a real LSC policy that will be enforced in the fall.
>
> LSC PARENT 4: We should write a clarification letter. Encouragement this year, and enforcement for next year. Letters for noncompliance this year will be kind of an FYI [for your information] about the upcoming policy for parents.
>
> SORENSON: I agree that "optional" should stick for the rest of this year.

In this way, the LSC detected a potentially harmful choice—the sudden enforcement of a uniform policy—and developed a new policy that averted unnecessary resentment and division. When the uniform policy is finally fully implemented, it may be that those who oppose the policy come to realize that many of their fears are unjustified. Sorenson remarks that this has been the experience at other schools: "Talking to other principals, the pattern seems to be that the first year 10–20 percent don't wear, second year 95-percent compliance, and by the third year everyone wants it." Conversely, it may turn out that continued resistance to the policy destroys the very harmony and order that motivates mandatory uniforms in the first place, and that LSC members come therefore to reverse the policy. If past processes indicate the quality of future governance, then the Traxton School LSC is likely to recognize and respond effectively to these developments.

5.5.3. Did Traxton Need Accountable Autonomy?

The discussion above describes how the Traxton LSC created an *effective* system of deliberative problem-solving that not only identified and addressed both existing problems in the curriculum and physical plant, but developed solutions to problems barely perceptible in most other Chicago schools, such as the isolation of teachers from one another. Beyond this, the LSC took great pains to insure that the formation and implementation of school policy *fairly* accounted for all points of view, as in the difficult advancement of the uniform policy. Through practical measures, as exemplified by the uniform code, pressing demands upon the CPS board, and developing joint resources with nearby schools, the Traxton LSC developed specific goals and took decisive steps to realize those goals. Finally, this high degree of mutually verifiable cooperation and its successes generated a similarly high degree of solidarity and trust between community members, parent, and professional members of the Traxton community. These successes are perhaps unsurprising given the favorable initial conditions of wealth and deep agreement at Traxton Elementary and they conform to the rough hypothesis about institutional performance depicted in figure 5.2.

It is more difficult, however, to make the comparative institutional assessment of whether salutary outcomes can be attributed to participatory-democratic governance structures. Did Traxton's students fare better than they would have under the prior institutions of hierarchical, bureaucratic school governance? There is substantial evidence to support the view that civic associations and regular volunteers had been performing monitoring and resource-acquisition functions prior to the 1988 school-reform law. In particular, one venerable organization called the Traxton Area Planning Association had an education group that had secured foundation grants that provided technical assistance and built networks between Traxton and other area schools for many years prior to reform. When the

LSCs were first implemented in 1988, for example, TAPA was the first group in the city, even before the CPS, to provide training in school management and budgeting to Traxton's newly elected LSC members. Beyond this, many in the Traxton Elementary governance group had been involved in school affairs as volunteers, parent advisors, or Parent-Teacher Association (PTA) members for decades—since the 1970s—and saw their election to the LSC as something of a nominal and formal change rather than a substantive one. One LSC member who sent three of her children to Traxton and is now a community representative recalls the city-wide popular movement demanding local school governance (see chapter 2) that resulted in the 1988 reform law: "We didn't really feel the need to get involved in the city-wide campaign. At [Traxton School], there has always been a lot of parental involvement, and the LSCs just validated that. [Molly Sorenson] has been principal since 1986, and things didn't really change much after [the 1988 reform law]." Sorenson herself recalls that "this is my ninth year as principal, and twenty-seventh year at [Traxton Elementary]. There has always been lots of parental involvement. Before the LSC it was the PTA and many other organizations." Though it is difficult to assess levels of informal contributions to school governance that occurred a decade ago, this testimony suggests that the benefits accruing to Traxton Elementary from school reform may not be as substantial as a synchronic assessment of its process might suggest. This finding, combined with a similar assessment of informal mechanisms that existed in West Traxton Beat prior to community policing (see chapter 6) indicate that relatively advantaged areas do well with participatory institutions, but that they also fare rather well without them. In our less advantaged contexts of Southtown, Central, and East Traxton beat, however, these reforms brought more dramatic gains because those areas lacked the machinery of voice, political power, and deliberative problem-solving that constitute accountable autonomy.

5.6. Poverty and the Character of Pragmatic Deliberation

Two general kinds of observations flow from experiences with deliberative problem-solving in these three South Side neighborhoods. The first is a definitional and methodological consideration regarding the scope of activities that should be considered as part of deliberation. Whereas most conceptual and empirical treatments of deliberation focus upon the discussion and maneuvering that yield particular collective decisions (Mansbridge 1980; Susskind and Cruickshank 1987; Cohen 1989; Forester 1999), the above experiences highlight the importance of components of public action that lie outside the narrow zone of particular decisions. In all three neighborhoods, for example, one major contribution of parents and other residents to public action was to *monitor* the implementation of group decisions, detect unintended consequences, and raise those concerns in subsequent, iterative participatory deliberations. In all three cases especially, lay citizens not only participated in agenda-setting and decision-making, but they contributed to the implementation of decisions in cooperation with police officers and school staff. In Traxton School, parents helped raise funds and design a school annex. In Central Beat, residents helped to "coproduce" neighborhood safety by organizing phone trees and Court Watch programs (Schneider 1987). While the formal and idealized deliberative problem-solving procedure developed above emphasized the contributions of public participation to implementation, monitoring, and assessment, the actual experiences described show how this idea has been realized in practice.[27]

A second set of summary observations concerns a limited assessment of the quality of the process and performance of accountable-autonomy institutions in these three neighborhoods, in particular how poverty—the absence of private and civic resources—affects pragmatic deliberation. First, how well did residents use new institutional opportunities for deliberation and participation to advance their interests and to solve problems fairly and effectively? The answer to this question is uneven and correlates with economic advantage. The impoverished cases of Southtown School/ Harambee Academy and Central Beat did exploit opportunities offered by participatory decentralization, but the deliberative processes in each of these cases fell short of the ideal of participatory deliberative governance in important ways. While Southtown/Harambee utilized the increased discretionary latitude provided by 1988 school-reform measures to reorient the school pedagogically and culturally toward an arguably more appropriate Afrocentric vision, school staff dominated processes of innovation and problem-solving. While they did not participate in the determination of priorities and development of strategies as an ambitious ideal of deliberation would have them do, they did monitor the performance of school staff and so utilized the participatory elements of school reform for a kind of bottom-up accountability.

In contrast, the residents of Central Beat took a leading role in identifying problems and developing solutions to them. They participated as equals with police officers not only in this collective decision-making, but also in implementing the strategies that were generated. We saw, however, that the defect in Central Beat's deliberative dynamics was its lack of sustained order. Rather than arising from a process of deliberative justification and prioritization, the public-safety agenda was set haphazardly through discussions that assumed a first-come–first-served style. The joint governance of Traxton Elementary, however, exhibited none of these defects. There, due in large measure to both deep consensus on educational goals and the social and economic advantages of participating parents, community members, and school staff developed very effective working relationships that included systematic deliberative problem-solving, monitoring of instructional and operational aspects of the school, and a working division of labor between the professional and lay participants in school governance.

It is perhaps unsurprising that the residents of Traxton Elementary were able to translate their social and economic advantages into more successful participatory and deliberative governance. Indeed, it would be remarkable if the multiple advantages of professional occupations, social status, abundant private resources, and a rich civic infrastructure did not enhance the quality of deliberative problem-solving. From the perspective of institutional choice, however, the second question posed at the outset of this chapter is equally important. What benefits did each neighborhood reap as a result of the shift from hierarchical and insular police and school governance to the participatory and deliberative forms of accountable autonomy? The benefits of local control to Traxton School seemed marginal in many respects. The school staff and parents there had already set into motion many of the elements of participatory problem-solving through informal agreements long before the Chicago school-reform law of 1988. By contrast, the impoverished residents of Southtown Elementary and Central Beat changed their relationships with local public officials and public institutions quite profoundly. Participatory and deliberative reforms to the CPS and CPD created new opportunities for interaction, communication, voice, and accountability that residents used with moderate success. We shall see that this pattern of poorer neighborhoods deriving greater benefits than the wealthier ones from institutional reforms like accountable autonomy repeats itself in the following chapter.

These cases generate an affirmative answer to the third question of whether the city-wide, formal institutional changes described in chapters 2 and 3 have resulted in concrete changes at the neighborhood level. Though the precise mechanisms varied, the reformed institutions (compared to the prior hierarchical bureaucracies) increased civic engagement and public participation, administration through deliberative problem-solving, increasing the accountability of local officials to residents, and building trust between these residents and their street-level public servants. The reforms yielded these successes despite sporadic and underresourced efforts of the CPS and CPD central administrations to perform the kind of mobilization, training, support, and accountability functions described in chapter 3. Some of the defects of participatory deliberation in Southtown/Harambee and Central Beat might well have been avoided, or repaired, given more investment and concerted effort from central administration.

6

Deliberation in Social Conflict

THIS chapter explores processes of participatory and deliberative problem-solving in politically conflicted contexts. The neighborhoods examined below were riven by four varieties of division: racial conflict, economic inequality, tensions between professional autonomy and citizen
control, and substantive policy disagreements. In such contexts, institutions designed to produce fair and effective deliberations may instead result in domination, paralysis, or chaos. Each case exhibits both the promise and dangers of participatory deliberation. In each, there were moments
when deliberation was inclusive, fair, and effective, and periods in which
discussion fell far short of these ideals. Examining the differences between
these moments of successful and failed deliberation illuminates the conditions and interventions that encourage deliberation. Appropriate external
supports can make participatory decision-making fair even under trying
circumstances of factionalism and inequalities of power.

6.1. Bridges across Race and Class in Traxton Beat

The fifteen-by-eight–block rectangle that forms Traxton Beat was one of
the more diverse areas of the city. More polarized than socioeconomically
plural, a fenced-off set of commuter railroad tracks segregated the well-
to-do west section from the lower-income east side. A brief drive-though
"windshield survey" of the area generated impressions that census statistics later confirmed. On either side of the smooth, wide streets of beat's
west side sat large, solid houses that had well-manicured lawns and shiny
new cars in their driveways. Its residents were among the wealthiest in
the city proper. The population of the west side was racially integrated
but predominantly white; economically, households were mostly upper
middle–class and professional.

By no means dilapidated, houses on the area's east side were nevertheless modest by comparison. While most of the houses were smaller but
still well maintained, the creep of urban decay was discernable from the
boarded-up and otherwise abandoned buildings that marred east side
blocks. In contrast to the west, east side residents were uniformly African-
American.

As a consequence of decades-old boundaries, these two very different
clusters of residents—each with its own distinct public-safety needs and

interests—shared the same set of policing resources. Since both sides composed a single police beat, these residents were served by the same set of patrol officers and squad car. Despite the conflicting demands that might be placed on them given such diversity of culture, race, class, and location, residents of the east and west sides had never come to loggerheads over policing issues, or over any issues at all, for that matter. The two groups lived in separate and parallel worlds, each with its own avenues, public services, commercial areas, and civic institutions. When residents from one side or the other had problems with public safety and police action or inaction, they would pursue standard channels of redress—perhaps by taking the matter up with individual officers, their supervisors, or local politicians—that did not require awareness of, much less interaction with, residents from the other side of the beat. The Chicago community-policing reforms of 1994 and 1995, however, removed this luxury of mutual ignorance by creating a common forum that threw residents from both sides of the tracks together. Perhaps idiosyncratically, given the common perception that political and administrative decentralization tends to engender parochial sentiments and balkanize polities, participatory policing reforms brought together these previously segregated neighbors.

6.1.1. Social Organization, Spatial Separation, and Socioeconomic Polarization

Neighborhood descriptive statistics confirmed and elaborated these rough impressions of socioeconomic disparity between the east and west sides of Traxton Beat. According to 1990 U.S. census figures, the west side was quite advantaged compared to the east. The median household income of west side residents was almost twice that of those on the east side, the percentage of female-headed households was approximately three times as great on the east side, the east side poverty rate was six times greater than that of the west side, and the east side unemployment rate in 1990 was four times as great.

The west side of Traxton Beat, then, was one of the most peaceful and well-off enclaves within the Chicago city limits. Many of these advantages can no doubt be attributed to the raw income power that west siders possessed. But Traxton Beat's west side was an oasis in the city not just because its residents enjoyed substantial material advantages, but because they had self-consciously organized themselves to deploy those resources to preserve the character of their neighborhood over the course of more than three decades.

The senior cohort of west side residents had moved into the neighborhood in the late 1960s and 1970s. Many of them were young, upwardly

TABLE 6.1
West versus East: Selected 1990 Census Figures for Traxton Beat

	West Side	East Side
White, non-Hispanic (%)	75	2
Black (%)	23	97
Median Household Income ($)	61,264	34,391
Female Head of House (%)	14	48
Housing Units Owner-occupied (%)	93	70
College-educated (%)	81	47
Poverty Rate (%)	1.6	10.5
Unemployment Rate (%)	6	28
Total Population	3,940	2,794

mobile white couples, at the beginning of their careers, who sought comfortable housing on a constrained budget. Fortunately for these young families, the fear of black encroachment and outward flight of established white families had depressed housing values and thus created fireside bargains for whites who were not terrified of racial integration. One neighborhood notable, call him Mr. Phillips, who was active in one of the west side's churches and president of the Traxton Improvement Association, reflected on his decision to live in the area: "In the late 1960s, we used to walk through [West Traxton] often. The [home] buys were great then because of white flight. After looking at many places [all over the South Side], we saw the place [we wanted in Traxton], closed the deal in two hours, and have been living there for twenty-seven years now. . . . Many [neighbors] said that they wouldn't live with blacks, and many of them could and did move out" (Anonymous subject, interview with author).

Almost as soon as Mr. Phillips and other families like his moved in, many began organizing mightily to transform West Traxton Beat into their vision of a livable urban community. Defying the logic that poverty and ghettoization radiate outward from city centers, West Traxton residents proudly claimed that they had created and maintained "a model of diversity and residential stability" through their clever and cohesive collective action.[1] These self-help efforts occurred through a web of associations that included neighborhood committees of two churches and an impressive number of civic associations, such as the Traxton Improvement Association (TIA), Traxton Area Planning Association (TAPA), the Traxton Arts Association (TAA), the 8th Street Business Association, and the Apple Avenue Business Association. These groups pursued neighborhood-stabilization strategies through independent civic action and by leveraging their connections with local politicians, agency officials, and local business people. Mr. Phillips recalls early strategies to stabilize the socioeconomic level of residents during the period of white flight:

I got involved right away at Traxton Church [and its] Social Action Committee, chaired by _____.[2] We took some definite steps in the early to mid-1970s to stabilize the population. We knew that we had to attract buyers to the area, and so we put together a professional brochure of homes. We went to the heads of corporate transfers of big corporations in Chicago, and made them aware of what great deals were available in Traxton, what a great place to live it was. We took interested potential buyers on tours. Based upon the steps he devised at the time, [local civic leader] was the person most responsible for the state of Traxton as it is today.

For decades, residents have maintained what they see as the quality and peace of their neighborhood through measures that some outside observers have found controversial and others horrifying. Home sales in West Traxton, for example, almost never appeared on the open market because they were passed down to acceptable potential neighbors through word of mouth. While West Traxton was itself quite racially integrated by Chicago's standards, the area had the reputation of being a white enclave within a city increasingly composed of people of color. The geographic contours of the neighborhood itself provide perhaps the most dramatic testimony to the boldness and effectiveness of West Traxton's residents. Attentive to the spatial determinants of the quality of neighborhood life, residents in Traxton's neighborhood organizations have used public resources to construct walls around their community to keep out what they perceive to be the chaos and crime of the surrounding urban environment. The map of Traxton Beat (figure 6.1) below shows the division between its east and west sides and several notable features of each.[3]

Residents effectively used public resources to create a walled community in the west; formidable barriers surrounded the area on all sides. Its eastern edge was defined by a set of commuter rail tracks running north-by-northwest. These tracks lay on an elevated berm and were protected by wire fence on both sides. A forest preserve with a single road through it defined the northern boundary of West Traxton. The wide streets that formed its western and southern edges would not obstruct access were it not for the large concrete planters—marked by the gray circles in the map—that block vehicular entry on all but two points to the south and one to the west. Another planter-barrier also closed the smaller street that ran through the northern forest preserve. To further slow traffic and make the area less navigable, concrete traffic barriers were erected on the interior streets of West Traxton—marked as diagonal lines on the map—to transform that traffic network into a circuitous maze of one-way streets. These cul-de-sac obstacles and other traffic barriers resulted from a successful effort in 1995 by several active residents and their aldermanic representative to capture city-wide traffic funds and use them to build barri-

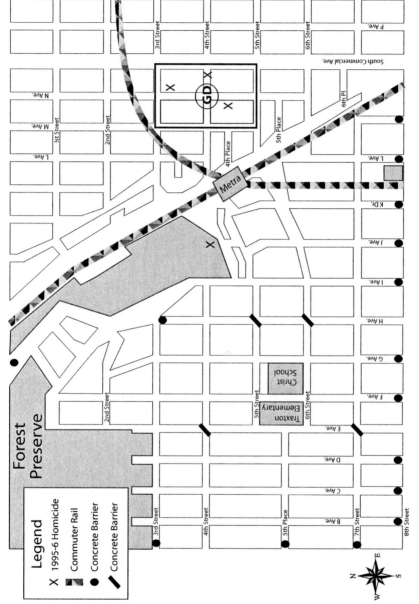

6.1. West and East Traxton.

ers that they hoped would reduce traffic and unwelcome visitors from outside the neighborhood.

The less well-off residents of East Traxton, by contrast, lacked the community capacities manifest in West Traxton. There were no durable civic or business associations beyond a handful of occasional block clubs. Discussions about the proper direction of neighborhood development occurred in isolated, private settings. Also in contrast to their westward neighbors, East Traxton residents lacked close relationships with their alderman, and so have leveraged few neighborhood-improvement resources from him.

Due in part to this dearth of independent organization and absence of outside connections, the physical structure and condition of the neighborhood bore little imprint of the conscious neighborhood self-help efforts found on the west side. The strip that ran north to south through the middle of East Traxton along Commercial Avenue (see figure 6.1) was dotted with convenience stores, liquor lounges, auto-repair operations, and one large grocery store located on the southern end of the avenue. Though the health of these businesses varied, owners and customers frequently complained about various kinds of minor disorder that ranged from street harassment to prostitution to shoplifting. Store owners and residents reported hearing occasional gunshots on this avenue. In stark contrast to West Traxton's style, residents and proprietors had taken no coordinated action to combat these widely felt neighborhood problems.

Consistent with Jane Jacobs's notion that lively streets make safe spaces, the most dangerous areas of Traxton Beat lay in the interior, residential neighborhood west of Commercial Avenue rather than on the busy avenue itself.[4] The Gangster Disciples (GD) street gang claimed as their turf a four-block area (marked on figure 6.1 above) bounded by 3d Street on the north, 5th to the south, M Ave. on the west, and Commercial on the east side. Spike, a mid-30s black male, allegedly operated a crack-house located in the center of this rectangle.[5] His elderly mother, who owned the house, was unable to control her son. At one Traxton beat meeting, a neighbor reported that "I asked Mrs. _____ [Spike's mother] to come to this [community-policing] meeting, but her health is not good. That is why Spike can do this [criminal activity]. John and Spike are the only ones that live there [other than their mother], but many others hang out."

This concentrated area of four square blocks suffered from the systemic violence that often accompanies the drug trade; three of the five homicides that occurred between 1995 and 1996 on this beat took place in this area (see figure 6.1). All three victims were black men who died by gunshot. Several less severe "hot spots" of violent threat dot East Traxton. On P Ave. between 3d and 4th Streets, just to the east of the GD hot spot, residents frequently complained about narcotics trafficking and sporadic automatic gunfire. Businesses on Commercial Avenue faced persistent armed robberies. Furthermore, 2d Street is a territorial boundary between GDs on the south and the Black P. Stone Nation on the north, but a truce between these groups kept this border quiet during the period of my observation.[6]

These considerations led to the classification of Traxton Beat as "intermediate" on the material-resource dimension and "more diverse" on the interest-dispersion dimension (see figure 5.3). The assessment of intermediate material resources comes straightforwardly from combining its wealthy west side with a solidly lower middle–class east side. On the second initial-condition dimension of interest dispersion, the public-safety concerns of east side residents differed considerably from those of west side residents in terms of location, severity, quantity, and general character. These divergent interests stemmed from material inequalities as well as the area's spatial contours. West side public-safety problems revolved around quality-of-life and disorder issues, whereas east side inhabitants faced narcotics trafficking, criminal burglary and robbery, and more serious physical threats.

6.1.2. Discussion and Domination: November 1996–February 1997

How did these racially and economically variegated residents and their public servants in the police department interact with one another in community-policing deliberations? Did they treat each other fairly, with respect, together developing and implementing effective solutions to public-safety problems? Or did discussion give way to domination and paralysis, as some of the critical perspectives put forward in the previous chapter would suggest?

Experiences in Traxton between November 1996 and August 1997 offer evidence for both hope and skepticism about deliberation. During the first four months, better-off west side residents set the community-policing agenda, east side residents were quiescent, and consequently west-siders dominated discussions about what the police ought to be doing and how they ought to be doing it. During the final six months of the observation period, however, the process included voices from both sides of the neighborhood in roughly comparable proportions. In this later period, both groups agreed that east side problems were more severe and they devoted the majority of policing resources to them. The prime explanation for this marked difference is that participants were reminded and guided by explicit deliberative norms and procedures in the second period, whereas meetings in the first period were free-form discussions that allowed the most articulate and aggressive speakers to dominate.

During an initial period, November 1996–February 1997, monthly community-policing beat meetings consistently exhibited several notable characteristics. First, though a substantial number of east side African-American residents attended, the majority of "civilian"—nonpolice—participants were white west side residents. Between fifteen and thirty residents and from five to ten police officers attended the average beat meeting over this period. This overrepresentation of better-off residents conforms to the expectations of the strong-egalitarian and social-capital perspectives in their criticism of accountable autonomy. Second, discussions were extremely orderly, well facilitated, and effective by the standards of community meetings. In Traxton Beat, community-policing participants have adopted the practice of electing one resident, chosen by majority vote, to serve as beat facilitator each year. Both of the facilitators who served in 1996 and 1997 were west side residents, and both possessed excellent group-process skills that they had gained in other community associations and in professional life. As a result of their facilitation, meetings moved very quickly, decisively, and possessed continuity from one session to the next. Third, within this context of fast facilitation and formally equal participation rights, west side residents effectively, though perhaps not consciously, controlled the agenda of priority-setting and problem-solving. West side problems received the majority of attention in both meeting discussions and community-policing attention. The most obvious, and accurate, explanation for this domination is that better-off residents enjoyed advantages of articulateness, education, and attitude in open discussions with those who are less well-off (Sanders 1997).

The November 1996 beat meeting was typical for this period. It was held in the community room of Christ School, a parochial school located on the west side of the beat, on a cold Wednesday night.[7] Traxton's beat meeting–participation rates are high compared to the rest of the city, and on this night twenty-nine adult residents (two or three brought their children) and eight police officers braved the cold to attend.[8] Twenty-one of the residents were white, while eight were African-American. Approximately half—a lower ratio than at the average Chicago beat meeting—were female.[9] Three of the police officers were black, and the rest white.

Residents and police officers sat in a large circle facing one another, to attenuate the distinction between law-enforcement professionals and residents. This simple practice is again distinctive; in typical beat meetings, police sat at a head table facing residents arranged as an audience. This effort to efface distinctions was not entirely successful, however, as police officers, white west side residents, and black east siders for the most part still tended to cluster together in their respective groups. Figure 6.2 depicts the seats that participants chose.

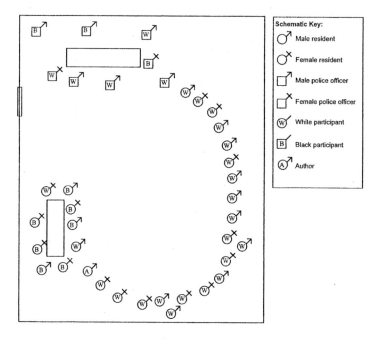

6.2. November 1996 Traxton Beat Meeting.

The beat facilitator, call him Leonard Jones, began by reading the minutes from the previous meeting. Various reports followed. A police sergeant read the crime report and arrest statistics for the beat. Emily Crenshaw, West Traxton resident and also an employee of CANS, updated residents on the organizing and training activities of her group. Again exhibiting an unusually high level of internal organization, the Traxton Beat group regularly invited aldermen and their representatives to request particular actions from the City Councilors' offices. At this particular meeting, a representative of the west side alderman's office reported that she had fulfilled several requests from prior meetings. There was no representative from the aldermanic office of East Traxton's ward.

The meeting then moved on to the direct discussion of public-safety problems by reviewing the problems raised at prior meetings and progress made in solving them. Residents had complained about illegal drinking by teens on the grounds of Traxton Elementary, located on the west side of the beat. In response, they formed an ad hoc school-safety committee that had met with school officials to urge them to post signs and install outdoor lighting. An abandoned building was the second problem brought forward from the prior meeting. The building had been a synagogue, but its institutional owners had left the property unoccupied and unsecured for several months. Trespassers subsequently used the building for drinking, possible drug use, and other illegal activities. In response to this problem, residents had formed another ad hoc committee that had met with the rabbinical owners of the property and persuaded them put a protective fence around the property. Several months later, the committee found a buyer to purchase and develop it for commercial use.

The third continuing problem was late-night noise emanating from a pancake diner located on the western edge of the beat. Residents living next to the structure had for months complained about horns, shouting, car alarms, occasional fights, and other noise. Some of the more militant and suspicious residents complained of substantial gang activity (called "gang loitering") inside the restaurant. As with the previous two problems, residents responded proactively. Those who lived near the area organized one another to call the emergency 911 number whenever disturbances occurred. Police devoted additional patrol attention. Residents organized yet another committee to meet with the franchise owner. Though he seemed stubborn initially, the owner grew more cooperative with time. He attended several community-policing meetings and eventually agreed to take measures that nearby residents would later report to be effective: he hired additional security guards, reduced operating hours in order to close earlier in the evening, and reconfigured his parking lot to reduce loitering.

The meeting then moved on to "new business"—the raising of new issues and suggestion of strategies to deal with them. In a first-come–first-served style, residents aired their safety concerns and public nuisances. Street peddlers operating on the avenue that formed the western edge of the beat bothered a few residents, and they pressed police to enforce vending-license requirements more strictly; police promised to do so. Various traffic issues—drivers hopping curbs to defeat the cul-de-sac planters and drivers cutting through traffic lights—caused several West Traxton residents to demand an additional traffic light at one of the busy corners of the beat and a stop sign on another corner. Police said they would target traffic surveillance at these points. The alderman's representative noted and promised to submit requests for stop signs and traffic lights to appropriate city departments.

The discussion then shifted from these relatively minor problems to more serious concerns of East Traxton residents. Unlike the discussions that involved proposals, sometimes demands, for action involving the police, the alderman, and other residents, the issues raised by East Traxton residents took the form of question-and-answer informational requests. One black East Traxton resident inquired about gunshots that he had heard one evening:

RESIDENT: What happened with the shooting that occurred on 1st and N
   Ave.? I heard that one guy got hit with a shotgun in his ear. A couple of
   houses down, someone got hit with a BB gun, as well.
POLICE OFFICER: That is right, but the people who got shot didn't see who
   did it. The same day, on the same corner, Officer Crusher and the gang
   guys picked up four guys with a MAC-10 in a car on that same corner.[10]

To his credit, the beat facilitator did attempt to delve a bit deeper into
this issue by establishing whether these shootings revolved around some
kind of "hot spot" or whether it was an isolated instance. No one else in
the meeting, however, accepted his invitation:

JONES: Has this house . . . been a problem?
POLICE OFFICER: Only that there is a loud dog there.

And so ended this meeting's discussion of the multiple shootings at the
corner of 1st Street and N Ave. No further action was taken beyond that
required standard police routines because none was imagined or demanded at this meeting. This inaction on the part of East Traxton residents stands in contrast to the coordinated and persistent efforts of west
side residents to solve what were, by comparison, quite minor problems.
This meeting's general pattern of effective west side action and east side
paralysis continued in the next two meetings, through January 1997. As
in this November meeting, residents from both sides of the tracks raised
concerns on their minds. Only West side residents, however, proposed
strategies to deal with issues raised. Table 6.2 shows the major problems
discussed in rough order of attention given them during these three
months in the left-hand column, and the actions taken in response to
those problems in the right-hand column. East side problems are listed
in bold faced type. As just described, west side residents and their allies
in the police department, city agencies, and city council made significant
progress on distinctively west side problems 1.1, 1.2, and 1.3. A fourth
problem that arose in meetings during this period, this one shared by
both east side and west side residents, was slow police response to 911
calls (problem 1.4). Residents frequently complained that police did not
appear until hours after a call had been placed. The group took action
on this problem in two ways. First, residents invited a representative of
the 911 office to explain the system, and to answer questions about tardy
response. The representative laid out the priority system of responding
to calls and placated resident complaints without changing the city-wide
system. As a second strategy residents and police short-circuited this system. Police began to carry personal pager units and publicized their numbers at beat meetings.

TABLE 6.2
Problems in Traxton Beat: November 1996—February 1997

ID#	Problem Raised	Strategies and Actions Taken
1.1	Abandoned Church Property	Increased patrol; Board of Education secures area, property sold to developer.
1.2	Noise at Pancake House	Issue noise citations; open discussions with owner, which resulted in operational changes that reduced noise and fighting.
1.3	Street Peddlers	Citations; intensified patrol.
1.4	Poor 911/Police Response	Presentation and tour of 911 center; police carry pagers
1.5	**Intrusive Police Surveillance**	(Request for evidence—which cars?)
1.6	**Brother Shot Dead**	(Police report ongoing investigation)

* East Traxton problems shown boldfaced.

In contrast to these fairly effective responses to targeted problems, two of the major issues that concerned East Traxton residents received much less sustained attention during the first observation period. In February 1997, black residents from East Traxton raised two recurring problems that directly questioned the competency, interest in public safety, and racial attitudes of the police. One woman suspected the police of conducting surveillance operations on her house (problem 1.5). She said that "whenever one of my friends comes over to visit, I [always] see police come ten minutes later. I always see them outside my house with binoculars." The police denied this accusation, she did not press the matter, and the meeting continued without addressing her concern. In a very similar comment in a meeting some months later, one woman complained that police harassed her son. This time, however, the beat facilitator (who at that meeting was Emily Crenshaw) pressed the matter further:

BLACK RESIDENT: I live on 3d Street and N Ave. We have an unusual number of plainclothes officers, and there is trouble [when they are around]. We are having trouble with those that are trying to protect us. Some of these officers harass the teens playing in the vacant lots. [You police should] make yourself useful.

EMILY CRENSHAW: Do you know how to identify police cars? On the top of the police cars are numbers with four digits, if you see something that is not right, then take down this number [and we can act on it].

BLACK RESIDENT: The kids say, "The police told us to go away, they took our ball." The police would stop my daughter from being on the street. I want to know what we can do [to stop police harassment].

EMILY CRENSHAW: You are going to have to ask your daughter to get the name, or the numbers on the cars. That is the only way we can do anything.

POLICE OFFICER: What lot is this that kids are being run off of and balls taken?

BLACK RESIDENT: There is an alley by my house, and a lot next to it.

EMILY CRENSHAW: The best thing to do is to ID them. If you bring license-plate numbers, then we can track it down.

BLACK RESIDENT: You have two cars in that neighborhod, and their badge numbers are not visible. I report them to city hall. I have reported them, and all they do is harass me more.

TACTICAL (PLAINCLOTHES) OFFICER: Why don't you give me their names?

BLACK RESIDENT: This won't do any good.

Unfortunately, this matter was never pursued further. The woman did not return with more detailed information.

At the same meeting, another African-American female resident of the east side raised a concern about her brother's murder:

FEMALE RESIDENT: On December 15, my brother was shot and killed at a store on the corner of [14th and Commercial]. I don't think that the police are doing anything about this. I have made many attempts to get some satisfaction, but nothing is being done to find the person who killed my brother. You would say that he was a young black man [and so deserved it], but you don't know me, and you don't know my brother.

DETECTIVE: Within two days of your brother's death, seven people were picked up. One woman gave us a name [of a suspect] and he was picked up, but no one ID'd him in a line-up. I have talked to other detectives, but we are having trouble turning up more leads.

Again, the matter was dropped after this exchange. East side residents, in contrast to their more persistent counterparts to the West, failed to advance their problem-solving efforts beyond the mode of complaint, question, and informational response. East Traxton participants never attempted, as west side residents almost certainly would have, to ascertain whether that corner was the site of recurring problems (it was) and to press for sustained action.

During the months between November 1996 and February 1997, then, west side residents dominated the community-policing process of Traxton in the sense that problems they raised received much more airtime in meetings, sustained attention from meeting to meeting, and follow-through on the part of police, city agencies, political officials, and the residents themselves. Thus during this period the formal deliberative institutions of community policing did not yield fair outcomes. The mechanisms of domination in effect in Traxton over this period were peculiar in three respects.

First, domination was not the intent or plan of west side residents, but rather an unintended consequence of a laissez-faire, first-come–first served style of discussion in which the most assertive and well-spoken participants guided proceedings. There were no heated arguments between east siders and west siders or police officers about what counted as a problem, or whether some course of action should or should not be taken. To the contrary, police and west side residents tried unsuccessfully to draw out problems raised by east siders.

Second, domination in Traxton did not operate according to conventional mechanisms that commonly describe the operation of power, conflict, and subjection. Consider the common typology of decision power that distinguishes between three "faces"—or modes—in which a stronger party can steer group decisions in its own interests, over the colliding interests of a weaker party. One party may dominate another through (1) achieving victory in outright conflict, (2) controlling the agenda of decision-making, or (3) subjecting the consciousness of the weaker to the degree he does not even recognize, and therefore cannot press, his own interests (Bachrach and Baratz 1962; Lukes 1983). None of these mechanisms, however, accurately describes the discussion and decision processes that engaged East and West Traxton residents. East Traxton residents had subjective interests in conflict with west siders, and so were not so subjugated that they accepted West Traxton's interests as their own. They repeatedly raised issues of particular concern to those who lived on their side of the tracks—police harassment, gun violence on the east side, and police inaction on east side crimes. Neither were East Traxton residents unable to place their items on the agenda, as they often spoke during the "new business" section of meetings, and west siders appeared to listen. Finally, it is not as if east siders lost discursive battles to those who lived west of the tracks or to the police officers who are supposed to serve them. Far from attempting to quash their contributions, west side residents sometimes attempted to elicit elaboration on various issues from East siders.

Not well described by the three faces of power, domination and the corollary failure of deliberation resulted from yet a fourth, straightforward, but untheorized, mechanism. Residents from the west side were able, even without trying, to dominate community-policing deliberative proceedings because east side residents were unable to address the issues they raised in a sustained manner. When different east side residents raised problems of murder and firearm violence, for example, they failed to articulate that these problems constituted systemic or recurrent patterns that warrant preventative attention and action or offer proposals to address these problems. When another resident raised the problem of police harassment, others questioned the factual basis of the allegations, and no one took the straightforward steps necessary to offer dispositive evidence or generated other proposals for resolving the issue.

Given this peculiar mechanism of domination—deliberative failures of east side residents and of the group as a whole—the third notable aspect of domination in Traxton Beat was its apparent fragility. Since the domination was for the most part unintended and operated according to a mechanism that seems much less robust than the more common three faces of power, small perturbations of the discursive process might have transformed it into the kind of deliberation that would have yielded more fair outcomes. Minor failures of the imagination and lack of persistence, rather than deep structural or psychological constraints, prevented east siders from offering modest proposals or additional evidence to articulate their complaints into fuller demands for collective action. If east siders had offered better arguments or proposals for action, west siders might well have used their greater numbers, resources, and education to perpetuate their domination of the proceedings through more common techniques, such as victory in open conflict or control of the agenda. Alternatively, they might have been guided by the deliberative norms of reasonableness even in situations where those norms required them to modify or sacrifice their own interests. A second period, March 1997–August 1997, offers additional evidence to assess the potential for fair and inclusive deliberation in Traxton.

6.1.3. Structured Deliberation: March 1997–August 1997

At the beginning of each year, Traxton Beat elects one of its residents to serve as beat facilitator. This person is responsible for preparing agendas, conducting beat-meeting discussions, and ensuring continuity from one meeting to the next.[11] The baton of beat facilitation moved from Leonard Jones to Emily Crenshaw at the beginning of 1997. While Jones had been a local civic leader active in several Traxton community organizations, he had no prior training in community policing prior to his participation in Traxton beat meetings. Crenshaw, as previously noted, had worked for CANS as a JCPT trainer over the prior year and half.[12] Out of this experience, Crenshaw enjoyed greater familiarity with both the distinctive procedures of deliberative problem-solving, substantive issues in public safety, and the particular difficulties that residents often encountered in working with police officers.

Though Crenshaw lived on the west side of Traxton, her commitments to social and racial justice impelled her to increase the involvement of east side residents. Concurring with the analysis above, she felt that those living on the east side needed community policing more than west siders, but had gained little from the existing process. When she began her tenure as beat facilitator, she independently started to organize east side residents to attend meetings through phone calls and a few visits to houses and commercial businesses of East Traxton. Beginning in February, these low-level efforts began to bear fruit, and the proportion of African-American, East Traxton residents expanded dramatically, as shown in figure 6.3.

In March 1997, Crenshaw shifted the meeting style from the laissez-faire, town-hall style described in the previous section to one that more

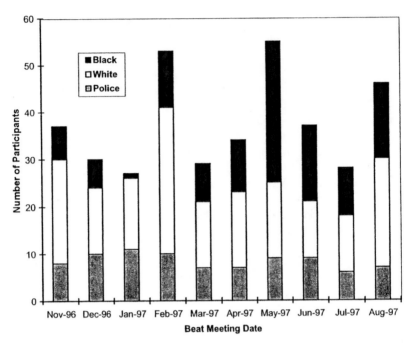

6.3. Traxton Beat Community-Policing Meeting Attendance.

closely followed the structured five-step deliberative problem-solving procedure described in chapter 2. The proximate cause of this transformation
of discursive style was a CPD administrative decree on community policing. Some months earlier, the CPD issued a general order to all police beat
teams directing them to produce "beat plans" containing a prioritized list
of public-safety problems and strategies to ameliorate those problems.[13]
As a community activist, Crenshaw felt strongly that residents, not police
alone, should determine the ordered list of priority problems. At the
March beat meeting, therefore, Crenshaw started the discussion of problems by announcing that: "We have got to put together a beat plan. This
will give the [Police] Commander some sense of what the top problems
[are]. Remember that a 'problem' is something that is ongoing, affects
more than one person, and something that we have the resources to deal
with. Why don't we start by making a list of all the problems?"

In response, a white male west side resident immediately raised the
alleged gang-related crack operation run by "Spike" as the beat's greatest
priority. Whether or not these allegations were true, his house, located
at 4th Street and N Ave. (see map in figure 6.1) was as a matter of fact
the center of gravity of criminal violence in Traxton. Two of the three
murders in 1995 occurred within one block of his house, as did the mur-

TABLE 6.3
Problems in Traxton Beat: March 1997—August 1997*

ID#	Problem Raised	Strategies and Actions Taken
2.1	**Spike's Drug Area**	Arrests around house; residents show themselves in relevant court cases.
2.2	**Burglaries and other disturbances at stores on 8th and Commercial**	Increased patrols; police work with (African-American) store owners to increase responsiveness.
2.3	Residential burglaries	Major perpetrator caught; prevention workshops for residents held.
2.4	**Loitering and harassment at Metra Station**	Increased police visibility.
2.5	Noise at Pancake House	Increased police patrols; negotiations with owner over operations changes to reduce disturbances.

* East Traxton problems shown boldfaced.

der of December 1996 that was heatedly discussed in the February 1997 beat meeting.

> WHITE MALE WEST TRAXTON RESIDENT: Is [Spike] still operating? That would be the number one problem.
> EMILY CRENSHAW: Yes he is. For those of you who don't know, he lives at _____ N Ave. Does everyone agree that he is a priority problem?

With quick assent and without further debate, everyone in the room—black and white, east and west side—agreed that criminal activity around Spike's house was the beat's number one problem. East Traxton residents and police testified in this meeting and others that Spike and his colleagues caused trouble. One woman reported that "when I got home at 9 P.M., there were about twenty of them standing there [blocking my path]. This was at 4th Street and N Ave. When I came back out to my car, they had 'fuck the police', and gang signs [written] on the car." Despite the fact that this problem received scant attention in previous meetings, everyone immediately assented when asked to name *the* most important issue. It would have been difficult indeed to publicly justify any other problem as a higher priority.

After agreeing that Spike's operation was the highest priority, participants discussed and settled upon four additional items:[14] loitering and harassment of passers-by at the Metra Station on the east side, late-night noise and fighting at the pancake diner, drug and firearms activity around the corner of 1st Street and N Ave., and teenage drinking in the forest preserve on Traxton's north side. Table 6.3 shows the order of urgency as established by residents in the left-hand column, and the actions taken to address these problems in the right-hand column. As with the previous table of problem priorities, East Traxton issues are shown boldfaced. Contrasting table 6.3 with table 6.2, the first major difference between this second phase of community policing in Traxton (March 1997–August 1997) and the first phase (November 1996–February 1997) was the group's consensus that the beat's most urgent problems lay on the east side. At the level of agenda-setting, the second phase was more fair than the first.

On the major problem of Spike's crack house and its surrounding blocks, the group developed and implemented two strategies. First, police increased their presence in that small area of the beat through more frequent patrols, the use of a controversial (but legal) technique called "field interviews," in which suspicious persons or persons in suspicious areas are stopped, questioned, and sometimes searched on the street. This technique resulted in several arrests for possession of crack cocaine and marijuana. Second, residents and police tracked relevant cases through its court watch committee. The assumption—widely accepted among Chicago community activists—behind this strategy was that judges and juries would issue harsher sentences if they heard the personal testimonies and perspectives of victims and other residents. These Court Watch groups also monitored the prison and parole status of people whom they considered threats to the neighborhood. They conveyed this information to beat-meeting participants and other neighborhood residents. Police worked with residents to use court watch to target particular individuals associated with Spike's operation:

> POLICE: [Last week, between Commercial and N] we arrested [Jerry Anderson]. This is his first arrest [he is only 13]. Another one for the Court Watch is [Spike's brother]. [Third and fourth suspects for Court Watch are] "Yummie," the guy who did a bunch of their shootings, who is under arrest, and so is Washington T.
>
> CRENSHAW: "You can't really show up because _____ is a minor, only 13 [and so proceedings are closed]. The best we can do is send a letter. We can call court advocacy and get them to send a letter. We should attend the rest of the hearings, though.

At a later meeting, an East Traxton woman active in Court Watch told the group that: "I have been going to the Court Watch, the judges have really been cooperative with the Court Watch cases. They would like more people to attend. When a crime is committed on a block, [I know that] the people from there don't like to go to that trial, because then they [those arrested] will pick on you, but it is important."

Did these measures yield progress on the crime and physical threats around the corner of 4th Street and N Ave.? During this period, Spike himself was not arrested for PCS.[15] The actions did elicit a reaction, however; Spike himself attended the June Traxton beat meeting along with two associates. He offered a brief statement denying any criminal activity: "[I] came here to say that I don't run nothing, don't do nothing. Everybody is saying that I am a big dope dealer, but I am not doing anything." East Traxton residents who lived near him were present at this meeting, but remained silent in the face of this denial. After the meeting, some residents said that they had been intimidated by his presence. Others speculated that he came precisely to spark such feelings. Both East Traxton residents and police reported enormous progress in reducing the fear and threat from Spike's alleged criminal operation, however, though both agreed that serious problems remained. At the May meeting, a tactical police officer reported that, "In the past three weeks, there hasn't been anyone out at 4th Street and N Ave. We seem to have moved that problem away from there for now." At the June meeting, a resident who lived near Spike said that "Sunday night, at three or four in the morning, I heard shots fired around [Spike's corner]. But that is about it [in terms of criminal activity there]. You guys are doing great work, and please keep up the good work."

The second priority problem (2.2) was commercial burglaries in the various stores that line Commercial Avenue, but especially on the corner of Commercial and 8th Street. The corner was a busy one because it received foot traffic from several stores and several major bus lines stopped there. In addition, school-age children frequently visited the stores in the afternoons. Store operators suspected that thieves came from both groups. The major strategy was straightforward. East Traxton residents asked police to patrol the area more frequently, to show greater presence, and to walk into the stores on foot from time to time. Police complied with all of these requests. In the May meeting, one East Traxton resident reported with satisfaction that "since the last meeting, the [police] visibility has been up 100 percent, and the boys are no longer on the corner of [4th Street and Commercial]." As with Spike's crack-house, however, this strategy did not eliminate the problem; according to other residents and store owners, the burglaries continued, though with less frequency.

In order to deal more systematically with this problem and others, several East Traxton residents and small-business owners formed the East Side Business Association in March 1997.[16] Participation in just a few beat meetings had made them more acutely aware of the crime problems on Commercial. Those who formed the association also realized that the east side had low participation and organization at beat meetings. The members therefore scheduled their monthly meetings to occur one week before the beat meetings, so that the group could raise its issues and proposals at the beat meeting.

Another priority problem revolved around the Metra Station on the tracks that separate the east and west sides of Traxton (see figure 6.1). The station itself and its parking lot are located on the east side, and residents who use the station and those who live near it allege that young people congregate around the area, drink, and harass passersby. The exchange that established the problem as a priority at the March meeting illustrates how an issue can be quickly identified, how open discussions can transmit detailed information, and how mutual commitments to act can build trust between parties—in this case police, west side residents, and new east side participants—unaccustomed to working with one another:

> BLACK FEMALE: The Metra parking lot gets pretty good monitoring in the mornings, but the path between the green and white house and the empty school is still attracting a lot of unwanted traffic. The gang members come and drink and hang out. As it gets warmer, it will become an even worse problem.
>
> EMILY CRENSHAW: What time does this happen?
>
> BLACK Female: [It is worse around] 5 P.M. or so, but happens at all times.
>
> POLICE OFFICER: Have you called the police when they come?
>
> BLACK Female: I have called the police, and I have gone out and talked to them directly.
>
> CRENSHAW: If we agree to work on it [the problem around the Metra Station] this month, will you come back next month to help?
>
> BLACK FEMALE: Yes, yes.

Like the burglary problem directly to the east, residents proposed and officers implemented the straightforward solution of increased police presence at times of the day that they identified as most problematic. According to field observations and residents who live near the area, the action substantially reduced the harassment after just a few weeks. One resident said, "Thank you for patrolling near the Metra station, I think that the [foot] traffic has gone down. I just want to say thanks. . . . It is dangerous in the lots . . . and they shouldn't be there."

6.1.4. Explaining Institutional Performance in Traxton Beat

Did Traxton residents use community-policing reforms to participate and deliberate in ways that advanced the fairness and effectiveness of policing in the beat?

The fairness of community-policing decisions and their effectiveness for east side residents was clearly greater in the months between March 1997 and August 1997 than in the earlier period from November 1996 until February 1997. This improvement was due to the shift from a laissez-faire, town-meeting, free-form mode of meeting discussion to one in which participants were asked explicitly to rank problems according their severity, and then to distribute their problem-solving energies accordingly. When asked to do so, Traxton residents did not self-interestedly press as most urgent those problems that were closest to them. Instead, they agreed on a consensus ordering despite differences in their "objective" interests.

In both the dominated and deliberative phases, residents and police developed and implemented quite *effective* strategies to solve problems (see tables 6.2 and 6.3). Indeed, Traxton Beat ranks among the most effective neighborhood-level groups in this series of six cases. The group was able to focus its attention on priority problems over time and develop strategies to significantly reduce the severity of all the problems on which it focused. The principal difference between the first and second phases was that outcomes in the first benefited primarily west side residents, despite the relatively benign character of their problems, while priorities, strategies, and results in the second phase served east side and west side residents more equitably.

Another important dimension of institutional performance is the generation of social solidarity. The institutions of community policing in Traxton served as handmaiden to the early development of two kinds of solidarity in Traxton. First, it is difficult to imagine how cooperation, consensus, and group action between residents of the east and west sides would have developed in the absence of bridging institutions constructed by community-policing reforms. Residents of the two neighborhoods hardly spoke to one another prior to these community-policing reforms; indeed, west siders had spent much collective energy barricading their neighborhood against interaction with their neighbors. Second, community-policing institutions drove east side residents to greater levels of organization—as manifest in the formation of the East Traxton Business Association and the informal self-mobilization of east side residents to participate in the beat meetings. An explicit motive of this community and social organization was to capture and direct the public-safety resources for east side problems, following the "civic engagement" mechanism (see chapter 1).

How, then, do we explain the bifurcated outcomes of institutional failure followed by success in Traxton Beat? The explanation is that the institutional design was more completely implemented in the second period than in the first. In particular, the first period exhibited decentralization without deliberation, while the second phase incorporated both critical elements of accountable autonomy. In both periods, policing activity was decentralized in that substantial operating autonomy devolved to the level of individual beats. Discussions in beat meetings were not, however, properly deliberative in the first phase; on the contrary, discussions were laissez-faire, town-hall affairs in which the most outspoken and articulate voices dominated. Against the unfavorable initial background conditions of material inequality and interest dispersion, this discursive style resulted in the domination of worse-off east side residents by better-off west-siders. This domination occurred according to just those dynamics specified by the four critical perspectives of rational choice, strong egalitarianism, social unity, and cultural difference. In the second period, however, group processes more closely and self-consciously followed the pragmatic deliberative procedure, and more equitable outcomes resulted.

Once implemented, the mechanisms and norms of deliberation overran the dynamics that pervaded the first period. Diverse participants from both the east and west sides quickly agreed on a single list of priorities, beginning with a west side resident who suggested that an east side crackhouse ought to be the beat's top concern. This experience shows how Traxton's west side residents did abide by deliberative norms. In particular they displayed the moral capacity to restrain pursuing their own narrow self-interest *when asked to do so*. In the laissez-faire discussions of the initial period, no one suggested, either implicitly or explicitly, that such norms ought to be followed. In the second period, however, these norms became effective in the process of prioritizing neighborhood problems.

The shift in Traxton Beat from domination and unfairness to a deliberative mode with more democratic outcomes may seem to rest on the improbable rise of a skilled facilitator with substantial social-justice commitments in the person of Emily Crenshaw. On one interpretation of these events, the move to structured deliberation depended upon the conjunction of her election to beat facilitator and her idiosyncratic combination of personal capacities and political inclinations. Without her, one might think, west siders might have been able to continue to assert their priorities over those of east side residents indefinitely because the decision process would have remained a discursive free-for-all.

The first response to this contention is that the operation of any institution—including markets, bureaucracies, and political parties—depends upon competent individuals who understand how those institutions ought to function and possess the capacities to work and lead within them. That such individuals can be found in our case studies is not an embarrassment for the institutional design but rather a point in its favor. Emily Crenshaw was that kind of person. Without denying her substantial skills as a facilitator and leader, her critical actions in moving Traxton to structured deliberation were *fully prescribed by the rules and institutions of community policing and not extraordinary actions of maverick leadership.* The move to prioritize problems rather than merely discussing them as they come up is an explicit part of the five-step problem-solving procedure (see chapter 2) and by the official Chicago community-policing materials. Furthermore, she suggested the prioritization procedure in order to generate group decisions that would fulfill her responsibility of helping to construct the "beat plan" required by the district office. None of this is to say, however, that people like Emily Crenshaw were easily found. The institutions were still young, she had participated almost since their inception, and the procedures developed so quickly that their requirements were sometimes ambiguous even to those quite close to the process. As this institutional reform matures, perhaps many more participants will gain the levels of knowledge and skill that Crenshaw exhibited.

A second response to the problem of overdependence on personality is that the institutional design of Chicago's community-policing program attempts to reinforce the kinds of deliberative procedures and motivations that made the second phase more successful than the earlier period.[17] Again, the structured deliberation that led to the generation of a fair agenda and collective action was not an accident of individual whim, but rather was designed as the fundamental, constituting, deliberative group-decision process (see chapter 2). While the implementation of this deliberative architecture may have come via the leadership of the beat facilitator in Traxton, many other mechanisms transmit the structure of this deliberative process, including the materials that organize these groups and efforts of central administration to provide training and other supports for participatory deliberation.[18]

6.1.5. Accountable Autonomy versus Hierarchical Bureaucracy in Traxton Beat

While community-policing processes in Traxton produced institutional and deliberative successes, were these outcomes any better or worse than those that would have been generated by nonparticipatory, bureaucratic policing? The answer to this question of institutional comparison differs for the two sides of Traxton. For those on the west side, community-policing added one institutional avenue to their already rich panoply of options for social and political action. Community-policing participation from West Traxton residents, therefore, probably substituted for or displaced other kinds of social action and engagement. In other words, problems in West Traxton that were handled through community policing might well have been solved through other channels if community policing had not existed.

Similar to the situation with Traxton Elementary, West Traxton residents had developed informal mechanisms of resident voice and participation. For example, formal mechanisms of *civic engagement* were not new to West Traxton residents. Many west side participants were already involved in neighborhood organizations—churches, the school, and/or local improvement associations. Through these organizations, some had developed connections with police officers that allowed them to utilize the tool of *directed discretion* with regard to the actions taken by police to remediate problems that these residents considered more important. Out of these working partnerships with police, residents and police had gained both healthy levels of trust and accurate skepticism about the motives and capacities of the others, and so the mechanism of *studied trust* was also operating prior to community policing. Finally, the effective and venerable associations of West Traxton had practiced the mechanisms of *institutional learning* and gained the ability to *cross-functionally coordinate* transactions among different parties in the public, private, and community sectors many years before CAPS. Since informal versions of all of these mechanisms existed in the absence of accountable-autonomy reforms, we say cannot say that West Traxton gained dramatic benefits from them.

Nevertheless, these formal and public institutions offer two important advantages over informal, associative mechanisms. First, the use of these mechanisms through the open meetings and other processes made them more accessible and fair to all residents compared to their relatively more hidden operation in civic organizations or private associations. Under the informal, associative version of directed discretion, for example, those who happened to know particular officers enjoyed the ability to focus otherwise discretionary police power. Second, the informal versions of these mechanisms sometimes operated in opposition to, sometimes independently from, the logic of command-and-control institutions. Since accountable autonomy changed the central logics of these public institutions, those mechanisms may be more effective compared to informal methods. Consider again the example of directed discretion. When asked by a resident to pay special attention to an area or to particular suspicious persons, an officer may rightly feel equivocal about doing special favors for a private friend and might indeed be punished for ethical violations if this interaction became public. When this request comes through an open community-policing meeting, it moves from the gray borders of policing to its center stage.

The benefits to East Traxton residents were greater and more clear. Since they lacked the associations, connections, and history of informal cooperation of their neighbors to the west, they also lacked the networks with which to construct these mechanisms. During the second, more successful period of observation, however, we saw East Traxton residents together with police and other residents utilize several mechanisms of participatory deliberation.

By far the simplest and most commonly used mechanism during the observation period was directed discretion. Prior to community policing, east side residents lacked working connections with police and so police power was distributed according to the logics of preventative patrol and emergency response. Through the community-policing process, east side residents gained the power to direct police attention to problems that they considered priorities. They focused police attention on all three of the east side priority problems shown in table 6.3, and in all three cases residents reported this increased presence and police activity was effective.

Community policing also set into motion the second mechanism of increased civic engagement in East Traxton. After hearing about opportunities to affect and deploy police action, East Traxton residents organized themselves to participate in the community-policing process. This participation, in turn, made possible the contributions of east side residents to problem-solving strategies, for instance advocacy in the Court Watch program and the formation of the East Traxton Business Association—the only business association in East Traxton.[19]

In terms of gains over the prior institutional context of bureaucratic policing, then, accountable autonomy generated small but substantial gains for West Traxton and much more dramatic gains for East Traxton. This result belies the common expectation, previously characterized as strong egalitarianism (chapter 4), that participatory-democratic arrangements primarily benefit those who are already well-off while leaving the worst-off behind.

One critical response to this neighborhood's experience is that Traxton Beat was not really such a hard case. Though the west side was wealthier than the east, the east side was far from poor by Chicago standards. Therefore Traxton does not test the hypothesis about material poverty. Another critic might argue, following Matthew Crenson's (1983; Oliver 2002) contention, that material inequality actually favors neighborhood collective action and so Traxton is actually an easy case rather than a hard one. The following two cases continue this exploration of deliberation and social conflict under conditions of severe poverty.

6.2. Translation and Trust in Southtown Beat

Southtown Beat, located on Chicago's far south side, is a low-income area of some forty square blocks that is home to Hispanics—many of them Spanish-speaking—and African-Americans. Though no impenetrable physical fences separated these two groups, as in Traxton, residents considered various blocks to be either black or Hispanic. The latter group lived for the most part in the northeast portion, with its rough boundary defined by the railroad tracks that run northwest and southeast through the beat. Though there were many exceptions to this pattern, most of the blocks that lie to the south of these tracks were inhabited by African-Americans.

Residents of the beat did share great vulnerability to crime. Southtown Beat's personal crime rate in 1996 was 111 crimes per 1000 persons, slightly lower than that for Central Beat,[20] but almost 50 percent greater than the city-wide rate and high enough to place it in the most violent quintile of Chicago police beats. There were a total of ten homicides in Southtown Beat between 1995 and 1996. One female victim died in domestic violence, and the other nine were young males between the ages of 15 and 40 who were shot down either in the streets or in automobiles. In 1994, sniper fire from suspected members of the Latin Kings gang disrupted a basketball game in Southtown Park, the neighborhood green space. Violence also often occurred on a territorial boundary between the Black Gangster Disciples and Latin Kings. In 1994 and 1995, several retaliatory murders flared on this boundary. In addition to this gun violence, there were several crack-houses on the beat. Finally, street-walking prostitutes solicited customers on a run-down commercial strip, and then took them to alleys, the abandoned buildings, or Southtown Park to complete their transactions.

6.2.1. The Contours of Poverty and Interest Dispersion in Southtown Beat

Southown residents faced severe barriers to dealing with these problems through self-help mechanisms. Poverty is the most obvious of these. As table 5.1 shows, the average household income in Southtown Beat was $14,074 in 1990, easily placing it in the poorest quintile of Chicago beats. In that same year, 38.6 percent of the families in the beat received some form of public aid, and one third of the beat's households that had children were headed by a female. The 1990 unemployment rate for residents living in the beat was 24 percent, about two and a half times the city-wide rate. The physical condition of the neighborhood's housing stock and commercial real estate mirrored these indicators. Approximately one-third of the commercial lots that lined once-thriving commercial boulevards lay vacant. Some of these lots were simply empty, the buildings that once stood there having been demolished. Unoccupied, boarded-up, and decaying buildings, however, still stood on much of this commercial strip.

Most of the residential interior was better maintained, but there were still substantial quantities of abandoned and boarded-up single and multiunit housing. Even by the lowered standards of urban America, Southtown Beat was a poor area.

Space, language, culture, and civic institutions separated African-Americans from Hispanics in Southtown. Though the neighborhood was small, blacks and Hispanics for the most part lived in separate blocks. Though plenty of African-Americans lived in Hispanic blocks and vice versa, these territorial designations nevertheless constituted powerful mental maps for those who live in the neighborhood. Many Hispanic residents considered the area south of the railroad tracks to be "black" and hence not to be crossed lightly or alone. Though most of the Hispanic households in the area had at least one member of the family who was fluent in English, many more spoke Spanish exclusively or were more comfortable in that language. Finally, African-Americans and Hispanics for the most part participated in parallel civic institutions. Though a large faction of both groups held deep Christian religious commitments, Spanish-speaking residents attended a nearby church called St. Peter's, while the African-Americans went to the First Baptist Church. Educationally, St. Peter's operated an excellent parochial school attended by many Hispanic children, while the majority of African-American families sent their children to one of two nearby public schools. Since many other social activities grow out of block, church, or school affiliations, these anchors of neighborhood life effectively segregated civic life along racial fissures in Southtown Beat.

This spatial and cultural segregation led residents to adopt live-and-let-live policies of noninterference and noncooperation and to perceive that they held quite separate interests. For the most part, these two groups saw little common ground, but neither was there much basis for outright conflict. Suspicions sometimes broke through this apathy, however. When members of the Latin Kings or the (black) Gangster Disciples shot at one another or across public areas populated with bystanders, African-Americans often commented that it was the "Mexicans shooting again" and vice versa. According to one long-time activist in the neighborhood, past attempts at racial coalition "all fizzled out" due to suspicions that various leaders were using these efforts to advance individual or racial agendas.

Relations between police and residents were even less congenial than between groups of residents. Both Hispanic and African-American residents held rather low opinions about the effectiveness of police and their willingness to engage in cooperative partnerships with those whom they supposedly served. One Hispanic resident, active in the community-policing effort, offered this critical observation:

CAPS is disappointing in our neighborhood right now because it is top-down [and the people at the top are giving the wrong message]. For a while we had two officers who both spoke Spanish and would come out of their cars and talk to people in the neighborhood about what was going on. The kids knew them; they extended themselves into the community. They left about six months ago, and things have gone back to the old ways. The police stay in their cars now and the only time I see them is at the beat meetings. At the meetings, I asked about this, about whether the officers can get out of their cars some more [and get to know us and what is going on]. One of the officers said that we should stop them when they drive by if we have something to say. But community policing is about taking the time to stop and say "hi." Officer _____ said that this would be too hard, and that different officers have different styles. But I know that in an organization, it comes from the top. We need to break through the [standard] police-officer mentality [if community policing is going to work]. Commander _____ needs to set a better tone for the community-policing style.

In contrast to Traxton Beat, where residents had officers' pager numbers, and the congenial police-resident relationships in Central Beat, Southtown residents wanted simply to open *some* lines of communication to their police officers. At one beat meeting, for example, an African-American resident asked despairingly but diplomatically, "Do you [officers] have cards? The majority of us don't know you, and we want to start building a working relationship." The officers responded that they did not have cards (much less pagers), but did provide their first names. A female Hispanic resident of Southtown commented at one beat meeting that "we only see you when there are shots fired. I called in an incident several nights ago when shots were fired, and within two minutes fifteen cars appeared. But the only time we see you is when shots are fired. Can we have a little more preventative policing—walk the streets and know the names of the kids?"

For their part, police officers acknowledged that residents could contribute effectively to public-safety efforts, but did not recognize them as equals in this enterprise. They were surprisingly ignorant of residents' suspicions and resentments against them and had no specific strategies to build more cooperative relationships. The sergeant in command of Southtown Beat offered the following assessment of civilian (resident) contributions: "They can be helpful in things like court processes, but you have to tell them where they are effective, and then they can be even more effective than the police." In contrast to the opinions of most involved residents, another sergeant thought that police-resident relations were quite good. When asked what could be done to improve matters, he responded that "for the most part, our officers are really good already."

6.2.2. The Mediating Center: Disembedded Deliberation

The prospects for participatory and deliberative problem-solving in Southtown Beat seem rather dim given these multiple axes of isolation, conflict, and the absence of conditions (e.g., trust, wealth, agreement) thought to be conducive to fair deliberation. Surprisingly, then, the community-policing problem-solving process was both fair and quite effective from August 1996 until December 1996. It included, for the first time in Southtown, both African-American and Hispanics in concerted group action. Over this period, police cooperated with residents and provided crucial problem-solving resources. This diverse group solved two important, long-standing neighborhood public-safety problems.

As with Traxton Beat, the strategic intervention of a skillful facilitator contributed enormously to this success. In Southtown, the facilitator and other helpful actors were dispatched from CPD headquarters to support local deliberation. These individuals, called community-policing trainers and organizers, operated in Southtown between August and December 1996 under the JCPT program.[21] The JCPT team performed three important functions that were especially critical in light of Southtown's adverse initial conditions. Its leader was a civilian trainer named Roger Sanchez. Sanchez was employed by the CANS.[22] A highly skilled, bilingual facilitator, Sanchez brought African-American and Hispanic residents together. Residents from both groups found him inviting and fair. In the presence of this intermediary, Hispanic residents, African-Americans, and police officers who lacked a prior history of cooperation avoided the deliberative breakdown that would likely have occurred without him. When asked why community policing seemed to spark a biracial effort when nothing else had done so, one long-time neighborhood resident responded that, "CANS bilingual staffing helped a lot. We tried to get some community-safety efforts going a couple of years ago, but it didn't work out because it [the effort] lacked leadership ability and this skill."

Second, trainers from JCPT and CANS provided residents with deliberative problem-solving skills and made them aware of opportunities for directing police power under the Chicago reforms. Several Southtown residents cited problem solving–skills training as a distinctive and critical feature of community policing in their area. One Hispanic resident, who had been active in several city-wide and neighborhood efforts, including the Chicago Empowerment Zone and a well-known community development corporation, commented that: "CAPS is the first time that I have seen a program empower people. CANS instructors were especially important in this. No one ever came out and taught us a whole process before. This is quite different from the Empowerment Zone, which was a war between different agencies." An African-American Southtown beat-meeting participant commented that "none of this [successful problem-solving] would have happened without CANS and the changes in the Chicago Police Department. The doors [to neighborhood improvement] would not have opened, as they are starting to do now. They helped bridge the African-American and Hispanic communities, and this is an unprecedented alliance. CANS training showed us what resources and talent exist in the community, and we never saw that before."

Third, the presence of JCPT trainers induced beat-level police officers in Southtown to cooperate with residents. The first two factors of bilingual facilitation and skills-training forged a unified voice with particular problem-solving plans. Police officers were largely content to fulfill the roles assigned to them by these resident-devised plans because they saw the JCPT Program as a legitimate authority associated with the police headquarters. After all, one member of the training team was a sworn officer.

Recall from chapter 3 that the JCPT program calls for a kind of situated training. Instructors teach community-policing skills and procedures by guiding resident and police trainees through the five steps of deliberative problem-solving as applied to actual neighborhood concerns. Training in Southtown began at a beat meeting, held in St. Peter's Church, in early September 1996. Though participation in community policing had been quite low prior to that, organizers mobilized residents for this event through posters and door-to-door canvassing. As a result, 112 residents attended the meeting, split about equally between African-Americans and Hispanics. They used the session, conducted with simultaneous bilingual translation by Mr. Sanchez, to develop a list of the priority problems on the beat and to select one for group attention over the next several meetings. Though residents initially raised shootings in Southtown Park, they eventually settled on what some might consider a relatively minor issue: unsanitary, loud, and occasionally violent residents who owned a house in the beat. Participants reported that they selected this house as a first target even though they didn't consider it to be the beat's most severe problem. They wanted to begin their biracial community-policing efforts, to "cut their teeth," on a manageable issue that lay within their limited capabilities.

The targeted problem consisted of two brothers, call them the Stilps, and their house. Neighbors had long complained about conditions in and around the house. They reported that noxious, odors issued from the house and complained that human feces and other raw sewage often lay in the front and back yards. Reports from city inspectors later validated these claims. Neighbors also reported that the Stilps owned a large number of junked automobiles that obstructed traffic and rendered the block unsightly. Another frequent complaint was that loud music came from the Stilps' house at all hours. The Stilps also owned two rottweiler dogs who occasionally roamed without leashes. Circumstantially, three of the nine nondomestic homicides in Southtown between 1995 and 1996 occurred within one block of the Stilps' house. Several neighbors tried for years to make the Stilps more neighborly, but nothing worked. One active resident reported that he had pursued many avenues over the years—including dealing directly with the Stilps, calling the police, and contacting various city agencies—without an iota of progress.

When the Stilps' house became the community-policing group's first target, however, actions became more strategic, persistent, and forceful. Following the next four steps of the problem-solving process (problem analysis, strategy development, implementation, and reevaluation), the group developed several simultaneous approaches to address the Stilps' house and assigned these steps to various participants. This strategy utilized the mechanism of cross-functional coordination whereby resident groups orchestrated the actions of multiple bureaucracies.[23] They invited the Stilps to discuss the problem, but received no response. They asked police officers to issue citations against immobilized and therefore illegally parked vehicles. They invited representatives from the Department of Streets and Sanitation to attend one of the group's meetings so that residents could learn about pertinent city regulations and possible routes of legal action. Initially, the department did not respond. After several petitions, however, the department finally sent an inspector who issued multiple citations to the Stilps after examining their property. Animal-control officials were contacted about the rottweiler dogs, but they failed to respond. Finally, the group requested that housing inspectors visit the building, and these city agents eventually brought the Stilps to housing court for code violations.

The area around the Stilps' house improved gradually as a result of these persistent efforts. Visible progress began when broken-down cars were towed away and noise violations ceased as a result of police citations. When citations from housing and sanitation inspectors brought the Stilps to housing court, two dozen residents organized themselves to testify about the property's blighting effect. The Judge ordered the Stilps to desist from unsanitary practices and to implement building repairs rapidly. The Stilps failed to respond to these court orders, and the judge eventually evicted them. Neighbors report that the area has greatly improved since their departure, and residents generally view cleaning up the Stilps' property as a quite substantial neighborhood victory.

This problem-solving example may seem to illustrate the dangerous potential of participatory governance to impose community norms in violation of individual rights. But the sequence of events that culminated in the eviction of the Stilps complied with deliberative norms, existing law, and pedestrian notions of reasonableness. The Stilps were invited repeatedly—first in community-policing meetings, then in housing court—to offer arguments as to why others ought to accept their obnoxious behavior. Again and again, they failed to do so and thus rejected opportunities to deliberate. Had they chosen to participate, it is doubtful whether they—or anyone—could have formulated reasonable arguments to justify their actions. Why should they justify their private behavior to neighbors? Because their actions had severe negative externalities and were, in the end, illegal. It should also be noted that they were only allowed to inhabit the house as long as they did due to lax enforcement of existing building and sanitary regulations. The eventual eviction was in many respects overdue. In this case, the deliberative efforts of the Southtown community-policing group *directed the existing legal discretion* of city agents to target a situation that they deemed problematic.[24]

After these signs of progress, the eighty or so regular participants in this community-policing group turned their energies to a larger neighborhood problem: violence around Southtown Park. Southtown Park was the neighborhood's primary public green space. The Park's grounds were small, amounting to only two city blocks. Its facilities included two asphalt basketball courts, a multiuse natural-grass athletic field, and a modest field house. In past years, staff from the Chicago Department of Parks and Recreation used the field house to teach various crafts and sports classes to children, working-age adults, and elderly neighborhood residents.

Like many other public spaces in inner-city neighborhoods, Southtown Park was a site of violence as well as leisure. In 1994, several children playing in the park were wounded by sniper fire, allegedly from Hispanic gang members. In response, the Parks District decided to defend the park by closing it down. The closure did not prevent residents from using the open space for basketball and other sports, but staff were pulled from the field house. But neither did the closure eliminate violence in and around the park. Police and neighbors alleged that substantial narcotics trafficking continued. Furthermore, of the three homicides in this beat in 1995, two occurred within one block of Southtown Park.

In response to this continued violence, the community-policing group selected Southtown Park as its second priority problem. Some Hispanic participants initially objected to prioritizing Southtown Park on the grounds that this space, which lies to the south of the railroad tracks that informally segregate Hispanics from African-Americans, was primarily a "black" problem. Solving it would principally benefit African-American residents. Black participants responded first that the park lay on the border between the two groups, and should therefore be a public space for both despite its past use patterns. Beyond this, they argued, the park was objectively one of the neighborhood's most urgent crime and safety "hot spots." Finally, black participants promised that they would devote energies to making the park accessible to everyone. These arguments persuaded Hispanic participants, and the group as a whole agreed that the park would be their next priority problem.

Residents and police developed two strategies to improve the park situation. First, they would increase police visibility and patrol around the area. Officers agreed to visit the park more often. Furthermore, the police maintained a "park car" devoted exclusively to patrol its many parks, and they arranged to have this car visit Southtown's park more frequently. Both police and residents report that this patrol-based strategy reduced narcotics activity. As the group's second strategy, they decided to make the park safe by turning it into a lively, oft-used public space. Criminal and violent individuals, they reasoned, prefer to conduct their activities in the shadows, and so increasing public use would also make the space safer. Residents organized a committee to meet with the nonprofit group "Friends of the Parks" to learn about how others in Chicago had dealt with dangerous parks. The committee petitioned several officials from the Parks District and organized large resident turnouts to several Parks District hearings to impress upon officials there the importance of reopening the park. Only one month after this initiative began, Parks District officials decided that they would open the park. Southtown residents trace the turning point in this campaign to open the park to a Parks District hearing in which a nine-year-old Hispanic boy from Southtown testified to city officials about the difference that open green space would make in his life.

The park officially opened at the end of October 1996. Shortly thereafter, the community-policing group spun off a portion of itself as the Southtown Park Council, charged with handling governance and public-safety issues concerning the park.[25] Staying true to the initial commitment to make the park accessible to Hispanic as well as African-American residents, the council used new parks funds to hire two full-time staff members, one Spanish speaking and the other African-American. In a continuing effort to make the park a safe space, council members petitioned the alderman for physical improvements, such as outdoor field lighting and new paving. More routinely, the council also channeled resident requests to parks officials for specific craft classes and after-school programs. After the park opened and officials began to staff it on a full-time basis, residents reported that both narcotics activity and violence dropped off as public use grew.

6.2.3. Retreat of the Center and Deliberative Breakdown

Just as Southtown beat participants were enjoying these victories, the JCPT team concluded its assigned period in Southtown Beat and moved on to other neighborhoods. Funding constraints limited each team to just a few trainers, short stays in each beat, and prevented them from offering ongoing assistance. Because the program had not yet set into place stable organizations or durably imparted deliberative skills, the JCPT team's departure severely crippled Southtown Beat's problem-solving process. This breakdown manifested itself in two ways. First, participation generally, but Hispanic participation in particular, declined precipitously. Between August and November, the period of JCPT presence, community-policing meetings numbered between 60 and 120 persons each. African-Americans and Hispanics participated in equal measure. After November, the number of residents at meetings ranged between 20 and 30 persons, and less than a half-dozen Hispanics attended each. Second, relations between police and citizens became suspicious and hostile. Police began to make unilateral decisions and their respect for resident contributions deteriorated.

Three factors precipitated the decline in Hispanic participation. First, a key community leader departed. In the last stage of the JCPT organizing process, two very active and enthusiastic residents, one African-American man and the other a Hispanic woman—call her Ms. Martinez—became beat facilitators. Soon after, however, Martinez decided to pursue community-organizing opportunities in other parts of Chicago and ceased her contributions to Southtown. No remaining participant possessed both the bilingual facilitation skills and procedural knowledge necessary to connect Hispanic residents to community policing.

Such an individual might have eventually turned up were it not for a second loss associated with the departure of JCPT: its community organizer. In Southtown Beat, much of JCPT's phone calling and door-to-door–organizing activity had been focused upon the Hispanic population. With the team's departure, the beat lost the "push" of a very active effort to mobilize Hispanic residents as well as the "pull" of effective leadership.

Third, no one worked to maintain high levels of Hispanic participation after JCPT staff left. As any community organizer will testify, a thousand small decisions make the difference between high and low participation. JCPT staff took deliberate and concrete steps to increase Hispanic participation. Meetings were held at St. Peter's Church, a central Hispanic neighborhood institution, they were facilitated in both English and Spanish simultaneously, and special efforts (follow up calls, home visits, et cetera) were directed toward sustaining Hispanic participation. Mr. Sanchez paid attention to these details, and hoped that Ms. Martinez would continue to do so after his departure. Since she, too, left the process, the remaining energetic paticipants consisted of the police and a handful of African-American residents. The police viewed their responsibility as administering community policing at a minimal level—attending meetings, scheduling them, and selecting locations—rather than mobilizing residents. In this ostensibly neutral role, they made decisions that had the unintended consequence of reducing Hispanic participation. In particular, some officers felt that the St. Peter's location was inappropriately religious for public meetings, and so they moved it to the Southtown Park field house. As mentioned above, many Hispanics felt uncomfortable and unsafe in this part of the neighborhood because it was located in the "black" section. Active African-Americans, for their part, felt that they had their hands full maintaining their own mobilization and improving relationships with police. When asked what he planned to do about the drop off in Hispanic participation, one black activist responded that "we have to consolidate the involvement of our own community, and then we [will] reach out to the Hispanics again."

A second major aspect of Southtown's deliberative breakdown was the erosion of cooperation between police and those residents who continued to participate. In the prior period, residents identified quite specific problems and strategies using a well-facilitated, deliberative problem-solving process. Each of these strategies featured specific roles for police action that officers themselves willingly fulfilled. When the trainers left, resident activists had not yet acquired the capacities to formulate precise, feasible proposals for dealing with sundry neighborhood public-safety concerns and to assert such proposals with confidence. Police officers similarly lacked the skill and imagination to develop the complex, novel strategies evident in the first period. Lack of training was one obstacle. When asked how he came to learn the techniques of community policing, the sergeant in charge of the Southtown Beat officers responded that "I didn't get any formal training. I just sort of read the general order to get the story on what to do."

With participants not yet inculcated into this problem-solving discipline, the previously deliberative process degenerated into the kind of laissez-faire discussion that occurred in both Traxton and Central Beats. Unlike those two cases, where residents exercised control or at least dealt on a par with police, Southtown officers frequently imposed their views upon residents and, more out of bureaucratic habit than purposeful design, made decisions for the group that truncated participatory problem-solving. Residents, lacking confidence in their own abilities and authority, often accepted these decisions when they might have questioned them. For example, a police offer announced at the February 1997 beat meeting that "we don't want to discuss drug-houses like we have in the past, because you never know who is at the meeting." They reasoned that gang members might attend these public beat meetings to gather intelligence and target vocal residents for retaliation. Instead, alleged drug-houses would be reported on a form, filled out by citizens and collected by police, and police would deal with the problem properties with their own methods and on their own recognizance. While it was true that many residents feared criminal retaliation and a few had even suffered intimidation for their participation in community-policing activities, there was no evidence that gang members or others involved in narcotics trafficking had attended Southtown beat meetings. More importantly, the flat prohibition on discussion of drug-houses erected a major barrier to deliberative problem-solving. There were at least two active crack-houses in Southtown, and residents had from time to time brought these up as potential priority problems. By submitting the location of these areas to police rather than devising solutions on their own, residents would be unable to monitor police progress, or determine whether the police had indeed exerted any effort at all.

The cooperative character of problem-solving also declined after November 1996. Police answered some resident calls for action with narrow police solutions—most often by increasing patrols—at the same time that they offered excuses to justify inaction on other problems. Residents, on the other hand, recognized the limitations in police responses but also failed to offer constructive proposals. An exchange that occurred at the March 1997 beat meeting illustrates the missed opportunities to develop joint solutions:

> BLACK FEMALE: On [Jefferson and 54th Street], I understand that there was a shootout and one person was shot. Why wasn't our community informed about this?
>
> POLICE OFFICER: We can't inform everyone about every crime. It's doesn't show up on this sheet because the guy didn't die. He was shot in the buttocks.[26]
>
> BLACK FEMALE: There have been approximately five shootouts and two homicides [near that address]. It seems like the police should be more involved. Its getting warm now. Those same people are still living there.
>
> POLICE OFFICER: There were shots fired yesterday. We are aware that there is a problem there and we are dealing with it with [increased] presence.

Had they been more experienced or better trained in the intended Chicago style of community policing, either the police or residents might have offered effective strategies like those developed by other beat groups to combat similar problem properties: search warrants, title-searches to identify owners, the nuisance-abatement enforcement, city inspections, and housing court. Unfortunately, no one proposed such strategies.

The following three-beat meeting exchanges between police and residents illustrate again the tension inherent in the relationship, as well as the unwillingness of the police to propose constructive solutions:

BLACK FEMALE: A while ago, there was a black man in a house [near mine], and a group of Latin Kings surrounded the house [and trapped him in there]. This was a month ago. I called 911, and a sergeant drove by in a truck, but he just kept going.

POLICE OFFICER: In that situation there is no complainant and there is nothing that we can do.

BLACK FEMALE: If you could listen to what I am saying. . . . I am looking at this out the window, and describing every detail to 911. The man could not call in because there was no phone in the house.

And:

BLACK FEMALE: They want my daughter to join a gang. They pulled a gun on her, and I don't know what to do about this. She doesn't want to call it in because she thinks that they will kill her.

POLICE OFFICER: There is nothing we can do unless there is a call. You have to take care of this yourself.

The height of unilateral police action in this period occurred when the district commander cancelled the July and August 1997 beat meetings in Southtown over the vocal objection of several active resident-participants. According to one frustrated activist:

Three weeks ago, I met with the commander for an hour and a half. He said that the meetings would be cancelled, partly because many officers were on furlough. He himself could not come because he was pretty busy. He would not move on this. . . . So I am looking at a dictator-type commander, a snide and unresponsive alderman, and I am wondering, "Is my effort really going down in flames?" I am stuck in a gear that I can't get out of here.

Last week, there was a drive-by shooting, on Sunday, at a house a block from mine. The house [sic] returned fire, and a woman's house who was in between had her windows shot out. On Monday [people in] the car came back for retaliation.

6.2.4. Uneven Institutional Performance in Southtown Beat

As in Traxton Beat, there were two distinct periods in Southtown's experience. Between August and November 1996, participatory problem-solving in community policing increased the fairness and effectiveness of public-safety institutions despite initial conditions of poverty and conflict. The latter period of deliberative problem-solving, marked by the departure of the JCPT training team, was far less successful.

In four short months, residents and police managed to solve two enduring problems that had plagued the neighborhood for years: they cleaned up the Stilps house and dramatically reduced crime and violence by reopening Southtown Park. Many mechanisms of effectiveness (see chapter 1)—directed discretion, institutional innovation, cross-functional coordination, and studied trust—explain this success. These action items were selected *fairly* through deliberative procedures of prioritization. Whereas in the prior regime, police energies were directed according to the unfocused logic of preventative patrol and emergency response, residents—both Hispanic and Black—and police agreed on particular priorities after full discussion and selected the Stilps house and Southtown Park.

Both deliberation and autonomy were substantially advanced in the first observation period because Hispanic and African-American residents and police officers participated robustly in problem-solving discussions and acted in good faith to implement the results of those deliberations. In the second period, Hispanic participation fell off substantially and the quality of deliberation between African-Americans and police decreased. Nevertheless, even in the second period, communication and highly constrained discussions between residents and police continued whereas the prior regime of command-and-control policing provided no such formalized interaction.

Does this drop-off in Hispanic participation validate the perspective of the difference theorist (see chapter 4), which doubts that constructive deliberation can occur in culturally diverse contexts? The experience of Southtown highlights how fragile deliberation across racial and professional divides can be. Nevertheless, the case also suggests important strategies for engendering commitment and participation. The keys to success in the first period included neutral facilitation, fair and open discursive procedures, training to develop the skills of participants, active mobilization of marginalized Hispanics, and top-down legitimation of community involvement for street-level police officers. In the first period, all of these were provided through self-conscious public policies designed to encourage deliberation. This dynamic follows the design of accountable autonomy. When these centrally provided supports for deliberation were withdrawn, the quality of participatory problem-solving declined. When offered, these supports brought Hispanic and African-American residents together in novel forms of cooperation that generated mutual respect and benefit to all participants.

6.3. The Discipline of Self-Reflection: Central Elementary under Probation

Central Elementary lies in the heart of Chicago's historic South Side. The school's total enrollment in the 1995–1996 school year was 727 students.[27] Reflecting the neighborhood in which it sits, the school's student body was quite poor, slightly more so than that of Harambee Academy: 92.4 percent of the students came from low-income backgrounds and 100 percent of them were black. The mobility rate of students in 1996 was a high 44.6 percent. In that same year, class sizes were substantially larger than Chicago averages, ranging between twenty-seven and thirty students.[28]

Though Central lacked the racial cleavages of the previous two cases, factions of its parents and community members had fought vigorously with one another and against school administrators over fundamental school issues, including principal-selection and the use of school funds. These conflicts prevented not only concerted deliberative action for school improvement, but even honest communication between parents, staff, and the school principal.

6.3.1. Conflict, Paralysis, and Principal-Selection

Between 1984 and 1994, the school enjoyed the popular and effective principalship of Marcy Gilson. According to participants who were active that period, she used the freedom brought by the 1988 reforms to lead problem-solving experiments that improved critical aspects of school operation and academic performance. Central initiated volunteer programs and created monetary stipends to increase the involvement of parents in the supervision and discipline of students. The school participated in a U.S. Department of Housing and Urban Development (HUD) program that brought college-educated teaching aids. In 1993, it joined a partnership with education experts at Northwestern University in their Total Schools Program. This effort applied business principles such as basic statistical quality control to various aspects of school performance—test scores, attendance, and classroom discipline. Though the causes of school improvement are difficult to determine, many in the school thought that these and other efforts produced better educational outcomes. Then-LSC Chair Nathan Bowles recalls that "1992 was the highest year [of student test scores], and we thought that we had turned the corner [of school improvement]."

Marcy Gilson's retirement for health and other personal reasons in 1994, however, cut short this experiment and sparked balkanization of this school community. The LSC faced the difficult task of selecting a replacement principal. Like some university tenure decisions, the discussion over this choice was heated—some say duplicitous—and many of those involved bore grudges for years afterward. The LSC began its search process by forming a committee, composed of twelve teachers and eighteen parents and community members, that reviewed applications over a six-week period. Beginning as deliberation should, the group first agreed on selection criteria. They wanted their next principal to (1) be an expert in reading instruction, (2) have charisma that could unify the diverse school community and provide a social model to students, and (3) demonstrate proficiency in administration.

One top candidate was a reading expert and disciplinarian. She angered some staff, however, by stating in her interview that if she were hired, teachers would have to pursue additional training. The other had been a principal at another Chicago school and had received her training in social work. Using the same criteria, teachers uniformly preferred the latter while parents favored the former. Some parent and community committee members suspected that teachers objected to the disciplinarian because they feared her harsh management style, but no one raised this point in public discussions. Participants complained that the selection process was dominated by unstated and unjustified preferences. One recalled that there was "lots of personal stuff . . . but this didn't come out in the discussion. None of their reasons came out in the discussion. [The teachers just said] 'We just don't like her [the disciplinarian].'" The second candidate, Principal Krauss, prevailed in a final vote in which all of the teachers and two parents supported her. After Krauss became principal of Central in 1994, many teachers left the school. One long-time LSC member who continued to oppose Ms. Krauss's candidacy noted with pyrrhic satisfaction that "I personally know. . . a lot of teachers on the [search] committee now think that they made a mistake."

In November 1996, the parties to school governance—active parents, community members, teachers, and Principal Krauss—were still divided along the factions that formed during the 1994 principal-selection decision. To some extent, these rifts reproduced themselves as older participants transmitted their biases to newer ones, but many of those who joined in the 1994 decision were still active but scarred by the conflict. As a consequence, the energies of the LSC between 1994 and 1996 were consumed with bureaucratic infighting and attempts by all sides to build complex coalitions: the principal with one section of the parent representatives, while one stable section of community representatives tried to ally themselves with parts of the school staff and with some parents against the principal.

Though the primary axis of contention was whether Krauss should continue to be principal of Central, no faction had attempted to explicitly remove her. Instead, they fought over nearly every other school decision. Staff and LSC morale plummeted. All sides were suspicious of maneuvering on the part of the others—changing committee meeting times to restrict attendance, using minute rules to move agenda items from full LSC meetings into closed executive sessions or to remove them from the agenda entirely, and withholding information. Much of the LSC discussion re-volved around these procedural issues rather than the substantive diffi-culties of governance or school improvement. Conflict paralyzed the body.

Consequently, the LSC had not embarked on any major systemic inno-vations since the departure of Principal Gilson in 1994. Many dimensions of the school's operation—including academic performance, discipline, and the condition of the grounds—suffered from this inability to act. The most visible signs of decay came from the building itself. Unlike the well-lit, clean rooms and halls of Harambee, Central's rooms and halls were ill-kempt and often dark. Though the building itself was overcrowded, the failure to repair water damage rendered three classrooms unusable and thus further exacerbated class-size limitations. Insufficient resources do not explain this inattention to the physical infrastructure of the school because Harambee and Central received comparable levels of per-pupil funding in their school budgets. The school also suffered from rather high chronic truancy rates; in 1996, 6 percent of its students missed more than 10 percent of the school days without excuse (Chicago Public Schools 1996).[29] Teachers and other school staff complained about being unable to discipline those children who attended class. Many classes were loud and unruly, and students often roamed the halls without supervision.

Perhaps the most damning indicators of failure were the low standard-ized test scores of Central's students. In 1996, only 14.6 percent of stu-dents met or exceeded national reading norms according to the ITBS, and only 13.4 percent met or exceeded math norms on that test. On this met-ric, Central fell within the lowest decile of worst-performing Chicago schools. While the significance of test scores, even ones as low as Cen-tral's, is a hotly contested matter among educational scholars, these scores brought grave consequences for the school's governance. The Office of Accountability at CPS used aggregate test scores to assess whether or not to intervene in a school's internal governance and administration. Begin-ning in 1996, it placed all city schools in which fewer than 15 percent of the students were able to meet national norms as measured by the ITBS on a special probation status. Central fell easily into this group of seventy-one failing elementary schools.

6.3.2. Probation as Supervised Deliberation

In the fall of 1996, school-governance participants at Central, and indeed knowledgeable observers of educational reform throughout the city, were unsure how this new program of academic probation would operate. Many feared central-office administrators would take back much of the autonomy that had been given to the LSCs under the 1988 law. How else would a team dispatched from the Office of Accountability at CPS headquarters put a failing school back on track other than by putting it in a kind of receivership? To the surprise of Central LSC members, the next few months under probation did not involve cessation of power to external authorities. Instead, the probation team forced LSC members and others in the school community to break through their entrenched lines of conflict and engage in serious deliberations about strategies that might improve the school. From October 1996 until June 1997, the probation team performed two urgent functions attributed to the supportive center (see chapter 3). First, facilitators from the team helped restore the integrity of deliberation in Central's LSC. Much like Roger Sanchez's team in Southtown Beat, they were perceived as a legitimate and neutral third party who could help school participants work through their entrenched conflicts. At least as importantly, they approximated the function of *networking inquiry* by apprising Central LSC members and school staff of administrative and classroom techniques developed in other, more successful Chicago schools so that Central might incorporate these practices into its own strategies.

When the probation team, consisting of several education and school-governance experts from CPS headquarters and an outside consultant hired to be a "Probation Manager," began its intervention in September, they did so by assessing the school's deficiencies. These included:[30]

1. Poor LSC budgeting decisions
2. Polarization and school politics interferes with implementation of instructional program
3. Teachers need intensive monitoring
4. School staff not effectively utilized
5. Lack of effective teaching strategies
6. Instructional techniques not keyed to learning styles of students
7. Teachers not trained to use existing technology
8. Staff sometimes loiter in halls when they should be in class
9. Poor classroom management
10. Poor housekeeping
11. Student work often not graded
12. Funded but vacant teacher positions
13. Poor physical plant

More fundamentally, they observed that constructive deliberations within the LSC had broken down completely. Of the many contentious issues in the LSC at the time, the continuation of parent stipends was the most controversial and heated. As mentioned above, Principal Gilson had established the practice of paying small stipends to parents who volunteered to work as hall monitors, disciplinarians, and escorts at the school. By

1995, the amount devoted to paying these parent stipends had grown to $70,000, a substantial portion of the school's discretionary budget. Members of the LSC were bitterly divided over whether they should continue to fund the stipend program. Opponents saw the program as a handout to low-income community members who contributed little to the school. They suspected that those on the LSC who supported the program had close friends or relatives who benefited financially from it, and so raised the specter of corruption. Supporters of the program, on the other hand, argued that it forged critical links between school and community and that the school could certainly use the help given the demonstrated inability of its staff to control students. Furthermore, stipend-supporters suspected that the program's opponents' real, unarticulated objections had more to do with protecting teacher job areas from volunteer encroachment and insulating the school from community monitoring than with professed interest in school improvement.

In its assessment of Central, the probation team sided with the opponents of parent stipends by stating that the "LSC approved funds for exorbitant ($70,000) parent stipend[s]." Stipend-supporters feared that this authoritative statement dictated the end of the program. In a February meeting at Central, an LSC member who supported the program asked the supervisor of the probation team whether this report was a command to end the program. In an articulate and unequivocal declaration that probation's purpose was not to direct school practices in command-and-control fashion, but rather to force the LSC to self-consciously deliberate about the best school-improvement strategies, the supervisor of the probation team responded that:

> I understand that some [in the Central community] were offended by the statement that the amount allocated to parent stipends was exorbitant. We have to call it like we see it. We normally see less than $10,000 in parent stipends [at the schools we visit]. . . . [Discretionary school funds] are supposed to be used for the kids' best interest. That same $70,000 could buy a summer school, grade-and-homework retrieval system, or an enrichment program. I am not saying that the $70,000 is being wasted, but I am asking whether you can spend it on something more effective. What you did in the past, and what worked in the past, may not be the best strategy now. You are supposed to see this [probation-assessment] report as a suggestion and use it for self-reflection. If you don't agree with it after self-reflection, then discard it.

> Each of us needs to examine what we have always done and see whether we can do something that is more effective. If you don't do things differently, you can't expect better outcomes. We have plenty of schools that move from 5 to 30 percent improvement [as measured by the percentage of students meeting national testing norms] and you should look at what they are doing. If you look

and reject, then fine. But at least you will be doing so from an intelligent and informed perspective.

With the help of the probation manager's facilitation and knowledge of best practices at other Chicago schools, several LSC members and school staff formed a committee to develop a "Probation Corrective Action Plan." This intensive version of the SIP discussed above considered the issue of parent stipends and other school strategies. Stipend-supporters eventually accepted arguments that the funds could be used more effectively and worked with previously opposed factions to develop a number of new strategies in their Corrective Action Plan (CAP).[31] Some of these strategies responded to the weaknesses identified in the probation team's assessment report, while others addressed issues that those inside the school knew to be problems but went unnoticed by the outside evaluators. Everyone at Central, including the staff themselves, realized that teachers there varied enormously in their quality. The first goal, then, was to improve the classroom performance of teachers. Strategies included monitoring the performance of teachers by comparing the test scores of their students across time and across teachers within Central, summer professional development for teachers, and formation of teacher teams to discuss lesson plans and teaching strategies. In the area of curriculum reform, teachers would concentrate on improving reading by adopting thematic teaching units, new instructional materials, and by experimenting with the popular computer-based "Writing to Read" program. To reduce chronic truancy, the LSC decided to create and fund a new position of "Attendance Coordinator" to visit the homes of truant students and to coordinate with social-service agencies. To increase school and classroom discipline, they decided to implement a hall-monitoring program, develop clear suspension procedures, and direct teachers to formulate and post clear rules for acceptable classroom behavior. Despite the severe factionization that had poisoned collective governance over the two years prior to probation, the CAP received wide endorsement. All sides viewed its strategies as promising avenues to building a more effective school and it was eventually adopted into Central's SIP without objection.

The cooperative experience of forming a CAP warmed relations among previously warring factions. Each began to recognize that the other was not simply interested in parochial gain or spiteful obstruction, but had a common interest in improving the school. The ice broke in the following humorous, but telling, exchange between the leader of the faction opposed to Principal Krauss, a black man, and a black woman who was one of her foremost supporters.

> MALE: We need some training on teamwork, and we can get training for free from [a Chicago nonprofit organization]. We aren't going to get much done unless we are a team.

FEMALE: What did you say?
MALE: I said that we aren't going to get much done unless we are a team.
FEMALE: Repeat that two more times and put it in the minutes.

By June 1997, LSC members had largely transcended their history of bitter conflict. They began to behave cordially to one another and, more importantly, to deliberate substantively on school-improvement issues rather than using meetings as occasions for gaining political position. In the last Central LSC meeting of that academic year, the agenda contained two potentially incendiary items: allocation of discretionary funds and appropriate indicators of school progress. All of the LSC members participated in a reasonable discussion of school needs, and reached a consensus on allocations that would, among other items: fund capital improvements to increase classroom space by repairing damaged rooms and to install fans in classrooms without them; fill shortages of instructional materials; extend the school's computer network; and purchase additional equipment for the science lab. Whereas a discussion of indicators of school progress such as test scores would have likely drawn accusations and defensive responses only six months earlier, LSC members used the June meeting as an occasion for thoughtful reflection on the school's weak grades—the third grade turned out to need the most attention—and on the particular grades that posed truancy and mobility problems. Finally, the principal-selection committee had agreed to renew Principal Krauss's contract for another three years. Their decision was unanimously approved by the LSC.

6.4. Beyond Decentralization: Structured Deliberation and Intervention

The deep conflicts in Traxton Beat, Southtown Beat, and Central Elementary—organized along spatial, economic, racial, cultural, and historical divisions—posed substantial obstacles to realizing fair and effective deliberative decision-making and problem-solving. But these obstacles were not insurmountable. In each case, particular external interventions altered the preferences, objectives, discussion methods, and relations of power among participants to transform domination and paralysis into constructive pragmatic deliberation. Left to their own devices, the pathologies of local governance would likely have continued to prevail. These cases illustrate not only the necessity of external support for local deliberation, but also illuminate the methodologies of appropriate intervention.

Deliberation-reinforcing interventions utilized three methods. In all three cases, facilitators imposed procedures of *structured deliberation* to improve the depth and quality of deliberations. In the community-policing cases of Traxton and Southtown beats, facilitators were themselves skilled in orderly participatory problem-solving processes from the JCPT program (see chapters 2 and 3). In Central Elementary, more reflective and structured discussion process was imposed by the CPS probation team. External pressure in all three cases, however, compelled local actors to step back from their immediate conflicts and objectives, reframe their interests in terms of longer-term and more inclusive goals, and to alter their positions in the course of reflection and justification.

In the community-policing cases, external agents also sought to *mobilize those who would have been underrepresented* in these processes. Emily Crenshaw went out of her way to organize the African-Americans who lived and worked on the west side of Traxton. Beyond mobilizing Hispanics in Southtown, Roger Sanchez also altered the meeting location and conducted the meetings in simultaneous English-Spanish translation to make community policing more inclusive.

Third, external facilitators also helped to equalize differences of power and status between local factions, and to increase the respect of each for the others. In Traxton and Southtown, the inclusion of African-Americans and Hispanics, respectively, into structured processes of deliberation helped to mitigate inequalities among residents stemming from economic, occupational, organizational, and linguistic advantages.[32] In Southtown, the legitimacy of the JCPT team and its support for resident participation in community policing tempered the professional impulse of police officers to minimize the influence of residents.

These interventions improved the integrity of deliberative problem-solving by effecting important changes within individual participants and in their relations with each other. Structured deliberation changed the goals and outlooks of participants themselves (Mansbridge 1992). Sometimes, participants enlarged their own preferences and expressed interests by becoming more inclusive of their neighbors and local institutions. In Traxton Beat, for example, west side residents expanded their conception of public safety to include not only the condition of their own area west of the rail tracks, but also crime and violence on the east side. When finally asked to do so by credible third parties, members of the Central LSC transcended historical animosities over principal-selection to collectively define a vision of their whole school and pursue it. In Southtown Beat, Hispanics and African-Americans maintained very distinct conceptions of their group interests and how community policing might relate to them. Over the course of their problem-solving deliberations, however, the two groups forged working relationships that involved compromise, cooperation, intergroup projects like the opening of Southtown Park, and the gradual construction of mutual respect and trust.

Two surprising features of these experiences should not escape notice. The first concerns the dynamics and objectives of centralized intervention.

Often, in Chicago and elsewhere, tensions between central authorities and local groups manifest themselves in attempts by the former to control the latter and the latter resisting for the sake of their autonomy. Importantly, external intervention in all three cases did not aim to impose centralized solutions or strategies, but rather sought to improve the character of local deliberation by making it more reflective and inclusive. Local governance would have been much less effective and fair were it not for these interventions. Second, a series of modest interventions and supports transformed division into fruitful deliberation. In each case, then, social conflict was not the result of intractably narrow conceptions of self-interest or immutable hatreds. Instead, at least for the purposes of school governance and community policing, participants adopted more reasonable and expansive objectives and built cooperative relationships with one another. These transformations would not, however, have occurred of their own accord in contexts of decentralized localism. They required external actors to mobilize the excluded, induce local participants to step back from their workaday conflicts and preoccupations, and ask them to deliberate in a reasonable and structured fashion rather than to simply engage in laissez-faire discussion and argument.

7

The Chicago Experience and Beyond

THIS volume opened with a puzzle: how can participatory democracy offer a feasible ideal for urban governance when the complexities facing modern administration create daunting barriers that prevent citizens from understanding, much less affecting, many of the public decisions that govern their lives? The experiences of two large municipal agencies in America's third-largest city suggest that deep citizen participation in structures of governance that empower their deliberations is indeed workable. Well-conceived forms of participatory- and deliberative-democratic governance can address some of the technical and democratic deficits of hierarchical bureaucracies that are insulated from public scrutiny and control. As an alternative to reshaping public provision into market forms, such as vouchers for public education or private security, participatory-democratic forms offer distinct advantages on the dimensions of accountability, control, and even innovation. At the end of the 1980s, the CPS and CPD developed a series of hopeful reforms that took seriously the ideals of direct resident involvement and voice, local control, and deliberative planning and problem-solving.

Reinvigorating the ideal of citizen participation required them to reinvent the institutions that constitute direct deliberation and engagement. None of the forms that we commonly associate with popular democratic decision-making—New England town meetings, town halls, blue-ribbon commissions, juries, simple devolution and local control, and the like—were suited to the distinctive challenges of drawing sustained, fair, deliberative citizen involvement in school and police governance. Therefore both the CPS and CPD engaged in a series of experiments to develop new methods to harness citizen participation and deliberation to public problem-solving. The chapters above have described that institutional design as accountable autonomy. Accountable autonomy addresses two major contemporary obstacles to strong citizenship.

The complexity of modern public action constitutes the first major challenge. Even the most basic tasks set to modern states—such as maintaining safety in a neighborhood or educating children—involve a bewildering thicket of intertwining variables, technologies, and actors. How can ordinary citizens hope to understand desirable courses of action amid this complexity, much less author effective strategies themselves? Accountable autonomy answers this challenge by developing a set of generative institutions—decentralized deliberative problem-solving processes and a supportive center that connects local groups like schools and police beats together and holds them accountable—that tie ordinary citizens to experts (e.g., police, educators) in mutually reinforcing partnerships that utilize local knowledge and elicit ingenuity. Social conflict, inequality, and outright material poverty—ubiquitous in urban areas—pose the second major challenge. How can anyone expect fair public deliberation to occur under such hostile circumstances? Accountable autonomy addresses this problem by constructing mechanisms in which civic engagement is above all a practical method of meeting the urgent needs of citizens who face such challenges. When participation and fair deliberation are rewarded with the power to improve the quality of their neighborhood schools and safety in their streets, individuals contribute to problem-solving and governance processes despite the obstacles of poverty and social conflict.

This chapter assesses the accomplishments and limitations of these CPS and CPD reforms by comparing the experiences of the six street-level case studies above, reviewing the democratic and technical achievements of these two reforms for the city as a whole, and reflecting upon their political dynamics and vulnerabilities. Two concluding sections draw out implications for theorists and practitioners. For the former, these highly situated investigations help to establish the range of application of deliberative- and participatory-democratic theory by exploring those high ideals under decidedly nonideal conditions. Furthermore, the quality of deliberation and participation depends crucially upon the institutions that constitute those activities. Abstract ideas like deliberation and participation are always made concrete by specific institutions. The character and eventual outcomes of discussion and decision-making—whether it is fair, inclusive, effective, or empowered—depend upon the details of those institutional designs. For practitioners, accountable autonomy offers a diagnosis of the ills of insular bureaucracy and strong democratic suggestions for moving forward. It potentially applies to many public-policy issues beyond urban education and public safety. The final section indicates this broad range of applicability by illustrating how the principles of accountable autonomy work in three diverse arenas: ecosystem management and the protection of endangered species; the formulation of municipal budgets in the Brazilian city of Porto Alegre; and village-level social and economic development planning in Kerala, India.

7.1. Lessons from the Street

The two preceding chapters presented six case studies in the neighborhoods of Traxton, Central, and Southtown. Those explorations assessed the extent to which institutional reforms in community policing and

school governance resulted in sustained citizen participation and problem-solving. They also examined whether such citizen engagement contributed to the fairness and effectiveness of public action and problem-
solving. We revisit those cases now by comparing their experiences and
outcomes to explore the relationship between particular initial conditions—poverty and social conflict—in those neighborhoods and the quality of participation, deliberation, and institutional performance.[1] Consider the cases in order of decreasingly favorable initial conditions.

Traxton Elementary benefited from very favorable conditions of wealth
and low social conflict. As one might expect given these advantages, the
quality of participatory problem-solving was higher in Traxton Elementary than in any of the other five cases: parents, school staff, and community members worked with one another to generate additional resources
for the school, monitor the performance of educational programs, and
support a highly competent principal. It is unclear, however, how much
the institutional reforms of accountable autonomy contributed to these
improvements in the effectiveness and fairness of school governance. Even
under the prior educational regime, before the creation of LSCs parents
at the school had developed informal mechanisms that perform many of
the same problem-solving and coordination functions as formal local
school governance.

Traxton Beat faced slightly less favorable initial conditions compared
to Traxton Elementary. Though the neighborhood enjoyed material advantages compared to the four cases in Central and Southtown, residents
were divided along lines of class and race into east and west factions. Out
of these initial conditions, two distinct periods of participation emerged.
In the first, the institutional performance of community policing was neither very fair nor effective because disadvantaged African-American participants from the east side of the beat were marginalized. In the second
period, however, problem-solving deliberations exhibited a remarkably
fair, effective, and systematic tone despite cultural and class differences.
How do these outcomes compare with policing in the command-and-control, nonparticipatory mode that preceded community-policing reforms?
As with Traxton School, residents on the better-off west side of the beat
had developed informal mechanisms to communicate with police even
prior to CAPS reforms, but these channels were not available to east side
residents. The institutional performance—the fairness and effectiveness of
policing—in Traxton Elementary, then, was slightly higher under accountable autonomy than under the prior regime of more hierarchical policing.

Central Beat and Southtown/Harambee had initial conditions in the
moderate range of favorability for participatory deliberation. Those cases
featured contexts of low resources but also low social conflict. In both,
accountable-autonomy reforms produced strong institutional perfor-

mance gains—again, in terms of the fairness and effectiveness of public problem-solving—over the prior bureaucratic regime. Before the creation of participatory channels of engagement and local autonomy, police officers in Central and educators in Southtown were insulated from residents in their communities. Residents used participatory-governance reforms effectively to address many chronic problems that persisted under the prior governance arrangements. The quality of participation and deliberative problem-solving in Central Beat and Southtown/Harambee, however, was more haphazard, less sustained and deep, than in Traxton Elementary and Traxton Beat. Confirming weak-egalitarian and perhaps social-capital perspectives, initial conditions matter. Residents in Traxton Elementary and Traxton Beat, due in no small part to their wealth, professional backgrounds, cultural self-confidence, and a host of other factors that correlate with material advantage, engaged more easily in focused deliberations with street-level officials. They solved more problems, were able to engage with officials on a more equal footing, and sustain these relationships over time in ways that poorer residents involved in community policing in Central and school improvement in Southtown were unable to do.

Finally, Southtown Beat and Central Elementary faced the most difficult initial conditions: low resources and high interest dispersion. The fairness and effectiveness of deliberative problem-solving for Southtown Beat was moderately high in the first period of observation under the assistance and facilitation of the JCPT team; African-Americans and Hispanics worked together systematically to eliminate a problem house and to reopen a neighborhood park. After this team left, however, Hispanics dropped out of the process and police officers became markedly more arrogant. Even in this period, police were still more responsive to residents than under the prior hierarchical, nonparticipatory regime of policing. This temporal sequence of intervention and high performance was reversed in Central Elementary. The first period of that case was marked by extreme paralysis and conflict. Later, however, a CPS probation team dramatically improved the quality of deliberation. Out of this process, the LSC generated a promising remedial CAP. When deliberation was bolstered through external support and facilitation in Southtown Beat and Central Elementary, the groups engaged in effective problem-solving that improved the fairness and effectiveness of policing and school governance. In these periods, the quality of participation and deliberation—and the consequent institutional performance of policing and school operations—was comparable to that of Central Beat and Southtown/Harambee; outcomes were superior to those under the prior regimes of command-and-control public administration here, but less good than in the well-off neighborhood of Traxton. In the periods where these interventions were absent, however, institutional performance in

Central Elementary and Southtown Beat was poor—perhaps not much better than policing and school governance under nonparticipatory, hierarchical governance forms.

Four conclusions arise from experiences of participatory governance in these six case studies. First, initial conditions bear importantly upon democratic performance. Participation, deliberation, problem-solving, and joint governance came most easily to participants at Traxton School, our most highly advantaged neighborhood with low interest dispersion and extreme wealth. These processes and outcomes seemed especially fragile in the two hardest cases of Southtown Beat and Central Elementary.

Second, inclusive participation and fair deliberation depend crucially upon the *implementation* of the centralized elements of accountable autonomy—the administrative provision of resources for mobilization, training, and facilitation to maintain the integrity of deliberations (see chapter 3)—especially under unfavorable initial conditions. The less-successful moments in Central Elementary, Traxton Beat, and Southtown Beat were all marked by incomplete implementation, and in particular by the absence of external correctives to foreseeable defects in participatory and deliberative processes. In the early developmental stages of these institutions, street-level participants such as residents and line-level public servants failed to grasp the basic procedures, concepts, and skills of deliberative problem-solving without guidance and training. Situations of high interest dispersion degenerated into factional competition and conflict absent such understandings. In the three high-conflict cases, the actions of a supportive center ameliorated these problems by reestablishing fair deliberation. In Traxton Beat, a beat facilitator transformed laissez-faire discussions into structured deliberation. In Southtown Beat, the JCPT team brought African-Americans and Hispanics together in joint cooperative action and tamed police arrogance. Finally, a CPS probation team transformed factional conflict into serious cooperative reevaluation of school priorities in Central Elementary. Far from a mere theoretical embellishment, these case studies show that the supportive center (see chapter 3) plays an indispensable role in the advance of democratic values under institutions of participatory deliberation.

Third, the institutional outcomes in all of the cases were higher under accountable autonomy than under command-and-control arrangements. Six cases cannot of course prove the hypothesis that accountable autonomy in these policy areas is generally superior to insular bureaucracy under any initial conditions. These experiences do, however, offer reasons to support that hypothesis. Under favorable circumstances where there are working relationships that link residents and public institutions, such as those that characterized Traxton Elementary, accountable-autonomy reforms improve governance by reinforcing and making transparent patterns of communication and cooperation between community members and local officials. Under less favorable circumstances, where relations between the local state and residents are hostile, nonexistent, or otherwise dysfunctional, accountable autonomy can create new opportunities for voice, cooperation, accountability, and popular control.

A fourth result disputes the conventional wisdom that the benefits of decentralized participatory institutions accrue primarily to wealthier and more homogeneous communities. While it is true that the most advantaged neighborhood, Traxton, was also the one in which deliberations were most fair and effective, all of the other cases gained much more from accountable autonomy *relative to what insular bureaucratic arrangements had given them*. Traxton Beat derived modest improvements from formalizing cooperative arrangements that had been in place informally for decades. The other cases, all less advantaged in terms of their initial conditions, benefited much more because accountable autonomy created new opportunities for voice and popular engagement.

7.2. System-wide Democratic and Administrative Accomplishments

Beyond the lessons of these six specific cases, have the CPS and CPD reforms been successful for the city as a whole, from system-wide perspectives?

Part of this judgment turns on whether the institutions of accountable autonomy have deepened democratic practices in school and police governance (Young 2000; Fung and Wright 2003). In this regard, the 1988 school-governance and 1995 community-policing reforms have succeeded on many dimensions. Most importantly, both reforms created new opportunities for citizens to participate in deliberations that both define the ends that these crucial local institutions should pursue and develop strategies to achieve those ends. As we saw in chapter 4, many Chicago residents have utilized these opportunities to participate in public life. On average, between five and six thousand persons attended community policing beat meetings each month (see figure 4.1) and fourteen percent of the adults in the city report that they have attended at least one beat meeting (Chicago Community Policing Evaluation Consortium 1999, 26). Similarly, more than four thousand residents serve on LSCs each year, and many more attend various meetings and committees associated with public-school governance. While these numbers comprise only a modest fraction of the total number of the city's residents, many more Chicagoans participate in pubic-governance decisions as a result of these reforms. Furthermore, policing and education constitute only a fraction of urban public life. If more sectors were made accessible to popular engagement and control in ways that the schools and police have been reformed, many others would participate.

Surprisingly, given the common wisdom that more intensive forms of political participation tend to exclude less well-off citizens, both the CPS and CPD reforms have increased the inclusion of disadvantaged residents. Participation rates in community policing, for example, were highest in low-income neighborhoods and in neighborhoods where residents were comparatively less well-educated because criminal victimization was most threatening in these areas (table 4.3). There was little difference in LSC-candidacy participation rates between schools with wealthy children and those with many poor ones. Exhibiting surprising gender inclusion, women participated more than men in both community-policing meetings and LSCs (figure 4.4).

Most explanations of participation (Verba, Schlozman, and Brady 1995) focus on the supply side of the account. On this understanding, socioeconomic advantages, skills, free time, or other resources that citizens possess determine their likelihood of participating in politics and public life. These Chicago experiences suggest that analysts and institutional designers should also be attentive to the demand side: What purposes do individuals seek through participation? Community-policing and school-governance reforms created opportunities to satisfy needs that were especially pressing for residents of poor neighborhoods. Their schools were typically less effective and their streets less safe than those in wealthy areas. Better-off citizens also often enjoy other, often private, opportunities to secure these goods and so public participation may be less attractive to them. In the instance of community policing, demand-side considerations overwhelmed supply-side factors; participation rates in poor neighborhoods were much greater than those in wealthy ones. Because the Chicago reforms targeted the needs of its disadvantaged citizens, it disproportionately attracted their participation.

Did their participation and deliberative problem-solving efforts improve safety in the streets or the effectiveness of schools generally? The case-level experiences showed how deliberative problem-solving can generate important innovations and institute accountable-governance processes at the level of particular neighborhoods. City-wide indicators of crime and educational achievement are consistent with the thesis that accountable-autonomy reforms have improved the effectiveness of policing and schools. Student test scores have risen consistently since school-governance reform and crime rates have dropped since the institution of community policing. These data do not show conclusively, however, that participatory-deliberative reforms *caused* these improvements. The technical and administrative benefits of these reforms are therefore more ambiguous than their democratic merits.

Standardized tests of students provide one common, if imperfect and controversial, measure of school quality. The ITBS in reading and mathematics is administered to CPS students on an annual basis. Students in all grades from third to eighth in both reading and mathematics increased their grade-equivalent performance over this period. Remarkably, there was steady, nearly monotonic progress at all grade levels in both subjects. While it is no surprise, given poverty and other disadvantages, that CPS students score less well than the nation's average at all grades, they have also narrowed this gap steadily over a decade. For example, while Chicago eighth graders tested at 7.3 grade equivalents in reading in 1992, they tested at 8.2 grade equivalents by 2000. Eighth graders tested at 7.5 grade equivalents in math in 1992, and 8.4 grade equivalents in 2000. Other researchers have concluded that these patterns are generally reproduced at various levels of disaggregation. So, the gap between black and Latino students and white ones has neither narrowed nor widened over this period. Beyond raw test scores, gain scores—the relative rise in student achievement over an academic year—also indicate that the CPS system has grown more effective as a whole since LSC governance was initiated (Bryk et al. 1998).

Similarly, incidents of serious crime have declined markedly since the initiation of community policing in Chicago. So called serious "index crimes" are divided into violent offences—murder, sexual assault, robbery, aggravated assault and battery—and property crimes: burglary, theft, vehicle theft, and arson. Index crime in all categories has declined since 1990 in Chicago. While property crime has declined steadily, dropping 25 percent in the last decade of the century, murder and other violent crime declined rapidly after the initiation of CAPS in 1995. Between 1990 and 1995, the number of murders declined 3 percent, from 851 to 824 incidents, while other violent crime decreased 11 percent. In the five years following 1995, the number of murders declined 23 percent, to 627 incidents in 2000, while other violent crimes dropped 29 percent.

These positive trends coincide with the institution of accountable-autonomy reforms to the CPS and CPD. Correlation does not demonstrate causation, however. Three considerations weigh against attributing these trends to participatory governance. First, student test scores have risen and crime rates have declined in many other American cities that lack Chicago's participatory structures. Therefore, other, more global factors, such as the economic prosperity of the 1990s, may explain these trends. Second, both the CPS and CPD have pursued an array of strategies beyond those associated with accountable autonomy over this same period. For example, the CPS has focused heavily on reducing social promotion through high-stakes standardized testing (Roderick et al. 1999). These strategies may also account for the observed system-wide performance gains. Third, these data give no purchase on the question of whether some other institutional choice would have produced still greater gains. Even if the CPD and CPS did improve outcomes in safety and education through participatory deliberation, strategies based upon market mechanisms or new-management "reinventing-government" techniques may have further improved the effectiveness of these organizations. For example, crime has declined dramatically in New York City. But police there pursued hierarchical and managerially oriented strategies rather than the participatory route taken in Chicago.[2]

While accountable autonomy generated clear city-wide gains on participatory and deliberative criteria, its benefits for the effectiveness of administration are more ambiguous. Though there have been substantial improvements in both areas, gains in public safety and educational outcomes cannot be definitively attributed to empowered participation and accountable autonomy.

7.3. Incomplete Politics and Institutional Instability

Recall from the historical discussion in chapter 2 that community organizations and civic associations played crucial roles in designing and establishing these deliberative and participatory reforms in the CPS and CPD. Groups like CANS, DFC, and PURE had three particular orientations and capacities that put school and police reorganization in Chicago on its distinctively democratic path. First, these community and civic coalitions possessed expertise in the fields of contemporary education and policing that enabled them to engage officials in sophisticated discussions about desirable courses of reform. Second, leaders in these coalitions were deeply committed to the principle that stronger neighborhood voice in the affairs of the municipal bureaucracies was an essential component of any reform. Finally, these groups mobilized broad constituencies throughout the city to support their positions. Though the presence of these community organizations was insufficient to determine the course eventually taken by CPS and CPD reformers, it was very likely necessary.

Once citizen participation and devolution had been established as planks of school and police reform, these secondary associations of community and civic organizations continued to contribute to the implementation of reform through their relations with both residents of neighborhoods and with high-level officials of the CPS and CPD (Cohen and Rogers 1992). Figure 7.1 depicts these functions and relationships schematically.

Under accountable-autonomy reforms, official action can be divided into the two levels shown in the left column. The 1988 school-reform and 1995 community-policing reforms devolved substantial power to street-level actors—principals, teachers, and police officers, shown in the lower

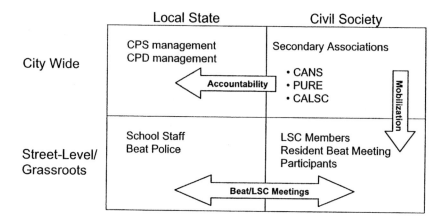

7.1. Secondary Associations in Accountable Autonomy.

left quadrant. CPS and CPD management, shown in the upper left quadrant, support, monitor, and hold these groups accountable (see chapter 3).

Initially, secondary associations (shown in the upper right quadrant) stabilized these arrangements politically by operating as watchdogs of public accountability and holding officials responsible for the implementation and development of participatory and deliberative reforms. In confidential dealings and public meetings, they criticized CPS and CPD officials when they sensed, for example, the old habits of professional control and secrecy gaining ground or when the pace of reform slowed. These groups also mobilized participants in neighborhoods, shown in the lower right quadrant, to participate in the new opportunities for civic engagement created by reform. They built civic capacity by raising awareness, providing training and technical assistance, and trying to give ordinary parents and residents the confidence and presence of mind to deal as equals with their street-level public servants in forums such as community beat meetings and LSC sessions.

In the late 1990s, cooperative relationships between public agencies and these secondary associations soured for predictable political reasons, and the role of community and civic groups in participatory reform consequently declined.[3] Looking forward, the exclusion of secondary associations has introduced two forms of institutional instability. First, these groups had been the voice of a popular constituency for participatory-democratic municipal organization. As such, they pushed the CPS and CPD to advance visions of school governance and policing that created substantial opportunities for public input and control. Absent these voices and the pressures they bring to bear, the course of reform may easily turn away from its participatory trajectory toward other, more insular and perhaps hierarchical paths. The CPS leadership attempted to reduce the scope of LSC authority in favor of more exclusively expert-driven reform strategies. Weakened but still formidable civic champions of LSCs, however, successfully defended many local prerogatives in the late 1990s. In community policing, CANS became so dependent on resources from city government that its eventual exclusion dramatically reduced its capacity to function as a watchdog. In contrast to the CPS, however, CPD officials remained steadfast in their commitment to participatory community policing. Even so, community-centered community policing rests on less secure political foundations when it lacks strong champions in civil society because its development relies upon the potentially fickle commitment of senior officials.

A second variety of institutional instability concerns the fairness and integrity of deliberative problem-solving. By mobilizing, training, and otherwise supporting individuals in neighborhoods, secondary associations conferred skills at the grassroots that increased the effectiveness of neighborhood deliberations. Since these organizations sought in part to build the capacities of residents and parents to criticize street-level officials and hold them accountable, it is natural that administrators might come to find their contributions uncomfortable and attempt to minimize their roles. Both the CPS and CPD at times tried to exclude civic organizations from the work of mobilizing residents. When civic groups are excluded or weak, however, the quality of local deliberation suffers for several reasons. Absent their assistance, some communities might never gain the capacities necessary to effectively deliberate and engage in problem-solving. City agencies might recognize the importance of building local capacity and assume responsibilities for mobilization from secondary associations. Because officials often lack grounded connections, however, they may be less effective than community groups. If official mobilization efforts overcome these obstacles, they are nevertheless unlikely to imbue the critical and oppositional sensibilities—perhaps necessary to avoid the kinds of official intimidation that occurred in Southtown Beat—that community organizations sought to instill in their training and support programs.

The CPD and CPS reforms were thus politically incomplete in the sense that they failed to set out a stable and constructive role for secondary associations in municipal governance. In the ideal of accountable autonomy, these civic groups would receive official cooperation and support for operating as watchdogs and builders of neighborhood capacity. The administrative and political reality of Chicago, however, lies far from that ideal. Its officials were unable to make a peace with coherent community actors. In one speculative future, changes could bring new leadership who would be willing to forge constructive, but still mutually critical, partnerships with civic organizations. In another hopeful future, these groups would gain the strength, perhaps with the aid of external allies or funding agents, to perform public-accountability and community-mobilization functions without official CPS or CPD sanction. Without robust secondary associations, however, accountable autonomy reforms in Chicago rest on shaky political foundations.

7.4. Bringing Practice Back into Participatory and Deliberative Democratic Theory

Whether or not these participatory reforms to the CPS and CPD endure, their experiences highlight the importance of applying the abstractions of democratic theory to concrete situations, and then revising theory in light of empirical observation. While few would disagree with this prescription in principal, democratic theorists too often neglect the lessons that practice offers them. The Chicago reforms highlight four general considerations that merit fuller attention in the development of participatory and deliberative democratic theory.

First, this exploration continues a thin strand of work in empirical democratic theory that explores attempts to realize ideals such as participation and deliberation in decidedly nonideal contexts.[4] With a few exceptions, much of the recent conceptual work in deliberative democracy has presumed or argued that such arrangements require demanding background conditions such as wealth, status or material equality, or homogeneity. Some of this work takes those favorable conditions for granted to focus on the question of whether deliberation is an attractive ideal compared to other methods of decision-making. Others advance an ideal of deliberative democracy and use it to criticize existing states of social and economic affairs. Still others criticize deliberation as an ideal for being insufficiently attentive to the demanding equality that it requires in order to produce desirable outcomes.

This exploration of deliberative democracy in Chicago has proceeded in a quite contrary direction. It examined participation and deliberation under some of the most unfavorable conditions that can be found anywhere in the industrialized world. Examining deliberation under trying circumstances advances the theory by exploring its range of application at the lower bound. If deliberation can be made to work despite such challenges, and some of the cases above suggest that it can, then the ideal of deliberation is more robust, and so more potentially attractive, than previously thought. More important than this conceptual consideration is a normative one. The subject of deliberative democracy is certainly more valuable if it can serve the least advantaged members of our society.

A second important conceptual lesson concerns the substance of deliberation. What are the appropriate subjects of deliberation? Unlike a Rawlsian account in which deliberation focuses on constitutional essentials, a Habermasian one in which public discussion generates large-scale criticisms of state action, deliberation aimed at settling moral disagreements (Gutmann and Thompson 1996), or even broad public-policy questions like the allocation of health care (Nagel 1992), Chicago residents and officials deliberated upon much more concrete and localized questions—how to make their neighborhoods safer and/or their schools more effective. Deliberation on these urgent and eminently tangible questions set distinctive dynamics in motion: who participated, what they did, and how effective they were. Ordinary participation biases were reversed—there were more women than men, and more poor people than wealthy ones. The subject of deliberation, therefore, importantly affects the normative character of its processes and thus its eventual outcomes.

Third, both theoretical and empirical students of deliberative and participatory democracy should pay much more attention to institutional designs. These concepts are abstractions without form or content until they are rendered into specific political, administrative, and civic rules and practices. Because deliberation and participation are constituted by particular institutions, the form and implementation of those institutions determines the quality and integrity of the resulting participation and deliberation. To their credit, the designers of Chicago school and police governance reforms recognized and attempted to overcome obstacles to effective deliberation and participation, such as the reluctance of street-level officials to engage with nonprofessionals, lack of skills and knowledge, and social conflict. The neighborhood case studies clearly showed how the quality of participation depended in part on the extent to which the institutions designed to support deliberative problem-solving were implemented. Accountable autonomy is one institutional structure for participatory deliberation. Democratic theory and practice would be well served with a richer menu of such alternative designs and assessments of their comparative strengths and limitations.

A fourth admonition is that students of participation and deliberation should extend their scope of investigation temporally to include not just the heated "political" moments of decisions, disagreement, and contest, but also the longer "administrative" stages of implementation, assessment, and revision. Most accounts of participatory democracy and deliberation are front-loaded in that they focus on the moments of initial decision. The pragmatically informed design of accountable autonomy and the participatory reforms in Chicago are self-consciously back-loaded. They provide substantial opportunities for continuing popular participation in the postdecision stages of local governance. In cases like those of

Traxton School and Southtown/Harambee, important contributions of participants involved implementation and monitoring. More generally, the quality of interaction in postdecision periods frequently affects the success of future iterations of deliberative decision-making. In this pragmatic action cycle, participants transform themselves in the course of decision-making, implementation, and reflection as they gain skills of deliberation and substantive knowledge, observe the trustworthiness of other parties, and perhaps embrace wider conceptions of self-interest. Because these transformations make fair deliberation more or less probable in successive encounters, accounts of deliberation are incomplete unless they include entire cycles of public decision, action, and reflection.

7.5. Beyond Chicago

The chapters above have developed a model for participatory-deliberative democracy and used two empirical cases to explore central elements of its operation. Two major factors drove the development and adoption of this model in Chicago school reform and community policing. First was broad frustration with the inability of hierarchical bureaucracies to meet the challenges set to them. Second, many felt that deeper popular participation in the governance of these agencies might improve the quality of local public action by increasing the legitimacy, accountability, inventiveness, fairness, and effectiveness of these administrative organizations. These two factors are not unique to education and policing in Chicago, nor even particular to urban governance. Three diverse recent public-sector experiments, each occurring far from Chicago's ghettos, illustrate how the elements of accountable autonomy—citizen participation, pragmatic deliberation, and centralized coordination and accountability—can contribute to the solution of a variety of vexing governance problems.[5]

7.5.1. Ecosystem Management and Habitat-Conservation Planning

Moving from municipal to federal government and from urban to environmental problems, one of the most dramatic recent examples of transformation from top-down administration to decentralized and participatory governance concerns the protection of endangered species in the United States. Since it became a national priority in 1973 with the Endangered Species Act (ESA), the federal strategy for ensuring the preservation of species has utilized extremely insular and hierarchical methods. Section 9 of that act prohibits the "taking"—killing or injuring—of wildlife designated as endangered. Federal experts thus determined which species would receive protection by constructing the federal endangered species list. They also determined the extent of each species' protection by designating its "critical habitat"—the area that must be preserved in order for it to survive. In practice, ESA regulation often prohibited development or resource-extraction activities of any sort near listed species.

This regulatory strategy has several defects. It affords some species too much protection by barring productive development that may have had marginal impact on their ultimate viability. But other species receive too little protection. The process of listing has become politicized and often drawn out because developers and property-owners often stand to suffer great economic loss. Furthermore, protection of listed species depends upon limited agency capacities. In 1999, almost 1,200 species were on the federal endangered species list, but only 120 of those had designated "critical habitats" (Darin 2000). As a result, too few species receive protection and some are nearly decimated by the time that they qualify. This regulatory process has also created intense and enduring conflicts between defenders of endangered species and those who seek to use the land on which they live.

In 1982, Congress created an option, called the "incidental take permit," within the ESA to escape these deep deadlocks (Sabel, Fung, and Karkkainen 2000; Thomas 2001). This provision opened the way for the development of a decentralized and participatory species-protection regime that exhibits the design principles of accountable autonomy. Under the amended ESA, an applicant can obtain a waiver from strict enforcement. In order to be exempted, however, the applicant must produce a "Habitat-Conservation Plan" (HCP). Analogous to the beat plans of Chicago community policing and SIPs of school reform, HCPs are often developed with the involvement of multiple stakeholders that include not only land-owners and federal agency staff, but also environmental groups and state and local regulators. These plans aim to devise durable ecosystem-management strategies that simultaneously protect endangered species and allow human development. They allow "incidental" take of species, but federal regulations also require HCPs to include measures to mitigate take and assure that human activity does not impair the chances for a species' survival and recovery.

The largest and best-managed HCPs result from participatory processes that include diverse and often conflicting interests. Unlike school reform and community policing, participants in these processes are typically professionals who represent agencies, companies, and environmental interests. As with urban civic engagement, opportunities for participation allow parties to inject important local knowledge, for instance about ecosystem features and about unforeseen consequences of management strategies, into planning processes. Including multiple parties in the formulation of plans also helps to secure their agreement and cooperation in their implementation. In stark contrast to the previous ESA regime, this process often convenes environmental and development partisans together to deliberate about the course of local action that can satisfy all of their priorities. The most advanced HCPs, for example large multispecies plans in Southern California, set out explicit numerical goals for species protection and habitat conservation, steps to achieve those goals, monitoring regimes to assess plan effectiveness, and funding mechanisms.

Though substantial power has devolved to regional and local groups under Habitat-Conservation Planning, federal agencies are responsible for supporting local efforts and holding them accountable to the legislative goal of protecting endangered species. At the most basic level, the U.S. Fish and Wildlife Service must review and approve HCPs. Responding to criticisms that it had devolved too much power without ensuring effective planning, the Fish and Wildlife Service proposed extending centralized supports for local conservation planning in 1999.[6] The agency suggested that all HCPs be required to contain certain fundamental elements, such as biological goals and monitoring methodologies.[7] They also proposed building an information infrastructure for HCPs that would improve the public and private monitoring of plans and allow sharing of best practices across localities.

This alternative regime expanded dramatically when then Interior Secretary Bruce Babbitt recognized its potential to reconcile deep political disputes. Only fourteen HCPs were produced between 1982 and 1992. Since 1993, however, these plans and their associated permits have proliferated. By April 1999, 254 plans covering more than 11 million acres had been approved and two hundred more were in various stages of development. In part because federal agencies lacked the capacity and will to impose demanding standards, the quality of plans approved over this period were uneven. A study of more than 200 HCPs revealed that less than half of them had basic features like clear biological goals, monitoring regimes, and adaptive management provisions (Kareiva et al. 1998). Just as the quality of participation and deliberation suffered from the absence of appropriate external supports and interventions in community-policing and school-governance reforms, close observers have noted serious defects in the opportunities for, and quality of, public participation in the formulation of many HCPs (Yaffee et al. 1998). Despite these considerable shortcomings in implementation, the accountable-autonomy structure of Habitat-Conservation Planning remains a promising strategy for species protection that utilizes civic engagement to enhance the capacity and legitimacy of public action in a technically complex and politically contested policy arena.

7.5.2. Porto Alegre's Participatory Budgeting Process

Whereas the two Chicago reforms and Habitat-Conservation Planning create opportunities for deliberative participation in relatively well-defined public-policy areas—education, public safety, and species protection—the city of Porto Alegre in Brazil has been the site of a more encompassing and ambitious program of participatory democracy (Santos 1998; Baiocchi 2001). The city is home to 1.3 million inhabitants and the capital of the state of Rio Grande do Sul. In 1989, a coalition of Left groups led by the Workers' Party, or PT, won the municipal executive.[8] The PT had long supported the notion of popular participation and neighborhood governance in the abstract, and their election allowed them to give institutional shape to this commitment. Their most substantial reform program was called "Participatory Budgeting" (PB). It aimed to place control over municipal capital investment decisions in the hands of ordinary city residents and civic associations. The PB is a bottom-up hybrid of participatory-democratic and representative arrangements that directly solicits the opinions and preferences of residents regarding city services and infrastructure and then aggregates those preferences into a municipal budget. Many supported this system as an alternative to allocating municipal budgets through a corrupt and clientelist city council.

At the lowest level, the PB begins in March of each year with a series of open plenary assemblies held in each of the city's sixteen regions. These meetings, often attended by more than one thousand residents, provide opportunities for direct popular review of the implementation of the prior year's budget as it affected each region. The mayor and his staff present progress on projects designated for each region, take feedback from the floor, and respond to questions and criticisms. Participants elect delegates to represent their neighborhoods at subsequent meetings. As an incentive to mobilize, each neighborhood selects a number of delegates that increases with the number of neighborhood residents that attend the March plenary. Specific neighborhood groups and civic organizations also elect their own delegates. Most regions select a total of forty to sixty delegates.

Over a series of subsequent meetings, delegates in each region meet with one another and with officials from various city departments to educate themselves about various technical details of public budgeting and infrastructure projects. They then deliberate about priority needs for their neighborhoods. They debate their relative needs across sectors such as transportation, sewage, pavement, health care, child care, and education and they discuss potential projects in each of these areas. At a second series of regional plenary meetings, delegates ratify the outcomes of these deliberations with a vote that establishes a schedule of priority sectors and projects for each region. At a third, still more representative level, two delegates from each region are elected to serve on a city-wide body called the Municipal Council of the Budget. This group is responsible for reconciling demands from each of the regions with available resources to develop a single city budget. Their deliberations take into account not only the schedule of priorities from each region, but also criteria such as each region's population and comparative need (e.g., regions with particularly low rates of paved roads would receive greater consideration in this sector). This city-wide council generates a final budget that the mayor submits to the legislative council. Because these budgets emerge from a painstaking and quite transparent process of popular participation, it difficult for city councilors to reject or amend them to capture resources for patronage purposes.

In pursuing its commitment to participatory democracy, the PT thus reinvented the central power of Porto Alegre's city government to constitute and facilitate the development of continuous neighborhood-level deliberations about how public money and authority should be deployed. Part of this local revolution required devolving substantial budget-making power to regional bodies. It also required reorienting muscular central authority in three crucial ways. As in Chicago community policing and school governance, officials from the mayor's office as well as city departments support local deliberation by training delegates and helping to facilitate their deliberations. Second, the PT has urged professional administrators in city agencies to adopt more transparent and receptive working methods and attitudes with respect to ordinary city residents. As Boaventura de Sousa Santos put it, the PT has attempted to transform municipal technocracy into "techno-democracy" (Santos 1998). Finally, the PT serves as a conduit that connects the novel structure of decentralized participatory deliberation to the older forms of city government. Through the Municipal Council of the Budget, the results of regional deliberations are aggregated into a proposal for the city as a whole, and then transmitted to the traditional structure of the city council.

Since its inception in 1989, the PB has increased civic engagement, improved the quality of municipal administration, and buttressed the electoral strength of the PT (Baiocchi 2001). Nearly fourteen thousand persons attended either the first or second round of formal regional plenary meetings of the PB in 1999. Many more—some estimate up to 8 percent of the adult population—participate in informal meetings related to participatory budgeting (Santos 1998). As in Chicago, participants from less-advantaged circumstances are overrepresented. In terms of its material accomplishments, Baiocchi reports that participatory decision-making has also been efficient and redistributive. Of the hundreds of projects approved, investment in the poorer residential regions of the city far exceeds investment in wealthier areas, and as a result of these public policies, 98 percent of all residences in the city had running water, up from 75 percent in 1988. Sewage coverage has gone up to 98 percent from 46 percent. Of the yearly 25–30 kilometers of road paved, almost all of it has been in the city's poor peripheries. In the years between 1992–1995, the housing depart-ment (DEMHAB) offered housing assistance to 28,862 families, against 1,714 for the comparable period of 1986–1988. Another example is the number of functioning public municipal schools today of 86 against 29 in 1988.

Finally, the PB has proved to be a strikingly successful electoral program for the PT. The Workers' Party has increased its margin of victory in every mayoral election since 1988, and most attribute this success to the popu-larity of the PB. Unlike the case with respect to the Chicago reforms or Habitat Conservation Planning, the PB is part of an explicit political pro-gram, in which the beneficiaries who participate in grassroots delibera-tions also potentially form a constituency to support the institution's long-term stability.

7.5.3. The Campaign for Democratic Decentralization in Kerala, India

A younger but still more ambitious project in direct, participatory-demo-cratic governance comes from the southern Indian state of Kerala. This state of 32 million inhabitants is perhaps best known internationally for its distinctive social-development trajectory. Despite being one of the poorest Indian states, its achievements in human development and well-being surpass those of other states and rival indicators in some industrial-ized countries. In 1991, for example, Kerala's adult literacy was 91 per-cent compared to an all-India rate of 52 percent. In 1995, life expectancy was 71 years compared to 62 for India as a whole. Kerala's infant mortal-ity was 13 per 1,000 live births, while the national figure was nearly an order of magnitude higher at 73 per 1,000 (Heller 2000, 8). Dreze and Sen (1995) and Ramachandran (1997) attribute these successes to the pursuit of "support-led" public policies that favor investment in infra-structural preconditions of growth—equality, education, public health, basic human needs—rather than prioritizing the construction of market mechanisms. After independence, left-wing parties, backed by robust so-cial and labor movements, incorporated these public policies into their political programs and created centralized administrative apparatuses to carry them out (Heller 2000).

Despite these impressive accomplishments, two shortcomings in the Kerala development model had become evident by the 1990s. First, the model failed to produce economic growth at the same time that it generated substantial equity. Even proponents of the Kerala model acknowledge that its progress in human development will be highly constrained absent stronger growth in the productive sectors of the economy. Second, the public bureaucracies that had created impressive redistributive, regulatory, and public health infrastructures had also become quite corrupt and unaccountable to either local residents or elected parties. Close observers decry the iron triangles of favoritism that connect politicians to government engineers and contractors (Isaac and Heller 2003).

In 1996, the Communist Party of India-Marxist (CPM) in Kerala initiated a dramatic program of participatory decentralization to address both of these major criticisms. Program architects hoped decentralized governance structures would improve productivity by injecting local information and preferences into the design and implementation of public projects in areas such as infrastructural development and agriculture. They thought that bringing the machinery of government closer to residents and making it more transparent would reduce public corruption by increasing the ability of citizens to monitor local officials and contractors.

This program was called the "People's Campaign for Democratic Decentralization." Its essential design followed the two-tiered center-locality relationships of accountable autonomy. The program devolved substantial governance authority and responsibility to planning councils located in the state's 990 villages, *panchayats*. Crucially, it shifted control over 40 percent of the state budget to these bodies, which had been without substantial revenue or power prior to the campaign. In order to receive and spend these monies, each panchayat group was required to adopt an elaborate participatory-democratic process whose stages followed the deliberative problem-solving procedure (see Chapter 2). The first stage consists of open assemblies (not unlike regional plenary meetings in Porto Alegre), or *Grama Sabhas*, in which citizens discuss collective priorities, called "felt needs." Then, more specialized groups in each panchayat form "development seminars" that assess resources, capacities, and problems of each area. Then, task forces in each panchayat develop particular project plans—including resources required, implementation details, and monitoring provisions—to fulfill felt needs in light of the contexts articulated in the development seminars. In each panchayat, the resulting projects are then combined into a village-level plan that is submitted for approval before the entire Grama Sabha. Subsequent committees and Grama Sabha meetings review the fairness and quality of plan implementation (Isaac and Franke 2000).

Because panchayat governments and residents for the most part lacked the capacities to formulate sensible plans and projects, these local planning initiatives were supported by a massive centralized education effort.

Between 1996 and 1998, 15,000 elected Panchayat representatives, 25,000 officials, and 75,000 volunteers were trained in the techniques of local planning and project development (Isaac and Heller 2003). In addition, 5,000 expert volunteers, for example retired engineers, formed into a "Voluntary Technical Corps" that worked with panchayat groups to vet their project proposals for their technical quality and feasibility. In the first two years of Democratic Decentralization, this VTC evaluated more than 100,000 projects.

In the short time since its initiation, the Campaign for Democratic Decentralization seems to have achieved impressive democratic and administrative gains on a large territorial scale.[9] In terms of popular participation and civic engagement, approximately 2.5 million people, more than 10 percent of the adult population and equivalent to one out of every three households, attended open Grama Sabha meetings in 1996. As with the reforms in Chicago and Porto Alegre, the poor were substantially over-represented. Participation patterns also reflected some traditional patterns of exclusion, however. Women and low-status individuals—those from Scheduled Castes and Scheduled Tribes (SC/ST)—were underrepresented.

Regarding administrative and technical impacts, decentralized planning has shifted the allocation of public expenditures toward basic needs such as housing, drinking water, and sanitation. Because planning processes require minimum allocations to projects that benefit historically disadvantaged individuals (SC/ST) and women, the reform progressively redistributed the allocation of public provision. Perhaps because leakage of funds from corruption was reduced and monitoring of officials by residents increased, the pace of public-project implementation seems to have accelerated. Isaac and Heller (2003) report that:

> the most readily measured physical achievements of the first two years of decentralised planning are, however, impressive. In the two years 1997 to 1999, 98,494 houses have been built, 240,307 sanitary latrines constructed, 50,162 wells dug, 17,489 public taps provided and 16,563 ponds cleaned. A total of 2,800,179 individual beneficiaries received support from the plan for seedlings and fertilisers. Nearly 8,000 k.m. of roads were built which is an astounding achievement by past standards.

The quality of local planning in the first year of the campaign was very uneven and quite low in many areas, however. Given the lack of prior local capacity and growing pains associated with any large-scale public policy of this sort, poor planning quality is perhaps unsurprising. Only time will reveal whether robust centralized training and mobilization programs can overcome these substantial difficulties.

Like Participatory Budgeting in Porto Alegre, the Campaign for Democratic Decentralization was initiated by a left-wing party not just because it was good public policy, but also because it seemed to be good politics. The electoral environment in Kerala is highly competitive and authority regularly rotates between left and center-Right governments. The campaign was in part a political innovation designed to gain popularity but also to shift the basis of political competition to lower levels of government, where the CPM felt that it had mobilization advantages. One aim, then, was to establish a reinforcing feedback loop between electoral and direct forms of political participation in which the shift to village-level participatory-democratic arrangements would create a constituency that recognized Left parties as the champions of participatory governance and thereafter support them as a way to stabilize participatory institutions. Unlike the Chicago reforms, then, the institutions of participatory democracy in Kerala have a potentially deeper self-reinforcing logic that does not depend on the fickle predilections of administrators or political elites. Since these reforms are still young and the popular perceptions about their efficacy not well articulated, it is unclear whether the CPM will be able to establish the virtuous circle connecting participatory-deliberative democracy and electoral victory that the PT seems to have built in Porto Alegre.

7.6. The Promise of Participatory-Deliberative Democracy

In his eulogy to countrymen killed in the first campaigns of the Peloponnesian War, Pericles famously said of Athens that "here each individual is interested not only in his own affairs but in the affairs of the state as well. . . . This is a peculiarity of ours: we do not say that a man who takes no interest in politics is a man who minds his own business; we say that he has no business here at all" (Thucydides 1954). That sentiment is even more peculiar, and less commonly realized at the dawn of the twenty-first century than in the fifth century B.C. The reasons are too familiar to rehearse. They include the eclipse of public life by private priorities, the complexity of government and administration and consequent necessity of conferring authority to guardians (Dahl 1989), and even the incoherence of popular rule (Riker 1982). Despite these and other challenges, commitments to deep democratic values, to popular sovereignty, participation, civic engagement, deliberation, and inclusion seem as broadly shared as ever.

The explorations above suggest that the complexities of modern governance do not antiquate these high ideals. Indeed, in some contexts, these ideals can inform distinctively effective methods of governance. The institutional space in which deeply participatory and deliberative forms of democracy can help meet the challenges of contemporary public action remains largely unexplored. Against a conventional wisdom that holds that such space is vanishingly small—perhaps empty—the experiences in Chicago, Porto Alegre, Kerala, and in Habitat-Conservation Planning indicate that this space may be much larger than commonly supposed. It may even be vast.

These chapters have mapped a small bit of that space by investigating the institutional forms, politics and operational logics, and consequences of two efforts to invent a kind of empowered participatory governance in urban public services. Fuller exploration requires first locating other innovative institutions of such deeply democratic public action, and then scrutinizing their creations empirically and conceptually. Only through this pragmatic cycle of action and reflection can we hope to understand the institutions that populate this space where practical needs meet democratic aspirations. Only with such knowledge can we advance our oft-professed but too seldom realized commitments to organize our public life together according to the principles of equality, respect, self-command, reason, and mutual understanding.

Notes

Chapter 1
Democracy as a Reform Strategy

References to sections in the notes indicate subheadings within chapters. For instance, Section 6.3 denotes the third subheading in chapter 6, whereas 3.6 indicates the sixth subheading of chapter 3.

1. The names of persons and institutions in this book have been changed to protect the identities of these protagonists.

2. Ninety-four percent of Harambee Academy students qualified for free and reduced lunches in 1998. To qualify, a student must live in a family whose annual income is less than one-and-a-half times the federal poverty line.

3. Though the bulk of education research focuses on resources or particular methods of school improvement—instructional techniques, management methods, systems of evaluation, and classroom size—several scholars have also emphasized the importance of a shared vision or "common good" among school staff, students, and parents. See Bryk et al. (1993) and Meier (1995).

4. See Bryk et al. (1993) and Meier (1995).

5. Information about this account was provided by John McDermott of the Chicago Alliance for Neighborhood Safety (CANS) and from sources of the CPD.

6. For other responses by counterexample, see Berry, Portney, and Thompson (1993) and Mansbridge (1980).

7. Albert Hirschman (1978) famously laid out the interactions between these two mechanisms in influencing organizational behavior and performance. Choice provisions and the availability of exit options may indeed enhance the quality of governance in forms of empowered participation.

8. Paul Hill, Lawrence Pierce, and James Guthrie (1997) have developed a proposal that they call "school contracting" in which public authorities would define educational missions that private charter operators would implement on retainer. This model is similar to the method of accountable autonomy, though more centralized because school missions and visions are not determined in the first instance by the citizens who use them, but rather by central school officials or by those who apply for charters and operate schools under them.

9. See John Buntin. "Assertive Policing, Plummeting Crime: The NYPD Takes on Crime in New York City," Parts A–D, Kennedy School of Government Case C16–99–1530.0 and C16–99–1530.1.

10. For an excellent review of four leading examples of state-level educational accountability, see Rhoten et al. (2000).

11. This objection is raised most forcefully by those who have examined the pernicious effects of democratic control upon racial segregation in education. See Hochschild (1984) and McDermott (1999).

Chapter 2
Down to the Neighborhoods

1. While this rough sequence of events enjoys something of a consensus among educational historians as the correct account, there is no such consensus regarding the ramifications of these events. Did the victory of the Progressive reformers constitute steps in "the development of American education as an unfolding series of triumphs, symbolizing the victory of democracy and modernity over aristocracy and error?" (Ravitch 1974, xi) Or, by contrast, was Progressive reform composed principally of white, male Protestants advancing their interests over those of less advantaged, working-class immigrants (Hays 1964)? Others see Progressive reform as driven by, and principally serving the interests of, capitalists in creating a docile, trained workforce (Bowles and Gintis 1976). Katznelson and Weir (1985) have responded to this view by providing a history that stresses working-class victories in both the content and structure of American public-education systems. Settling these difficult questions of "who benefited?" from these organizational changes lies outside of the scope of this chapter and this project. Here, we seek only to lay out the content of those organizational changes and describe the bases of their stability.

2. The account draws heavily on O'Connell (1991) and Hess (1991).

3. Warren Bacon, then executive director of Chicago United, said that "we thought of it as a cooperative relationship: the Board of Education was the client and we were there to assist them." See O'Connell (1991, 5).

4. It should be noted that the New York program broke the system into some 33 "community" districts, each averaging 20,000 students. The sense in which these districts offer local control is unclear, as each of New York's small districts is still larger than 98 percent of the school districts in the United States. For a comparative political history of the New York and Chicago school-reform movements, see Gittell (1994).

5. Data from Gallup Poll, various years, as stored in Lexis-Nexis polling results electronic archive.

6. These figures were kindly provided to me by the Epidemiology Program at the Chicago Department of Health. They are based upon the records of the CPD.

7. Source: United States Department of Health and Human Services, various years. Figures for the United States are based upon coroners' reports that are collected nationally by the Centers for Disease Control.

8. To be clear, the city as a whole is divided into twenty-six police districts, each of which is divided into between eight and twelve beats. There are 279 beats in the entire city. Each beat is numerically designated with four digits, DDBB, where DD gives the district number and BB gives the beat number.

9. So, John Dewey suggests that "policies and proposals for social action be treated as working hypotheses, not as programs to be rigidly adhered to and executed. They will be experimental in the sense that they will be entertained subject to the constant and well-equipped observation of the consequences they entail

when acted upon, and subject to ready and flexible revision in light of observed consequences" (1927, 203).

10. On this *epistemic* conception of voting, see J.-J. Rousseau in *The Social Contract*: "When a law is proposed in the people's assembly, what is asked of them is not precisely whether they approve or reject, but whether or not it conforms to the general will that is theirs. Each man, in giving his vote, states his opinion on the matter, and the declaration of the general will is drawn from the counting of votes" (1987, IV.2.viii). See also Cohen (1986).

11. This procedure is a pragmatic version of the more general deliberative procedure offered by Joshua Cohen (1989).

12. *Illinois Compiled Code of Statutes*, Chapter 105, Article 34, para. 2.4, "School Improvement Plan" (1996).

13. John Dewey, "The Economic Basis of the New Society," in *The Political Writings*, ed. Debra Morris and Ian Shapiro (Cambridge, MA: Hackett Publishing Co., 1993), 171.

Chapter 3
Building Capacity and Accountability

1. See section 2.8.

2. See section 2.10.

3. Described in section 2.9.

4. Parts of this template are illustrated in section 2.9.

5. J.J. Rousseau. *Social Contract*, I.7.8

6. This case of Central Elementary is examined in chapter 6.

7. Patricia Harvey's statement was recorded by the author at an LSC meeting on 18 February 1997.

8. Illinois Compiled Statutes, 720, Sec. 37–4 (1996).

9. The ordinance described in this paragraph went into effect on 11 November 1996. See "Amendments of Titles 8 and 13 of Municipal Code of Chicago Concerning Liability of Property Owners and Management for Unlawful Activities on Property." *Chicago City Council Journal* (31 July 1996): 27730–27735.

10. The state statute was originally targeted against prostitution.

11. This case is discussed in detail in chapter 5.

12. So, one of the most robust findings of empirical political science is that individuals of a lower socioeconomic status participate less frequently in all democratic channels. Verba and Nie write that "citizens of higher social and economic status participate more in politics. This generalization has been confirmed many times in many nations. And it generally holds true whether one uses level of education, income, or occupation as the measure of social status." See Verba and Nie (1987), especially chapters 6 and 8.

13. See section 3.2 above.

14. See section 2.3 above.

15. Illinois Public Act 89–15.

16. Illinois Compiled Statutes 105, 5/34-2.1 Local School Councils-Composition-Voter-Eligibility-Elections-Terms.

17. Letter on file with author.

18. Letter on file with author.

19. Letter on file with author.

Chapter 4
Challenges to Participation

1. Since the Chicago school-reform legislation was passed in 1988, the Consortium on Chicago School Research (based at the University of Chicago) has generated a series of high-quality reports that document the progress of LSC governance from many perspectives. Even prior to its official roll out in 1993, the state of community policing in Chicago has been painstakingly documented by the a group led by Wesley Skogan at the Institute for Policy Research at Northwestern University (formerly the Center for Urban Affairs). The author worked in this research group in 1996 and 1997.

2. See, for example, Riker (1982).

3. For an attempt to reconstruct rational-choice explanations of participation, see Verba, Schlozman, and Brady (2000).

4. Interview with Dr. Rodolfo Serna, Deputy Director of School and Community Relations, Office of Community, Chicago Public Schools, 20 November 1997.

5. Jane Mansbridge (1992). For a game-theoretic treatment of the biases in information that parties would reveal, and the skepticism with which listeners would treat information brought by adversaries, see David Austen-Smith (1992).

6. For a classic rational-choice discussion of a preference that consists of "compliance with the ethic of voting," see Riker and Ordeshook (1968).

7. This example is simply a scaled down version of the psychological account of political stability given by John Rawls (1972): "Since a well-ordered society endures over time, its conception of justice is presumably stable: that is, when institutions are just . . ., those taking part in these arrangements acquire the corresponding sense of justices and desire to do their part in maintaining them." (454)

8. Nearly every study of American voting verifies this point. See, for example, Rosenstone and Hansen (1993).

9. For a discussion of resources for political participation, see Verba, Schlozman, and Brady (1995, 270–72). On the structural-resource constraint, see Cohen and Rogers (1983, chap. 3). On the idea of falling below an absolute resource-threshold necessary to participate in democracy, see Justice Thurgood Marshall's dissent in *San Antonio* versus *Rodriguez* and Amy Gutmann (1987).

10. For an application of this idea in local democratic contexts, see Jane Mansbridge (1980). On the dubiousness of "bracketing" background inequalities in deliberative situations, see Nancy Fraser (1992).

11. See chapter 3.

12. Skogan (1988, 53). As will become clear below, Professor Skogan has recently altered his view on this point based largely upon the distinctive community-policing institutions in Chicago. See Skogan and Hartnett (1997).

13. This data set was very kindly provided by Wesley Skogan at the Institute for Policy Research at Northwestern University.

14. Personal crime rate is given as incidents-per-1,000 population annually, and includes murder, assault, battery, rape, and robbery.

15. In our sample of 270 beats, however, percentage of neighborhood that is college-educated turns out to be uncorrelated with percentage home-ownership, with a simple correlation coefficient of –0.07. Percentage home-ownership and median income, however, are fairly strongly correlated with a correlation coefficient of 0.66. The magnitude of the standardized regression coefficients (*betas*) rise from –0.18 to –0.20 for percent college-educated, and from 0.18 to 0.20 for median income.

16. When percent home-owners is removed from the list of regression variables, both percent college-educated and median income become statistically significant at the 0.01 level, indicating multicolinearity between these variables.

17. Recall from chapter 2 that each LSC has six parental seats, two community seats, two staff seats, and a position for the school principal.

18. Candidate and turnout data were very kindly provided by Mr. Doug Dillon of Management Information Services at the Chicago Public Schools. Demographic information on schools was taken from Chicago Public Schools (1996).

19. A student is classified as "low-income" if he or she is from a family receiving public aid, lives in an institution for neglected or delinquent children, is supported in a foster home with public funds, or is eligible to receive free or reduced-price lunches. In 1996, approximately four-fifths of Chicago students are classified as low-income, while less than one-fifth of the students in the state of Illinois are classified as low-income. (Chicago Public Schools 1996, 3).

20. Student mobility at a school is defined as the number of students enrolling in a school or leaving that school during a single school year. Students may be counted more than once.

21. Recall that each LSC provides six positions for parent representatives.

22. Parent turnout is given as the percentage of parents eligible to vote in the election who actually do vote.

23. There were 468 elementary schools in the city of Chicago in 1996. Election data for three of these schools were not available.

24. Fifty-six schools ranged from 0–59.9 percent low-income students, 53 schools had 60–79.9 percent, 93 schools had 80–89.9 percent, 144 schools had 90–95.9 percent, and 119 schools fell into the most distressed category, with 96–100 percent of students classifiable as low-income.

25. See Rosenstone and Hansen (1993, 275) and Verba, Schlozman, and Brady (1995, 233).

26. Ryan et. al. (1997, 31) Note that 41 percent of the adults in Chicago had at least some college education in 1995. Forty-six percent percent of LSC members surveyed in schools with over 90 percent low-income students had at least some college education.

27. See Putnam (1993), esp. chap. 4 on "Explaining Institutional Performance." On the difficulty of building social capital in areas where it is absent, see chaps. 5 and 6, esp. 177–81.

28. Measured by a survey question that asked whether a respondent would be likely to interfere if she witnessed incidents such as teenagers spray-painting graffiti, teenagers harassing an elderly person, and fights in front of her home.

29. Measured as a combination of voter turnout rate and survey-respondent likelihood of mobilizing against a neighborhood "take-away"—such as the closing of a district police station.

30. See discussion in Chicago Community Policing Evaluation Consortium (1997, 108–110). This metric of "community capacity" was the consortium's best effort to operationalize the concept of social capital in the context of community policing.

31. Chicago Community Policing Evaluation Consortium (1997, 130). Compare the figure on page 129 of that report to the figures in Putnam (1993, 151). Both figures plot cases in a two-dimensional space with social capital on the horizontal axis and institutional performance on the vertical axis. While all of Putnam's cases fall along the line $Y = X$, there is no obvious correlation in the figure from the Institute for Policy Research report.

32. See Aristotle (1891), sec. 26; Davies (1993).

33. See chapter 2.

34. In her study of a town meeting, Mansbridge (1980, 113) found a statistically significant attendance bias with respect to gender, though her theory might have predicted this. Mansbridge does write, however, that "women attend town meeting[s] as often as men, but they say much less."

35. See discussion in chapters 2 and 3.

36. Personal communication with Susan Ryan, Consortium on Chicago School Research, 18 June 1998, regarding unreleased data sets from LSC member surveys.

37. See discussion of the justifications of bureaucracy in chapter 1. See also the discussion of the constraint of complexity at section 2.3. Robert Dahl (1989, 333) has written that this distinction between expert and layperson poses a greater obstacle to democracy than even inequalities of economic class.

38. Robert Dahl calls this system "guardianship."

39. Because those procedures and methods, in turn, are widely perceived to be ineffective.

40. So far as I know, this matter has not been studied in decentralized democratic contexts. It does, however, roughly mirror concerns about "demand overload" in mass democracies as articulated by Samuel Huntington (1975), among others.

41. Of course, the self-reported attitudes of elites may portray the role of lay-participants more generously than reality warrants because the experts themselves are charitable or because they do not wish to disappoint researchers or supervisors. The surveys reported below did not control for nor attempt to detect these potential deceptions.

42. The response rate to this survey was 83 percent. Survey results appear in Consortium on Chicago School Research (1992).

Chapter 5
Deliberation and Poverty

1. Two varieties of this general criticism were examined using city-wide neighborhood comparisons in chapter 4: the "strong-egalitarian" criticism to accountable autonomy and the "social-unity" perspective.

2. These neighborhoods and their aliases also appear in several reports of the Institute for Policy Studies at Northwestern University. I was in a research group directed by Wesley Skogan, and assigned to conduct empirical investigations of community-policing activities in the three neighborhoods that appear below.

3. This discussion and related table are drawn from 1990 Census data.

4. This schema of cases is too rough to warrant further quantification, but one might think of "poor" neighborhoods as those in the bottom quintile for median family income in a particular context (Chicago neighborhoods, elementary school districts, police beats), "rich" ones as being in the top quintile, and the others residing in the middle band.

5. Data in this paragraph was drawn from the Chicago Public Schools (1996).

6. The average Chicago elementary school mobility rate was 29.0 percent in that year (ibid.).

7. See Spielman and Lawrence (1998).

8. An alternative to standard American English discussed in the Oakland, California, school system. Throughout this chapter I have relied on interviews I conducted in Chicago between 1997 and 2002.

9. Both of these names are fictitious in order to conceal the identity of the case. The school in this case, however, did have a rather generic name which it changed in 1996 to an Afrocentric name.

10. Druffin (1996).

11. The Harambee Technology Plan is on file with the author.

12. The School Improvement Plan (SIP) is a long-term planning document that each school must revise and submit every year to the CPS central office. See chapter 2 for a discussion of SIPs.

13. See figure 5.3.

14. 1996 murder descriptions taken from Chicago Tribune website; web package on 1996 murders in Chicago.

15. See the discussion of these mechanisms in chapter 1.

16. See chapter 3 for a discussion of this ordinance, the Corporation Counsel program, and central administration's role in creating background conditions conducive to successful problem solving.

17. Residents of this block had seen the author in the company of both police officers and Mrs. Rivers, and so considerations of personal safety prevented firsthand verification of these allegations of narcotics and gang activity.

18. Discussions with police later revealed that this fire-bomb was a Molotov cocktail incendiary device.

19. Tactical officers in Chicago dress in ordinary street clothes rather than police uniforms.

20. At this time in Chicago community policing, many beats had semiofficial "beat facilitators," residents responsible for facilitating community-policing beat meetings. In some beats, facilitators were chosen through elections while others were appointed by police officers. Some beats had no civilian facilitators at all.

21. In chapter 6, this mode of discussion is described as "laissez-faire" and contrasted with orderly and structured deliberation.

22. See chapter 1.

23. Letter on file with author.

24. See chapter 6 for a description of Traxton's extensive civic structure and capacity.

25. Name changed.

26. Note that both Harambee Academy and Central School had mandatory uniform policies. In both of those cases, in contrast to Traxton School, LSC members and others in the school community seemed to unanimously favor this measure, and so it was not in either case a contentious matter that required deliberation.

27. See section 2.8.

Chapter 6
Deliberation in Social Conflict

1. See, for example, Downs (1994).

2. Throughout, I have used aliases to conceal resident identities.

3. Street names on this map have been modified to conceal the location of this neighborhood.

4. On theories that busy areas tend to be safer than quiet ones, see Jacobs (1993), Merry (1981), and Murray (1983).

5. While riding with police during the observation period, I witnessed patrol officers stop several African-American youths between thirteen and fifteen years of age in this area who had previously been identified as GD lookouts for "Spike." While police did not find narcotics in the kid's possession, one did have $150 in his pocket.

6. The Black P-Stone Nation was an organization in Chicago headed by Jeff Fort on Chicago's West Side in the 1970s. In the 1980s, they changed their name to the El Rukins, but activists in Traxton still referred to the group as the P-Stones.

7. Community beat meetings in Traxton are held on the first Wednesday of each month so that residents and police can plan their schedules far in advance; most Chicago beats use some such regular scheduling practice.

8. Recall from chapter 4 that the average beat meeting in Chicago has eighteen participants, and that the figure is seasonally sensitive with most participation occurring in summer months.

9. See chapter 4.

10. The MAC-10 is a submachine gun accurate at short range.

11. In this simple process, candidates are nominated prior to the December meeting. Nomination requires only one vote, so in practice anyone who wants to stand for election may do so (he could simply nominate himself). Elections are

held in the December meeting, and the winner is the candidate who receives the plurality of votes. This process is distinctive to Traxton Beat. As of this writing, not all beats have designated facilitators, and those that do have each devised their own selection procedures. Some facilitators are appointed by their police district commanders while others are volunteers who serve by the assent of the rest of the participants.

12. Recall from the discussion of the JCPT program in chapters 2 and 3 that these trainers—from both civilian and police backgrounds—roved throughout Chicago to organize residents around community-policing issues and teach them the techniques of participatory community policing.

13. See section 7.2 for the description of beat plans and Fung (1997c).

14. Refer to the map of Traxton in figure 6.1 to locate these problems.

15. Spike was arrested in 1998, after these observations, for attempting to sell crack cocaine to an undercover police officer in a sting operation.

16. The name of this association has been changed to preserve anonymity.

17. See the discussion of cognitive templates for deliberation and problem-solving in chapter 3.

18. See chapter 3 and the discussion of Central School in section 6.3 for a discussion of how mechanisms to correct deliberative breakdown can reinforce structured deliberation.

19. For related notions of citizen coproduction of public goods, see Schneider (1987).

20. See chapter 5.

21. See chapters 2 and 3 for further descriptions of JCPT.

22. See chapter 2 for discussion of this activist organization and its role in the Chicago community-policing reforms.

23. On cross-functional coordination, see chapter 1.

24. On the mechanism of directed discretion, see chapter 1.

25. Though far less elaborate, the Parks District offers neighborhood-governance opportunities that roughly parallel those of community policing and school governance; if a neighborhood has the wherewithal to organize a local Parks Council, officials in charge of administering the park will follow their direction in programming, operations, and some staffing decisions.

26. The officer is referring to a list of most frequent crimes on the beat that is passed out at each beat meeting.

27. Statistics in this paragraph were drawn from Chicago Public Schools (1996).

28. Central kindergarten classes averaged 28.2 students, first-grade classes averaged 29.6 students, the average third-grade class had 29.3 students, and there were 27.3 students in Central's average sixth-grade class (Chicago Public Schools 1996).

29. The Chicago-wide chronic-truancy rate in that year was 4.7 percent, and the rate at Harambee Academy (see chapter 5) was 3 percent.

30. Office of Accountability, Department of School Intervention, Chicago Public Schools. "School Report," October 30, 1996. Document on file with author.

31. On file with author.

32. On the importance of having diverse group perspectives represented in deliberations, see Young (2000, 121–53).

Chapter 7
The Chicago Experience and Beyond

1. See sections 5.1 and 5.2 for a review of the expected relationships.

2. For a discussion of New York City's COMPSTAT program, see chapger 1.

3. See section 3.9.

4. In her path-breaking book *Beyond Adversary Democracy*, Jane Mansbridge highlights the pathologies of decision-making processes that presume consensus as a goal under conditions of material and psychological inequality. Lynn Sanders (1997) has explored the ways in which deliberative decision-making processes can generate unequal outcomes due to cultural and social differences between participants. Rather than abandoning the ideals, however, both theorists attempt to rescue the attraction of these strongly democratic perspectives. Mansbridge recommends a combination of adversarial and unitary methods, while Sanders offers "testimony" as an alternative to deliberation.

5. For more detailed studies of these cases, see Fung and Wright (2003).

6. Federal Register, Vol. 64, No. 45 (March 9, 1999), 11485–90.

7. See the discussion in chapter 3 on centralized provision of cognitive templates for local groups.

8. Partido dos Trabalhadores.

9. These figures are drawn from Isaac and Franke (2000) and Isaac and Heller (2003).

Selected Bibliography

Ackerman, Bruce. *We the People: Foundations*. Cambridge, MA: Harvard University Press, 1991.

Apple, R. W. "States of Mind: You Say You Want a Devolution." *New York Times* 29 January 1995.

Arato, Andrew, and Jean Cohen. "Civil Society and Social Theory." *Thesis Eleven* 21 (1988): 50–67.

Aristotle, *The Athenian Constitution* (350 B.C.). Trans. by Sir Frederic G. Kenyon. London: George Bell, 1891.

Arnstein, Sherry R. "A Ladder of Citizen Participation." *American Institute of Planning Journal* (July 1969): 216–24.

Arrow, Kenneth. *Social Choice and Individual Values*. New York: John Wiley and Sons, 1951.

Austen-Smith, David. "Strategic Models of Talk in Political Decision Making." *International Political Science Review* 13, no. 1 (1992): 45–58.

———. "Information and influence: lobbying for agendas and votes." *American Journal of Political Science* 37, no. 3 (August 1993): 799–833.

———. "Strategic transmission of costly information. (Notes and Comments)." *Econometrica* 62, no. 4 (July 1994): 955–63.

Bachrach, Peter, and Baratz, Morton. "Two Faces of Power." *American Political Science Review* 56 (Dec. 1962): 947–52.

Baiocchi, Gianpaolo. "Participation, Activism, and Politics: The Porto Alegre Experiment in Deliberative Democratic Theory." *Politics and Society* 29, no. 1 (March 2001): 43–72.

Banas, Casey, and Michele Norris. "Vaughn Says Byrd Still Fighting Last War." *Chicago Tribune*, 12 September 1987.

Barber, Benjamin. *Strong Democracy: Participatory Politics for a New Age*. Berkeley: University of California Press, 1984.

———. *An Aristocracy of Everyone: The Politics of Education and the Future of America*. New York: Ballantine Books, 1993.

Beadsley, Dan, Terry Davies, and Robert Hersh. "Improving Environmental Management: What Works and What Doesn't." *Environment* 39, no. 7 (Sept. 1997): 6–35.

Becker, Gary. *The Economic Approach to Understanding Human Behavior*. (Chicago: University of Chicago Press, 1976).

Beitz, Charles. *Political Equality: An Essay in Democratic Theory*. Princeton: Princeton University Press, 1989.

Bellah, Robert, Richard Madsen, William M. Sullivan, Ann Swidler, and Steven M. Tipton. *The Good Society*. New York: Vintage Books, 1991.

———. *Habits of the Heart: Individualism, Commitment, and American Life*. Berkeley: University of California Press, 1996.

Berlin, Isaiah. "Two Concepts of Liberty." In *Four Essays on Liberty* 118–72. New York: Oxford University Press, 1969.

Bernstein, Richard. "The Resurgence of Pragmatism." *Social Research* 59, no. 4 (Winter 1992): 813–40.

Berry, Jeffrey M., Kent E. Portney, and Ken Thompson. *The Rebirth of Urban Democracy.* Washington, DC: Brookings Institution, 1993.

Bohman, James. "Complexity, Pluralism, and the Constitutional State: On Habermas's *Faktizitat und Geltung.*" *Law and Society Review* 28, no. 4. (Dec. 1994): 897–930.

———. *Public Deliberation: Pluralism, Complexity, and Democracy.* Cambridge, MA: MIT Press, 1996.

Booz, Allen, and Hamilton, Inc. *Organization Survey: Board of Education, City of Chicago.* Chicago: Board of Education, 1967.

Bowles, Samuel, and Herbert Gintis. *Schooling in Capitalist America: Educational Reform and the Contradictions of Economic Life.* New York: Basic Books, 1976.

Brest, Paul. "Further Beyond the Republican Revival: Toward a Radical Republicanism." *Yale Law Journal.* 97, no. 8 (July 1988): 1623–31.

Bryan, Frank M. "Direct Democracy and Civic Competence: The Case of Town Meeting." In Stephen L. Elkin and Karol Edward Soltan, eds. *Citizen Competence and Democratic Institutions.* University Park, PA: Pennsylvania State University Press, 1999, 195–223.

Bryk, Anthony S., Valerie E. Lee, and Peter B. Holland. *Catholic Schools and the Common Good.* Cambridge, MA: Harvard University Press, 1993.

Bryk, Anthony, Yeow Meng Thum, John Q. Easton, and Stuart Luppescu. *Academic Productivity in Chicago Public Elementary Schools: A Technical Report* Chicago: Chicago Consortium on School Research, March 1998.

Bryk, Anthony S., John Q. Easton, David Kerbow, Sharon G. Rollow, and Penny A. Sebring, *A View from the Elementary Schools: The State of Reform in Chicago.* Chicago: Consortium on Chicago School Reform, July 1993.

———. *Charting Chicago School Reform: Democratic Localism as a Level for Social Change.* Boulder, CO: Westview Press, 1998.

Buntin, John. "Assertive Policing, Plummeting Crime: The NYPD Takes on Crime in New York City." Parts A–D, Kennedy School of Government Case C16-99-1530.0 and C16-99-1530.1.

CALFED. San Francisco Bay Delta Program. *Phase II Interim Report.* Sacramento, CA: 1998.

Callahan, Raymond E., *Education and the Cult of Efficiency: A Study of the Social Forces that Have Shaped the Administration of Public Schools.* Chicago: University of Chicago Press, 1962.

Carte, Gene E., and Elaine H. Carte, *Police Reform in the United States: The Era of August Vollmer, 1905–1932* Berkeley: University of California Press, 1975.

Catalyst Staff. "Local School Council Elections." *Catalyst: Voices of Chicago School Reform* 7, no. 8 (May 1996): 26.

———. "New Teachers Sink or Swim." *Catalyst: Voices of Chicago School Reform* 7, no. 8 (May 1996): 1.

———. "Chicago Accountability Timeline." *Catalyst: Voices of Chicago School Reform* 9, no. (June 1998): 8–10.

———. "More Candidates Sign Up for LSCs Despite Drop in Recruiting Funds." *Catalyst: Voices of Chicago School Reform* 13 (May 2002).

Chicago Civil Service Commission. *Final Report, Police investigation. Inquiry Conducted by Authority of His Honor Carter H. Harrison.* Chicago: 1912.

Chicago Community Policing Evaluation Consortium. *Community Policing in Chicago, Year One: An Interim Report.* Illinois Criminal Justice Authority, July 1994.

———. *Community Policing in Chicago, Year Two: An Interim Report.* Illinois Criminal Justice Authority, June 1995.

———. *Community Policing in Chicago, Year Three: An Interim Report.* Illinois Criminal Justice Authority, November 1996.

———. *Community Policing in Chicago, Year Four: An Interim Report.* Illinois Criminal Justice Authority, November 1997.

———. *Community Policing in Chicago, Years Five and Six: An Interim Report.* Illinois Criminal Justice Authority, May 1999.

———. *Community Policing in Chicago, Year Seven: An Interim Report.* Illinois Criminal Justice Authority, November 2000.

Chicago Department of Public Health Epidemiology Program. *The Epidemiology of Homicide in Chicago.* Chicago: January, 1994.

Chicago Police Department. *The Chicago Police: A Report of Progress, 1960–1964.* Chicago: Chicago Police Department, 1964.

———. *Together We Can: A Strategic Plan for Reinventing the Chicago Police Department.* Chicago: Chicago Police Department, October 1993.

———. "General Order 96–3: Patrol Division Strategy to Address Chronic Crime and Disorder Problems." Chicago: 29 April 1996.

———. *Joint Community Police Training Handbook* Chicago: 1996.

Chicago Public Schools, Office of Accountability. *The Illinois State School Report Card Data Book for 1995–96: An Analysis of Student, School, District, and State Characteristics.* Chicago: Chicago Public Schools, 1996.

———. Office of School Improvement Planning. *Guidelines and Format 2001–2002: School Improvement Plan for Advancing Academic Achievement Through Quality Assurance Internal Review.* Chicago: Chicago Public Schools, 2000.

Chicago Tribune Staff. "College Group Threatens Bar on City Schools, Demands Revisions to Stay on Accredited List." *Chicago Tribune:* (31 March 1946): 21.

———. *Chicago Schools: "Worst in America:" An Examination of the Public Schools that Failed Chicago.* Chicago: Chicago Tribune, 1988.

Chicago United. *Reassessment of the Report of the 1981 Special Task Force on Education.* Chicago: Chicago United, July 1987.

Children First. Exemplary Schools Program, Recognition Subcommittee. *Program Design, 1995–1996, Exemplary Schools Program.* Chicago Public Schools, 1995.

Chubb, John E., and Terry M. Moe. *Politics, Markets, and America's Schools.* Washington, DC: Brookings Institution, 1990.

Cohen, Joshua. "An Epistemic Conception of Democracy." *Ethics* 97 (Oct. 1986): 26–38.

Cohen, Joshua. "Economic Basis of Deliberative Democracy." *Social Philosophy and Policy* (1988): 25–48.

———. "Democratic Equality." *Ethics* 99 (July 1989): 727–51.

———. "Deliberation and Democratic Legitimacy." In Alan Hamlin and Phillip Pettit eds., *The Good Polity: Normative Analysis of the State.* Cambridge, MA: Basil Blackwell, 1989, 17–34.

Cohen, Joshua. "Procedure and Substance in Deliberative Democracy." In Selya Benhabib, ed. *Democracy and Difference: Contesting the Boundaries of the Political.* Princeton: Princeton University Press, 1996, 95–119.

Cohen, Joshua and Rogers, Joel, *On Democracy.* New York: Penguin Books, 1983.

———. *Associations and Democracy.* London: Verso, 1995.

———. "Secondary Associations and Democratic Governance." *Politics and Society* 20, no. 4 (Dec. 1992): 393–472.

Cohen, Joshua and Charles Sabel. "Directly Deliberative Polyarchy." *European Law Journal* 3, no. 4 (December 1997): 313–42.

Cole, G.D.H. *The Social Theory.* New York: Frederick A. Stokes Company, 1920.

Committee on Political Parties. "Toward a More Responsible Two-Party System." *American Political Science Review* 44, no. 3 pt. 2 (supplement) (Sept. 1950): 1–98.

Consortium on Chicago School Research. *Charting Reform: The Principals' Perspective.* Chicago: Consortium on Chicago School Reform, December 1992.

———. *A View from the Elementary Schools: The State of Reform in Chicago.* Chicago, July 1993.

Counts, George S. *School and Society in Chicago.* New York: Harcourt, Brace, and Co., 1928.

Crenson, Matthew. *Neighborhood Politics.* Cambridge, MA: Harvard University Press, 1983.

Dahl, Robert. "Decision Making in a Democracy: The Supreme Court as a National Policy Maker." *Journal of Public Law* 6, no. 2 (Fall 1957): 279–95.

———. "The City in the Future of Democracy." *American Political Science Review.* 61, no. 4 (Dec. 1967): 953–70.

———. *Polyarchy: Participation and Opposition.* New Haven: Yale University Press, 1971.

———. *A Preface to Economic Democracy.* Berkeley: University of California Press, 1985.

———. *Democracy and Its Critics.* New Haven: Yale University Press, 1989.

Dahl, Robert A. and Edward R. Tufte. *Size and Democracy.* Stanford: Stanford University Press, 1973.

Darin, Thomas F. "Designating Critical Habitat Under the Endangered Species Act: Habitat Protection Versus Agency Discretion." *Harvard Environmental Law Review* 24, no. 1 (2000): 209–35.

Davies, J. K. *Democracy and Classical Greece.* Cambridge, MA: Harvard University Press, 1993.

Davis, Mike. *City of Quartz: Excavating the Future in Los Angeles.* New York: Vintage Books, 1990.

Designs for Change. *The Bottom Line: Chicago's Failing Schools and How to Save Them.* Chicago: Designs for Change, 1985.

———. *Shattering the Stereotypes: Candidate Participation in the Chicago Local School Council Elections.* Chicago: Designs for Change, 1989.

———. *The Untold Story: Candidate Participation in the 1991 Chicago Local School Council Elections.* Chicago: Designs for Change, October 1991.

Devine, Edward T. "The Social Unit in Cincinnati: An Experiment in Organization." National Social Unit Conference. Cincinnati: 1919.

Dewey, John. "The Reflex Arc Concept in Psychology." *Psychological Review* 3 (1896): 357–70.

———. *Democracy and Education: An Introduction to the Philosophy of Education.* New York: Free Press, 1916.

———. *The Public and Its Problems.* Athens, OH: Ohio University Press, 1927.

———. *Liberalism and Social Action.* New York: G. P. Putnam's Sons, 1935.

Dorf, Michael, and Charles Sabel. "A Constitution of Democratic Experimentalism." *Columbia Law Review* 98, no. 2 (March 1998): 267–473.

Downs, Anthony. "An Economic Theory of Political Action in a Democracy." *Journal of Political Economy* 65 (1957): 135–50.

———. *Inside Bureaucracy.* Boston: Little, Brown, 1967.

———. *New Visions for Metropolitan America.* Washington, DC: Brookings Institution, 1994.

Dreze, Jean, and Amartya Sen. *Hunger and Public Action.* Oxford: Clarendon Press, 1989.

———. *India: Economic Development and Social Opportunity.* New York: Oxford University Press, 1995.

Druffin, Elizabeth. "Direct Instruction Making Waves." *Catalyst: Voices of Chicago School Reform* 7, no. 1 (September 1996).

Druffin, Elizabeth. "Spotlight Brings Focus: One School's Probation Story." *Catalyst: Voices of Chicago School Reform* 9, no. 9 (June 1998): 12–15.

Dryzek, John. *Discursive Democracy: Politics, Policy, and Political Science.* Cambridge: Cambridge University Press, 1990.

Dworkin, Ronald. *Taking Rights Seriously.* Cambridge, MA: Harvard University Press, 1977.

———. "Liberalism." In Stuart Hampshire, eds. *Public and Private Morality* (Cambridge: Cambridge University Press, 1978), 113–43.

———. "The Forum of Principle." *New York University Law Review* 56, nos. 2–3 (May–June 1981): 469–518.

———. "What is Equality? Part 4: Political Equality." *University of San Francisco Law Review* 22, no. 1 (Fall 1987): 1–30.

Easton, John Q., Todd Rosenkranz, and Anthony S. Bryk. *Annual CPS Test Trend Review, 2000.* Chicago: Consortium on Chicago School Research, 2001.

Ely, John Hart. *Democracy and Distrust: A Theory of Judicial Review.* Cambridge, MA: Harvard University Press, 1980.

Erie, Stephen P. *Rainbow's End: Irish-Americans and the Dilemmas of Urban Machine Politics, 1840–1985.* Berkeley: University of California Press, 1988.

Etzioni, Amitai. *The Spirit of Community: The Reinvention of American Society.* New York: Touchstone, 1993.

Evans, Karen G. "Reclaiming John Dewey: Democracy, Inquiry, Pragmatism, and Public Management." *Administration & Society* 32, no. 3 (July 2000): 308–28.

Fearon, James D. "Deliberation as Discussion." In *Deliberative Democracy*, ed. Jon Elster. Cambridge: Cambridge University Press, 1998, 44–68.

Fishkin, James. *Democracy and Deliberation: New Directions for Democratic Reform*. New Haven: Yale University Press, 1991.

———. *Voice of the People: Public Opinion and Democracy*. New Haven: Yale University Press, 1995.

Fogelson, Robert M. *Big-City Police*. Cambridge, MA: Harvard University Press, 1977.

Follett, Mary Parker. "Community is a Process." *Philosophic Review* 28, no. 6 (Nov. 1919): 576–88.

———. *Creative Experience*. New York: Longmans, Green, and Co., 1930.

Forester, John. *The Deliberative Practitioner: Encouraging Participatory Planning Processes*. Cambridge, MA: MIT Press, 1999.

Foucault, Michel. *Power/Knowledge: Selected Interviews and Other Writings, 1972–1977*. Trans. and ed. Colin Gordon. (New York: Pantheon, 1980).

———. *Discipline and Punish: The Birth of the Prison*. Trans. Alan Sheridan. New York: Vintage Books, 1995.

Fraser, Nancy. "Rethinking the Public Sphere: A Contribution to the Critique of Actually Existing Democracy." In *Habermas and the Public Sphere*. Ed. Craig Calhoun, 109–42. Cambridge, MA: MIT Press, 1992.

Friedman, Milton. *Capitalism and Freedom*. Chicago: University of Chicago Press, 1962.

Friedman, Warren. *Building on the Progress: Reason for Hope/Room For Doubt—The Community Role in Community Policing*. Chicago: Chicago Alliance for Neighborhood Safety, 1996.

———. "Research, Organizing, and the Campaign for Community Policing in Chicago (Case Study 23)." In *Building Community: Social Science and Action*. ed. Philip Nyden, Anne Figert, Mark Shibley, and Darryl Burrows. Thousand Oaks, CA: Pine Forge Press, 1997, 202–9.

Friedman, Warren, and Karen Matteo. *Police Service in Chicago: 911, Dispatch Policy, and Neighborhood Oriented Alternatives*. Chicago: Chicago Alliance for Neighborhood Safety, August 1988.

Friedrich, Carl. *Constitutional Government and Democracy*. Boston: Ginn and Co., 1950.

Fukuyama, Francis. "The End of History?" *National Interest* 16 (Summer 1989): 3–18.

Fung, Archon. "Build Them Up or Tear Them Down? Solving Problem Buildings." *Neighborhoods* 3, no. 2 (Summer 1997a): 1, 8–9.

———. "Englewood Residents, Police Clean Up Nuisance Building." *Neighborhoods* 3, no. 2 (Summer 1997b): 5.

———. "Residents Can Use Police General Order to Solve Specific Neighborhood Problems." *Neighborhoods* 3, no. 1 (Spring 1997c): 1, 5, 9–10.

———. "District Advisory Councils Searching for Community Policing Roles." *Neighborhoods* 3, no. 1 (Spring 1997d): 6–8.

———. "Contract Expired: Is Chicago Poised to Take the Community Out of Community Policing?" *Neighborhood Works* (March/April 1997e): 8–9.

Fung, Archon, and Erik Olin Wright. "Deepening Democracy: Innovations in Empowered Participatory Governance." *Politics and Society* 29, no. 1 (March 2001): 5–42.

———. *Deepening Democracy: Institutional Innovations in Empowered Participatory Governance.* London: Verso Press, 2003.

Galston, William A. "Salvation Through Participation: John Dewey and the Religion of American Democracy." *Raritan* 12, no. 3 (Winter 1993): 144–55.

Gardner, Howard. *Multiple Intelligences: The Theory in Practice.* New York: Basic Books, 1993.

Gastil, John. *Democracy in Small Groups: Participation, Decision Making, and Communication.* Philadelphia: New Society Publishers, 1993.

Geuss, Raymond. *The Idea of a Critical Theory: Habermas and the Frankfurt School.* Cambridge University Press, 1981.

Gittell, Marilyn. "School Reform in New York and Chicago: Revisiting the Ecology of Local Games." *Urban Affairs Quarterly* 30, no. 1 (Sept. 1994): 136–51.

Glendon, Mary Ann. *Abortion and Divorce in Western Law: American Failures and European Challenges.* Cambridge, MA: Harvard University Press, 1987.

———. *Rights Talk: The Impoverishment of Political Discourse.* New York: Free Press, 1991.

Goldstein, Herman. *Problem-Oriented Policing.* Philadelphia: Temple University Press, 1992.

Graham, Patricia Albjerg. "Assimilation, Adjustment, and Access: An Antiquarian View of American Education." In *Learning from the Past: What History Teaches Us About School Reform.* Baltimore: Johns Hopkins University Press, 1995.

Greenberg, Edward S. *Workplace Democracy: The Political Effects of Participation.* Ithaca: Cornell University Press, 1986.

Griffin, Jean Latz, and Thomas Hardy. "A Lesson Learned At Last? Old School-Strike Tactics Likely To Backfire This Time." *Chicago Tribune*, 13 September 1987.

Grinc, Randolph M. " 'Angels in Marble': Problems in Stimulating Community Involvement in Community Policing." *Crime and Delinquency* 40, no. 3 (July 1994): 437–68.

Guinier, Lani. "Second Proms and Second Primaries: the Limits of Majority Rule." *Boston Review* 17, no. 5 (Sept.–Oct. 1992): 32–34.

Gunderson, Adolf. *The Environmental Promise of Democratic Deliberation.* Madison: University of Wisconsin Press, 1995.

Gutmann, Amy. *Democratic Education.* Princeton: Princeton University Press, 1987.

Gutmann, Amy, and Dennis Thompson. *Democracy and Disagreement: Why Moral Conflict Cannot Be Avoided in Politics, and What Can Be Done About It.* Cambridge, MA: Harvard University Press, 1996.

Habermas, Jürgen. *Legitimation Crisis.* Trans. Thomas McCarthy. Boston: Beacon Press, 1975.

———. *The Structural Transformation of the Public Sphere: An Inquiry into a Category of Bourgeoise Society.* Cambridge, MA: MIT Press, 1989.

———. "Further Reflections on the Public Sphere." In *Habermas and the Public Sphere*, ed. Craig Calhoun, Cambridge, MA: MIT Press, 1992), 421–61.

———. "Three Normative Models of Democracy." In *Democracy and Difference: Contesting the Boundaries of the Political,* ed. Seyla Benhabib. Princeton: Princeton University Press, 1996, 21–30.

———. *Between Facts and Norms: Contributions to a Discourse Theory of Law and Democracy.* Trans. William Rehg. Cambridge, MA: MIT Press, 1996.

Hamilton, Alexander, James Madison, and John Jay. *The Federalist Papers.* Edited with an introduction by Garry Wills (New York: Bantam Books, 1982).

Handler, Joel F. "Dependent People, the State, and the Modern/Postmodern Search for the Dialogic Community." *UCLA Law Review* 35, no. 6 (Aug. 1988): 999–1113.

———. *Down from Bureaucracy: The Ambiguity of Privatization and Empowerment.* Princeton: Princeton University Press, 1996.

Harper, William R., Chairman. *Report of the Educational Commission of the City of Chicago.* Chicago: R. R. Donnelley and Sons, 1898.

Havighurst, Robert J. *The Public Schools of Chicago: A Survey for the Board of Education of the City of Chicago.* Chicago: Board of Education of the City of Chicago, 1964.

Hayek, Fredrick. "The Constitution of a Liberal State." *Il Politico* 32, no. 3 (1967): 455–60.

Hays, Samuel P. "The Politics of Reform in Municipal Government in the Progressive Era." *Pacific Northwest Quarterly* 55 (Oct. 1964): 157–69.

Heard, Jacquelyn, and John Kass. "Skyway Money to Aid City; Use of Police Grant Ripped." *Chicago Tribune.* 2 October 1996.

Heller, Patrick. *The Labor Of Development: Workers and the Transformation of Capitalism in Kerala, India.* Ithaca: Cornell University Press, 2000.

Herrick, Mary. *The Chicago Schools: A Social and Political History.* Beverly Hills, CA: Sage Publications, 1971.

Hess, G. Alfred. *School Restructuring Chicago Style.* Newbury Park, CA: Crown Press, 1991.

Hill, Paul T., Lawrence C. Pierce, and James W. Guthrie. *Reinventing Public Education: How Contracting Can Transform America's Schools.* Chicago: University of Chicago Press, 1997.

Hirschman, Albert. *Exit, Voice, and Loyalty.* Cambridge, MA: Harvard University Press, 1978.

Hirst, Paul. *Associative Democracy: New Forms of Economic and Social Governance.* Amherst, MA: University of Amherst Press, 1994.

Hochschild, Jennifer L. *The New American Dilemma: Liberal Democracy and School Desegregation.* New Haven: Yale University Press, 1984.

Hofstadter, Richard. *The Age of Reform: From Bryan to F.D.R.* New York: Alfred A. Knopf, 1956.

Horkheimer, Max, and Theodor Adorno. *Dialectic of Enlightenment.* New York: Continuum, 1972.

Huntington, Samuel P. *Crisis of Democracy.* New York: New York University Press, 1975.

Illinois Department of Education. *Annual Report of the Superintendent of Schools.* Chicago: 1924.

Illinois State Police. Illinois Uniform Crime Reporting Program. *Crime in Illinois.* Springfield: Illinois State Police, 2000.

Isaac, T. M. Thomas, with Richard Franke. *Local Democracy and Development: The People's Campaign for Decentralized Planning in Kerala.* New Delhi: Left World Books, 2000.

Isaac, T. M. Thomas, and Patrick Heller. "Democracy and Development: Decentralized Planning in Kerala." In Archon Fung and Erik Olin Wright, eds. *Deepening Democracy: Institutional Innovations in Empowered Participatory Governance.* London: Verso Press, 2003. 77–110.

Jacobs, Jane. *The Death and Life of Great American Cities.* New York: Modern Library, 1993.

James, Frank. "Community Policing Program Expanded to Entire City." *Chicago Tribune.* 8 March 1994.

James, William. "Pragmatism." In *Pragmatism and the Meaning of Truth.* Cambridge, MA: Harvard University Press, 1975.

Jones, M. Gail, Brett D. Jones, Belinda Hardin, Lisa Chapman, Tracy Yarbrough, and Marcia Davis. "The Impact of High Stakes Testing on Teachers and Students in North Carolina." *Phi Delta Kappan,* November 1999: 199–203.

Kareiva, Peter et. al. *Using Science in Habitat Conservation Planning.* Santa Barbara: University of California, Santa Barbara, National Center for Ecological Analysis and Synthesis, 1998.

Kateb, George. "The Moral Distinctiveness of Representative Democracy." *Ethics* 91 April 1981: 357–74.

Katz, Michael B. *Reconstructing American Education.* Cambridge, MA: Harvard University Press, 1987.

Katznelson, Ira, and Margaret Weir. *Schooling for All: Race, Class, and the Decline of the Democratic Ideal.* New York: Basic Books, 1985.

Keith Mckenzie, et al. v. City Of Chicago, et al., United States Court of Appeals for the Seventh Circuit. 118 F.3d 552 (1997) U.S. App. LEXIS 18832.

Kelling, George L., Tony Pate, Duane Dieckman, and Charles E. Brown. *The Kansas City Preventative Patrol Experiment: A Summary Report.* Washington, DC, 1974.

Kelling, George L., and Catherine M. Coles, *Fixing Broken Windows: Restoring Order And Reducing Crime In Our Communities.* New York: Martin Kessler Books/Free Press, 1996.

Kotler, Milton. *Neighborhood Government.* New York: Bobbs-Merrill, 1969.

Kozol, Jonathan. *Savage Inequalities: Children in America's Schools.* New York: Crown Publishers, 1991.

Kymlicka, William. *Contemporary Political Philosophy: An Introduction.* Oxford: Clarendon Press, 1990.

Lasch, Christopher. *The Revolt of the Elites and the Betrayal of Democracy.* New York: W. W. Norton, 1995.

Lawrence, Curtis. "They'd Bag Cul-de-Sacs: North Beverly Newsletter Airs Neighbors' Anger." *Chicago Sun-Times*. 4 January 1988.

Levi, Margaret. "Social and Unsocial Capital: A Review Essay of Robert Putnam's 'Making Democracy Work'," *Politics and Society* 24 (1996): 45–55.

Lijphart, Arend. "Unequal Participation: Democracy's Unsolved Dilemma." *American Political Science Review* 91, no. 1 (March 1997): 1–14.

Lindberg, Richard C. *To Serve and Collect: Chicago Politics and Police Corruption from the Lager Beer Riot to the Summerdale Scandal*. New York: Praeger, 1991.

Lindblom, Charles. "The Science of Muddling Through." *Public Administration Review* 19, no. 2 (Spring 1959): 78–88.

Lippman, Walter. *The Phantom Public: A Sequel to "Public Opinion."* New York: Macmillan Company, 1925.

Lipset, Seymour Martin. *Political Man: The Social Bases of Politics*. Garden City, NY: Doubleday, 1960.

Lipsky, Michael. *Street-Level Bureaucracy: Dilemma of the Individual in the Public Services*. New York: Russell Sage Foundation, 1980.

Locke, John. *Two Treatises of Government*. Ed. Peter Laslett. New York: Cambridge University Press, 1960.

Lowi, Theodore. *The End of Liberalism: The Second Republic of the United States*. New York: W. W. Norton, 1979.

Lukes, Steven. *Power: A Radical View*. New York: Macmillan Press, 1983.

Mahtesian, Charles. "Handing the Schools to City Hall: Desperate to Bring Some Accountability to Their School Systems, Cities are Turning back to a 19th-Century Idea: Put the Mayor in Charge." *Governing Magazine* 10 (October 1996): 35–38.

Mansbridge, Jane. *Beyond Adversary Democracy*. New York: Basic Books, 1980.

———. "A Deliberative Theory of Interest Transformation." In *The Politics of Interests: Interest Groups Transformed*. Boulder, CO: Westview Press, 1992, 32–57.

———. "Practice-Thought-Practice." In Archon Fung and Erik Olin Wright, eds. *Deepening Democracy: Institutional Innovations in Empowered Participatory Governance*. London: Verso Press, 2003, 175–99.

Maple, Jack. *The Crime Fighter: Putting the Bad Guys Out of Business*. New York: Doubleday, 1999.

March, James G. "Bounded Rationality, Ambiguity, and the Engineering of Choice." *Bell Journal of Economics* 9 (1978): 587–608.

Martin, Andrew. "Daley Defends Gang-Loitering Crackdown." *Chicago Tribune*. 16 July 1998.

Martinez, Michael. "Probation on Trial. One School's Journey." *Chicago Tribune*. 1 December 1996.

Mattson, Kevin. *Creating a Democratic Public: The Struggle for Urban Participatory Democracy During the Progressive Era*. University Park, PA: Pennsylvania State University Press, 1998.

McCubbins, Mathew D. and Thomas Schwartz. "Congressional Oversight Overlooked: Police Patrols versus Fire Alarms." *American Journal of Political Science* 28 (1984): 165–79.

McDermott, Kathryn A. *Controlling Public Education: Localism vs. Equity.* Lawrence: University Press of Kansas, 1999.

McKersie, William S. "Private Funding Down for LSC Elections" *Catalyst: Voices of Chicago School Reform* 7, no. 6 (March 1996): 15.

McNeil, Linda, and Angela Valenzuela. "The Harmful Impact of the TAAS System of Testing in Texas: Beneath the Accountability Rhetoric." Unpublished manuscript, Harvard University Civil Rights Project, January 6, 2000.

Meier, Deborah. *The Power of their Ideas.* Boston: Beacon Press, 1995.

———. *Can Standards Save Public Education?* Boston: Beacon Press, 2000.

Merry, Sally E. "Defensible Space Undefended: Social Factors in Crime Control through Environmental Design." *Urban Affairs Quarterly* 16, no. 4 (June 1981): 397–422.

Michels, Robert. *Political Parties: A Sociological Study of the Oligarchical Tendencies of Modern Democracy.* Introduction by Seymour Martin Lipset, translated by Eden and Cedar Paul. New York: Free Press, 1962.

Mill, John Stuart. *Utilitarianism.* Indianapolis: Hackett Publishing Co., 1979.

———. "On Liberty." In *On Liberty and Other Writings.* Ed. Stephan Collini. Cambridge: Cambridge University Press, 1989, 1–116.

———. *Considerations on Representative Government.* New York: Prometheus Books, 1991.

Mirel, Jeff. "What History Can Teach Us About School Decentralization." *Network News and Views,* 9, no. 8 (1990): 40–47.

Montesquieu Charles-Louis de Secondat, *The Spirit of the Laws.* Trans. and ed. Anne. M. Cohler, Basia Carolyn Miller, and Harold Samuel Stone. Cambridge: Cambridge University Press, 1989.

Mooney-Melvin, Patricia. " 'A Cluster of Interlacing Communities': The Cincinnati Social Unit Plan and Neighborhood Organization, 1900–20." In *Community Organization for Urban Social Change: A Historical Perspective.* Westport, CT: Greenwood Press, 1981, 59–88.

Moore, Donald E. *The Case for Parent and Community Involvement.* Chicago: Designs for Change, Oct. 1991.

Murray, Charles A. "The Physical Environment and Community Control of Crime." In James Q. Wilson ed. *Crime and Public Policy.* New Brunswick, NJ: Transaction Books, 1983: 107–22.

Nagel, Jack H. *Participation.* New York: Prentice Hall, 1987.

———. "Combining Deliberation and Fair Representation in Community Health Decisions." *University of Pennsylvania Law Review* 140, no. 5 (May 1992): 1965–85.

National Center for Health Statistics, Centers for Disease Control. *Monthly Vital Statistics Report* 45, no. 3(S)2 (4 October 1996).

National Commission for the Defense of Democracy through Education of the National Education Association of the United States. *Certain Personnel Practices in the Chicago Public Schools: Report of an Investigation.* Washington, DC: National Commission for the Defense of Democracy through Education of the National Education Association of the United States, 1945.

National Commission on Excellence in Education., *A Nation at Risk.* Washington, DC: Government Printing Office, 1983.

National Research Council. *High Stakes: Testing for Tracking, Promotion, and Graduation.* Ed. Jay P. Hubert and Robert M. Hauser. Washington, DC: National Academy Press, 1999.

Nozick, Robert. *Anarchy, State, and Utopia.* New York: Basic Books, 1974.

O'Connell, Mary. *School Reform Chicago Style: How Citizens Organized to Change Public Policy.* Chicago: Center for Neighborhood Technology, Spring 1991.

Okin, Susan Moller. *Justice, Gender, and the Family.* New York: Basic Books, 1989.

Oliver, Eric. *Democracy in Suburbia.* Princeton: Princeton University Press, 2001.

Olsen, Mancur. *The Logic of Collective Action: Public Goods and the Theory of Groups.* Cambridge, MA: Harvard University Press, 1965.

Orfield, Gary, and Mindy Kornhaber, eds. *Raising Standards or Raising Barriers: Inequality and High-Stakes Testing in Public Education.* New York: Century-Foundation Press, 2001.

Osborne, David, and Ted Gaebler. *Reinventing Government: How the Entrepreneutrial Spirit Is Transforming the Public Sector.* Reading, MA: Addison-Wesley, 1992.

Pateman, Carole. *Participation and Democratic Theory.* Cambridge: Cambridge University Press, 1970.

Pearson, Rick, and John Kass. "GOP Drop Schools in Daley's Lap." *Chicago Tribune.* 25 May 1995.

Peirce, Charles S. "The Fixation of Belief." *Popular Science Monthly* 12 (November 1877): 1–15.

———. "How to Make Our Ideas Clear." *Popular Science Monthly* 12 (January 1878): 286–302.

Pelletier, David. "Shaping of Collective Values Through Deliberative Democracy: An Empirical Study from New York's North Country." *Policy Sciences* 32, no. 2 (1999): 103–31.

Pennock, J. Roland. *Democratic Political Theory.* Princeton: Princeton University Press, 1979.

Peterson, David. "Racism is the Reason for Traffic Barriers." *Chicago Sun-Times* 19 January 1998: 28.

Peterson, Paul E. *School Politics Chicago Style.* Chicago: University of Chicago Press, 1976.

Peterson, Virgil W. *Report on Chicago Crime for 1959.* Chicago: Chicago Crime Commission, 1959.

Phillips, Anne. *Democracy and Difference.* University Park, PA: Pennsylvania State University Press, 1993.

———. "Dealing with Difference: A Politics of Ideas, or a Politics of Presence." In *Democracy and Difference: Contesting the Boundaries of the Political,* ed. Selya Benhabib. Princeton: Princeton University Press, 1996, 139–52.

Phillips, Wilbur C. "The Social Unit in 1920: A Presentation of the National Program, and the Discussion." National Social Unit Conference. Cincinnati, 1919.

Pick, Grant. "Central Office Gets More Money, Power." *Catalyst: Voices of Chicago School Reform* 8, no. 4 (December 1996): 13–14.

Piore, Michael J. and Charles F. Sabel. *The Second Industrial Divide: Possibilities for Prosperity.* New York: Basic Books, 1984.

Pitkin, Hanna Fenichel. "Justice: On Relating Public and Private." *Political Theory* 9, no. 3 (Aug. 1981): 327–52.

Pitkin, Hanna Fenichel, and Sara Shumer. "On Participation." *Democracy* 2, no. 4 (Fall 1982): 43–54.

Piven, Francis Fox and Richard A. Cloward. *Poor People's Movements: Why They Succeed, How They Fail.* New York: Pantheon, 1977.

Przeworski, Adam. *Capitalism and Social Democracy.* Cambridge: Cambridge University Press, 1985.

Putnam, Robert D. *Making Democracy Work: Civic Traditions in Modern Italy.* Princeton: Princeton University Press, 1993.

———. "Bowling Alone: Democracy in America at the End of the Twentieth Century." Paper Presented at the Nobel Symposium on Democracy's Victory and Crisis, Uppsala, Sweden, 1994.

———. "Bowling Alone: America's Declining Social Capital." *Journal of Democracy* 6, no. 1 (January 1995): 65–79.

———. "The Strange Disappearance of Civil Society." *The American Prospect* 24 (Winter 1996): 34–49.

———. *Bowling Alone: The Collapse and Revival of American Community.* New York: Simon and Schuster, 2000.

Rakove, Jack N. *Original Meanings: Politics and Ideas in the Making of the Constitution.* New York: Vintage Books, 1997.

Orfield, Gary, and Mindy Kornhaber, eds. *Raising Standards or Raising Barriers? Inequality and High-Stakes Testing in Public Education.* Washington, DC: Brookings Press, 2000.

Ramachandran, V. K. "On Kerala's Development Achievements." In *Indian Development: Selected Regional Perspectives.* Ed. Jean Dreze and Amartya Sen. New York: Oxford University Press, 1997, 205–356.

Rawls, John. *A Theory of Justice.* Cambridge, MA: Harvard University Press, 1972.

———. "Justice as Fairness: Political not Metaphysical." *Philosophy and Public Affairs.* 14, no. 3 (Summer 1985): 223–51.

———. *Political Liberalism.* New York: Columbia University Press, 1993.

Ravitch, Diane. *The Great School Wars. New York City, 1805–1973: A History of the Public Schools as Battlefield of Social Change.* New York: Basic Books, 1974.

Rhoten, Diana, Martin Carnoy, Melissa Chabran, and Richard Elmore. "The Conditions and Characteristics of Assessment and Accountability: The Case of Four States." Paper delivered at the meetings of the American Educational Research Association, New Orleans, April 2000.

Riker, William, *Liberalism against Populism: A Confrontation between the Theory of Democracy and the Theory of Social Choice.* Prospect, IL: Waveland Press, 1982.

Riker, William H., and Peter C. Ordeshook. "A Theory of the Calculus of Voting." *American Political Science Review* 62, no. 1 (March 1968): 25–42.

Roderick, Melissa, Anthony Bryk, Brian Jacob, John Easton, and Eliane Allensworth. *Ending Social Promotion: Results from the First Two Years.* Chicago: Consortium on Chicago School Research, 1999.

Rose-Ackerman, Susan. *Rethinking the Progressive Agenda: The Reform of the American Regulatory State.* New York: Free Press, 1992.

Rosenberg, Gerald N. *The Hollow Hope: Can Courts Bring about Social Change?* Chicago: University of Chicago Press, 1991.

Rosenstone, Steven J. and John Mark Hansen. *Mobilization, Participation, and Democracy.* New York: Macmillan, 1993.

Rousseau, Jean-Jacques. *The Basic Political Writings.* Trans. and edited by Donald A. Cress. Indianapolis: Hackett Publishing Co., 1987.

Royko, Mike. *Boss: Richard J. Daley of Chicago.* New York: Signet, 1971.

Ryan, Susan, et. al. *Charting Reform: LSCs—Local Leadership at Work.* Chicago: Consortium on Chicago School Research, December 1997.

———. *A Theory of Democratic Localism in Schools: Human and Social Capital as Keys to LSC Effectiveness.* Unpublished Ph.D. Diss., University of Chicago, School of Education, 1997.

Sabel, Charles. "Studied Trust: Building New Forms of Community in a Volatile Economy." *Human Relations* 46, no. 9 (1993): 1133–71.

———. "Learning by Monitoring: The Institutions of Economic Development." In Niel Smelser and Richard Swedberg, eds. *Handbook of Economic Sociology* 137–65. Princeton: Princeton University Press, 1994.

Sabel, Charles, Archon Fung, and Bradley Karkkainen. *Beyond Backyard Environmentalism.* Forward by Hunter Lovins and Amory Lovins. Boston: Beacon Press, 2000.

San Antonio Independent School District v. *Rodriguez. U.S. Supreme Court Reports* 411 (1972): 1–137.

Sandel, Michael. *Liberalism and the Limits of Justice.* New York: Cambridge University Press, 1982.

Sanders, Lynn M. "Against Deliberation." *Political Theory* 25, no. 3 (June 1997): 347–76.

Sartori, Giovanni. *The Theory of Democracy Revisited.* Chatham, NJ: Chatham House Publishers, 1987.

Santos, Boaventura de Sousa. "Participatory Budgeting in Porto Alegre: Toward a Redistributive Democracy." *Politics and Society* 26, no. 4 (Dec. 1998): 461–510.

Saxenian, Anna Lee. *Regional Advantage: Culture and Competition in Silicon Valley and Route 128.* Cambridge, MA: Harvard University Press, 1994.

Scheid, Dan. "Board Bumps Reform Groups from LSC Training" *Catalyst: Voices of Chicago School Reform* (September 1998): 1, 20–21.

Schlosberg, David. "Communicative Action in Practice: Intersubjectivity and New Social Movements." *Political Studies* 43, no. 2 (June 1995): 291–311.

Schneider, Anne L. "Coproduction of Public and Private Safety: An Analysis of Bystander Intervention, 'Protective Neighboring,' and Personal Protection." *Western Political Quarterly* 40, no. 4 (Dec. 1987): 611–30.

Schumpeter, Joseph A. *Capitalism, Socialism, and Democracy.* New York: Harper and Row, 1942.

Sen, Amartya. "Individual Freedom as a Social Commitment." *New York Review of Books* 37, no. 10 (14 Jun. 1990): 49–55.

———. "The Economics of Life and Death." *Scientific American* (May 1993): 40–47.

Senge, Peter. *The Fifth Discipline: The Art and Practice of the Learning Organization.* New York: Currency Doubleday, 1994.

Silverman, Eli B. *NYPD Battles Crime: Innovative Strategies in Policing.* Boston: Northeastern University Press, 1999.

Simon, David. *Homicide: A Year on the Killing Streets.* New York: Ivy Books, 1991.

Simon, Herbert. "A Behavioral Model of Rational Choice." *Quarterly Journal of Economics* 69 (1955): 99–118.

Skocpol, Theda, and Morris P. Fiorina, eds., *Civic Engagement in American Democracy.* Washington, DC: Brookings Institution Press, 1999.

Skogan, Wesley. "Community Organizations and Crime." In *Crime and Justice: A Review of Research*, ed. Michael Tonry and Norval Morris, Chicago: University of Chicago Press, 1988, 39–78.

———. *Disorder and Decline: Crime and the Spiral of Decay in American Neighborhoods.* New York: Free Press, 1990.

Skogan, Wesley G. and Susan M. Hartnett. *Community Policing: Chicago Style.* New York: Oxford University Press, 1997.

Skogan, Wesley, Susan Hartnett, Jill DuBois, Jennifer T. Comey, Marianne Kaiser, and Justine Lovig. *On the Beat: Police and Community Problem Solving.* Boulder, CO: Westview Press, 1999.

Skolnick, Jerome H., and David H. Bayley. *The New Blue Line: Police Innovation in Six American Cities.* New York: Free Press, 1986.

Sparrow, Malcom K., Mark H. Moore, and David M. Kennedy. *Beyond 911: A New Era for Policing.* New York: Basic Books, 1990.

Special Task Force on Education. *Chicago School System: Recommendation Summary.* Chicago: Special Task Force on Education, March 1981.

Spielman, Fran. "Police Report." *Chicago Sun-Times.* 23 July 1992.

Spielman, Fran, and Curtis Lawrence. "City School Test Scores Climb for Third Year." *Chicago Sun-Times.* 18 May 1998.

Stever, James A. "Technology, Organization, Freedom The Organizational Theory of John Dewey." *Administration and Society* 24, no. 4 (Feb. 1993): 419–43.

Stewart, Monica Faith and Judson Hixson. "Chicago School Reform Reinvents Central Support System." *Education and Urban Society* 26, no. 3 (May 1994): 285–92.

Susskind, Lawrence, and Jeffrey Cruikshank. *Breaking the Impasse: Consensual Approaches to Resolving Public Disputes.* New York: Basic Books, 1987.

———. "Progress Through Mischief: The Social Movement Alternative to Secondary Associations." *Politics and Society* 20, no. 4 (Dec. 1992): 521–28.

Szasz, Andrew. *Ecopopulism: Toxic Waste and the Movement for Environmental Justice.* Minneapolis: University of Minnesota Press, 1994.

Taylor, Michael. *The Possibility of Cooperation.* Cambridge: Cambridge University Press, 1987.

Teixeira, Ruy A. *The Disappearing American Voter.* Washington, DC: Brookings Institution, 1992.

Thomas, Craig. "Habitat Conservation Planning: Certainly Empowered, Somewhat Deliberative, Questionably Democratic." *Politics and Society* 29, no. 1 (March 2001), 105–32.

Thomas, Karen M. and Jean Latz Griffin. "Teachers May Bend for School Reform." *Chicago Tribune* 15 June 1988.

Thucydides. *History of the Peloponnesian War.* Trans. Rex Warner. New York: Penguin Classics, 1954.

Tiebout, Charles M. "A Pure Theory of Local Expenditures." *Journal of Political Economy* 64, no. 5 (Oct. 1956): 416–24.

Tocqueville, Alexis de *Democracy in America.* Ed. J. P. Mayer, trans. George Lawrence. New York: Harper and Row, 1969.

Tullock, Gordon. "Federalism: Problems of Scale." *Public Choice.* 6 (Spring 1969): 19–29.

Tversky, Amos, and Daniel Kahneman. "Rational Choice and the Framing of Decisions." *Journal of Business* 59, no. 4, part 2: 251–78.

Tyack, David B. *The One Best System: A History of American Urban Education.* Cambridge, MA: Harvard University Press, 1974.

Unger, Roberto. *False Necessity: Anti-Necessitarian Social Theory in the Service of Radical Democracy.* Cambridge: Cambridge University Press, 1987a.

Unger, Roberto. *Plasticity into Power: Comparative Historical Studies on the Institutional Conditions of Economic and Military Success.* Cambridge: Cambridge University Press, 1987b.

United States. Department of Health and Human Services. Public Health Service. Centers for Disease Control and Prevention. National Center for Health Statistics. *Vital Statistics of the United States.* Hyattsville, MD: National Center for Health Statistics, various years.

United States Department of Justice. Federal Bureau of Investigation. *Crime in the United States.* Washington, DC: U.S. Government Printing Office, various years.

Verba, Sidney, and Norman Nie. *Participation in America: Political Democracy and Social Equality.* Chicago and London: University of Chicago Press, 1987.

Verba, Sidney, Kay Lehman Schlozman, and Henry E. Brady. *Voice and Equality: Civic Voluntarism in American Politics.* Cambridge, MA: Harvard University Press, 1995.

———. "Rational Action and Political Activity." *Journal of Theoretical Politics.* 12, no. 3 2000: 243–68.

von Neumann, J. and Oscar Morgenstern. *The Theory of Games and Economic Behavior.* Princeton: Princeton University Press, 1944.

Weber, Max. *From Max Weber: Essays in Sociology.* Trans. and ed. H. H. Gerth and C. Wright Mills. New York: Oxford University Press, 1946.

Weeks, Edward C. "The Practice of Deliberative Democracy: Results from Four Large-Scale Trials." *Public Administration Review* 60, no. 4 (Jul./Aug. 2000): 360–72.

Weir, Margaret. "Urban Poverty and Defensive Localism." *Dissent* 41, no. 3 (Summer 1994): 337–40.

Westbrook, Robert B. *John Dewey and American Democracy.* Ithaca: Cornell University Press, 1991.

Whyte, William Foote, and Kathleen King Whyte. *Making Mondragon: The Growth and Dynamics of the Worker Cooperative Complex*. Ithaca, NY: Industrial Relations Press, 1988.

Williams, Deborah. "Probation Promotes Collaboration at Riis, Harper." *Catalyst: Voices of Chicago School Reform* 7, no. 7 (April 1997): 20.

Wilson, James Q. *Varieties of Police Behavior: The Management of Law and Order in Eight Communities*. Cambridge, MA: Harvard University Press, 1968.

———., *Thinking About Crime*. New York: Basic Books, 1983.

———., *Bureaucracy: What Government Agencies Do and Why They Do It*. New York: Basic Books, 1989.

Wilson, James Q., and Kelling, George L. "Making Neighborhoods Safe: Sometimes 'Fixing Broken Windows' Does More To Reduce Crime Than Conventional 'Incident-Oriented' Policing." *Atlantic Monthly* 263, no. 2 (Feb. 1989): 46–52.

Wilson, Orlando W. *Police Administration*. New York: McGraw-Hill, 1950.

Wilson, William Julius. *The Truly Disadvantaged: The Inner City, the Underclass, and Public Policy*. Chicago: University of Chicago Press, 1987.

Yaffee, Stephen L., Peter Aengst, Jeremy Anderson, Jay Chamberlin, Christopher Grunewald, Susan Loucks, and Elizabeth Wheatley. *Balancing Public Trust and Private Interest: Public Participation in Habitat Conservation Planning*. Ann Arbor: University of Michigan, School of Natural Resources and Environment, 1998.

Yates, Douglas. *Bureaucratic Democracy: The Search for Democracy and Efficiency in American Government*. Cambridge, MA: Harvard University Press, 1982.

Young, Iris Marion. *Justice and the Politics of Difference*. Princeton: Princeton University Press, 1990.

———. "Communication and the Other: Beyond Deliberative Democracy." *Democracy and Difference: Contesting the Boundaries of the Political*. Ed. Selya Benhabib. Princeton: Princeton University Press, 1996, 120–36.

———. *Inclusion and Democracy*. Oxford: Oxford University Press, 2000.

Zolo, Danillo. *Democracy And Complexity: A Realist Approach*. Cambridge: Polity Press, 1992.

Index